ERLING
HAALAND

ERLING HAALAND

MANCHESTER CITY'S STRIKING VIKING

MARK METCALF AND SIMON MULLOCK

First published by Pitch Publishing, 2023

Pitch Publishing
9 Donnington Park,
85 Birdham Road,
Chichester,
West Sussex,
PO20 7AJ
www.pitchpublishing.co.uk
info@pitchpublishing.co.uk

ISBN 978 1 80150 656 4

Typesetting and origination by Pitch Publishing
Printed and bound in Great Britain by TJ Books, Padstow

Contents

Dedications

From Simon Mullock: For my grandson, Teddy.

From Mark Metcalf: To Iris Swift, Frank Swift's biggest fan.

Foreword

By John Cross

THERE HAVE been some very special winners of the Football Writers' Association Footballer of the Year down the years.

But with the likes of Thierry Henry, Cristiano Ronaldo and Robert Pires, we did not see them at their best until at least their second season in English football.

That is what makes Erling Haaland so exceptional. He was simply unstoppable in his first year at Manchester City, winning the Treble for his club and the Golden Boot for his remarkable tally of 52 goals in all competitions.

No one is supposed to be able to do that. Certainly not someone so young. And that is a tribute to Haaland's professionalism, brilliance and determination.

He is not just a prolific goalscorer but a scorer of spectacular goals. His strength and power make him unstoppable.

But he is also a humble human being. And that's one of his greatest qualities and something that shines through in the story of his first season in English football.

When I was lucky enough to present him with his FWA award in May 2023, it was the 75th anniversary of our Footballer of the Year.

He was in the presence of some truly great previous winners with the likes of Alan Shearer and Gary Lineker in the room. And here was Haaland, a young player but someone genuinely interested in the history, in the previous winners and someone, when you speak to him, you quickly realise is a passionate student of the game.

Haaland was fascinated by the list of previous winners, was clearly overwhelmed by the respect in the room and happy to chat about his dislikes and likes about the game. It is so obvious that he thinks he can get even better and is determined to work at his game.

What a prospect for opposing defenders! I love his mischievous smile. His frustration and anger when he misses a chance. Why? Because he wants to improve and be ready to take the next one.

He is steely-eyed and determined. But he's also set on winning more trophies and more accolades both for his team and on a personal level.

We are witnessing one of the great strikers of his generation. He has the ability to become the best in the world. With a determination to get there.

John Cross,
FWA Chair

Introduction

ERLING BRAUT Haaland's first season in English football saw him tear up the record books. Manchester City's striking Viking eclipsed modern goalscoring legends like Alan Shearer, Andy Cole and Mohamed Salah as Pep Guardiola's Sky Blues ensured their place among the game's greatest-ever teams by winning a Premier League, Champions League and FA Cup Treble.

Haaland found the back of the net an astonishing 52 times, becoming the first top-flight player to rack up half a century of goals in over 90 years.

His incredible contribution also secured him the Premier League's prized Golden Boot as well as the Football Writers' Association Footballer of the Year Award – at the age of just 22.

The Leeds-born number nine had his pick of Europe's top clubs when he was deciding on his future during an injury-hit final season with Borussia Dortmund in 2021/22.

He rejected offers from Real Madrid and Bayern Munich to come 'home'. Haaland's father, Alfie, joined Manchester City in the same summer his youngest son was born.

Haaland's decision to sign for a team that had won four of the previous five Premier League titles under Guardiola was not based on sentiment.

This book details why the 6ft 5in Norwegian felt moving to Manchester to help City become European champions for the first time in their history made perfect sense for a player who has mapped out his career with the same precision he demonstrates in front of goal.

It also documents a debut season which saw Haaland set new standards in Premier League excellence as City were confirmed as football's most dominant force, both at home and abroad.

Mark Metcalf and Simon Mullock

1

Leaving Germany

WHEN SUPER-AGENT Mino Raiola negotiated the deal that took Haaland from RB Salzburg to Borussia Dortmund in the summer of 2019, he drove a bargain so hard that Manchester United decided against pursuing the Norwegian striker.

Dortmund paid €22.5m (£19.23m) to trigger a clause in Haaland's contract, just a year after the Austrian club had signed him from Molde.

The Germans also agreed to pay a €10m commission that was shared between Raiola's company and the player's father, Alfie. The agent then lived up to his nickname of 'Mr Three Hundred Million' by pushing the envelope a little further – and was rewarded when Dortmund declined to walk away again despite being told that Haaland wanted another release clause and that his arrival would also hinge on Raiola taking a cut of any subsequent transfer fee.

His buy-out at Signal Iduna Park would be €60m, a significant sum – but a bargain should Haaland take a wrecking ball to Bundesliga defences in the way he had done to those in Norway and Austria. The only slither of leverage Dortmund were able to negotiate was that the clause could not be triggered until the summer of 2022.

Manchester City, Real Madrid, Barcelona, Bayern Munich, Chelsea, Arsenal and Atlético Madrid were among the 20 clubs who felt that Raiola was asking too much for too little.

And so did United, despite the urgings of manager Ole Gunnar Solskjær, a man who had been instrumental in Haaland's rise to prominence at Molde and might have been able to recognise a natural-born goalscorer when he saw one given his own impeccable pedigree. United didn't want to do business with an agent who had played them like the proverbial fiddle in the past.

Raiola was also Paul Pogba's adviser. In the summer of 2012 he took the Frenchman away from Old Trafford when his contract expired. At the turn of that year, United manager Sir Alex Ferguson had persuaded Paul Scholes to come out of retirement rather than put his faith in Pogba as his team unsuccessfully tried to overcome rivals City in the closest title race in Premier League history.

When Raiola met Ferguson to discuss a new contract, he knew Juventus were willing to meet his demands because the midfielder would cost them nothing more than a €1m compensation fee because of his age.

Raiola recalled, 'Mr Ferguson thought that our value of Paul was exaggerated and that he should be happy to sign. I told him that for this money my chihuahua would not walk on the grass of the training centre.' Ferguson called Raiola a 'shitbag' as the meeting came to a close – and Pogba duly left for Turin.

When he returned to Old Trafford in the summer of 2016, it was to play for new boss José Mourinho. United were so desperate to keep Pogba out of the clutches of new Manchester City manager Pep Guardiola that they paid a world-record price.

According to Juventus director general Giuseppe Marotta, speaking at the club's AGM in October 2016, United agreed to pay €105m, including add-ons, to re-sign their academy graduate. Raiola's cut of the deal was an eye-watering €27m.

Solskjær, who was sacked by United in November 2021, later claimed that he urged his former club to sign Haaland for just £4m when he was his manager at Molde and Raiola had not yet ingratiated himself with the striker and his family.

Speaking at the 'An Evening with Ole Gunnar Solskjær' event in Manchester, the Norwegian said, 'I got in contact with United because we had this talented striker who they should have had. But they didn't listen, unfortunately. Four million, I asked for. But they never signed him. Four million! Don't ask.'

Haaland's escape clause at Dortmund was the worst-kept secret in football – because Raiola wanted it that way. It appeared the German club would be forced to cash in as early as the summer of 2021 when it seemed they would not qualify for the following season's Champions League – and a transfer then would have banked them in excess of €100m.

But they ended the campaign by winning their last seven games to finish third in the Bundesliga, with Haaland scoring six times in that sequence. He also scored twice in a 4-1 victory over RB Leipzig in the DFB-Pokal Final.

Dortmund were knocked out of the Champions League in the quarter-finals by Manchester City, losing both legs 2-1. Haaland was so well marshalled by City defenders Rúben Dias and John Stones that he didn't have an effort on goal in either game, with Guardiola's side limiting Dortmund to just over 38 per cent possession in both matches.

But that didn't stop City's players from starting a charm offensive that would last for a year, with Phil Foden covering his mouth with his hand as he gave the striker his opinion at the final whistle at the Etihad.

Haaland recalled, 'I'll be completely honest, when we played City about 15 people came to me and said I should join them. Stones, Rúben Dias and [İlkay] Gündoğan said so. Foden as well and [Kevin] De Bruyne. So many of them.

'Then I met [Riyad] Mahrez on holiday that summer and he started talking as well. It's nice when players want you to join their club. It is the club that is the most important thing [when you're making a decision], but it's also important when the players want you.'

Mahrez really did crank the rumour mill into top gear when he tweeted a short video of him dancing with Haaland in a restaurant on the Greek island of Mykonos in June 2021 with the message 'Agent Mahrez on duty'.

Raiola met with Dortmund's sporting director Michael Zorc at the end of the season to determine whether there was a potential escape route for his client that summer. Dortmund had already banked £73m by selling Jadon Sancho to Manchester United after refusing to budge on a commitment to only sell the England winger for an even higher price when the Old Trafford club first registered their interest 12 months earlier. Their stance on Haaland was just as steadfast.

'I can confirm I was in Dortmund to talk,' said Raiola. 'Michael Zorc let us know very clearly that Borussia Dortmund don't want to sell Haaland this summer. I respect that opinion but it doesn't mean that I agree with it. Borussia were very clear about their mindset and approach.'

That gave Team Haaland 12 months to plot their next move with absolute precision. Raiola and legal adviser Rafaela Pimenta would be the go-betweens for Haaland, Dortmund and interested clubs. The player, his father, and fixer and confidante Ivar Eggja would then weigh up which clubs and lifestyle would offer the best fit. Egil Østenstad, the former Southampton and Blackburn striker who also had a brief loan spell at Manchester City, was available for financial advice having moved into banking after hanging up his boots.

Eggja's role in Haaland's rise cannot be underestimated. Alfie's best friend is a personal trainer who also acts as a facilitator, arranging all the small details in the player's life from grocery deliveries to car insurance so that Erling can concentrate totally on what he does best.

When Haaland signed for City, he moved into the same city-centre apartment block that was also home to Jack Grealish, Rúben Dias and Julián Álvarez. It was fully furnished, the fridge fully stocked with the best food, while a chauffeur-driven car had been arranged to take him to City's state-of-the-art £200m training ground the next morning.

Haaland's tastes have become more expensive as he has progressed. When he signed for Dortmund, Eggja simply called into the local IKEA store to stock up on furniture. 'I think if I had been all alone and had to choose my own apartment and go shopping in IKEA, I wouldn't have scored three goals against Augsburg on my Dortmund debut,' admitted Haaland.

* * *

Pick of the top clubs

When Raiola gauged the level of interest it was clear that his client would have his pick of the top clubs in the summer of 2022. Viaplay, a Swedish video streaming service which held rights to screen Premier League games at the time of publication, was given access to the process that would determine Haaland's future for a documentary called *The Big Decision*. It would be part of an official long-term media link-up between the company and the Norwegian striker, including an arrangement that would see Alfie Haaland employed as a pundit for Premier League games shown in Norway, Sweden, Denmark, Finland, Estonia, Lithuania, Poland and the Netherlands. Formula One world champion Max Verstappen had a similar agreement.

Alfie would also play a starring role in the documentary after drawing up a points system to help his son determine which club would be the best fit. Former Norway striker Jan Åge Fjørtoft, who became a respected broadcast journalist following his own playing career, was given fly-on-the-wall access to the Haaland camp. *The Big Decision* was compelling viewing.

Haaland senior outlined how seven serious contenders – Manchester City, Real Madrid, Paris Saint-Germain, Bayern Munich, Liverpool, Chelsea and Barcelona – were initially whittled down to three. 'I would say there are five or six options,' he admitted on 21 February. 'But, to be honest, I can cut it down to three.

'We ask who is the best team at this moment. The next criteria is who needs a number nine? We have Liverpool right up there, but they don't need a nine. City scored ten for that one. They need a number nine.

'Real Madrid score only five or six because they have [Karim] Benzema. And also, will they get [Kylian] Mbappé? Bayern Munich have one point. They don't need a number nine because their best player is a number nine. But if he [Robert Lewandowski] goes, they have no one else.

'It would be controversial to go to Munich. But when we went through the points system, they are one of the best teams. Right now, they are number two on our list. I think City is the best team, Munich is second. We have Real Madrid at number three and Paris Saint-Germain as number four.'

Other factors were also considered. Alfie added, 'Some of the things we looked at were consistent. Like the size of the club, the stadium and the fans. Then there is the quality of the league. We consider England as the best league and Spain as the second.

'Then there is the economy of the club – and this can change. What type of a team are they? This can also change.

Do they need a number nine? This changes with injuries or transfers. I think it was one point separating the top two after our last calculations.'

One thing that Team Haaland were wary of taking into account was who would be Erling's next manager. But the prospect of lining up for Pep Guardiola and working with the best coach in the world was tantalising – even if the player allowed himself to do some thinking with his heart rather than his head. Erling said, 'It is better that a club is eager to get you rather than a manager. In the end, it is the club you transfer to. I have never joined a club because of the manager. He can get fired three weeks later and I would be sat there thinking, "What now?"

'But it is a big plus that Guardiola is at City. He is the best manager in the world. Ultimately, it is how well I can do in the team and how well I can deliver the goods over the next five years. The Premier League is the hardest in terms of tempo – and there are more matches in England due to the League Cup and FA Cup, as well as the Champions League.

'If you play for a top team, you have 60 matches a year, plus more for the national team. That makes it 70 matches if you play them all – which I hope to do. But if you play in every match, you can get injured if you can't handle it.

'There is nothing that can go wrong. It is going to be damn good whatever I choose. I think in the end, it's a gut feeling that has to decide – a bit like when I signed for Dortmund. I think what it would be like to wear the shirt? I ask myself if I score and celebrate, how good would it feel? I try to visualise things like that.'

Fjørtoft asked Haaland how he could reject an offer from Real Madrid. 'It is a good question,' was his answer. 'It is really not possible.' But the Spanish giants already had Ballon d'Or winner Benzema and were continuing to court PSG's brilliant Frenchman Mbappé. Haaland would only go where he felt wanted – and that meant Bayern Munich or Manchester City.

Bayern tried to distance themselves from the bidding, briefing several German newspapers and media outlets that they weren't interested in signing Haaland. The Bundesliga champions had made a habit of taking Dortmund's best players to Bavaria. In the build-up to Bayern's Champions League Final meeting with Dortmund at Wembley in 2013, they announced they would be triggering the €37m clause in Mario Götze's contract that summer. Defender Mats Hummels made the same move in 2016.

In between, Bayern also signed Dortmund's brilliant Polish striker Robert Lewandowski at the end of his contract – and while Haaland was deciding on his next move, they were in talks about extending the two-time Ballon d'Or Striker of the Year winner's contract.

Alfie Haaland insisted at the time, 'Bayern are interested. I understand that clubs will position themselves so that if he doesn't end up with them, they can say he was never an option. Lewandowski is still the best striker in the world, I think. But he is 34 years old.'

Lewandowski knew Bayern were courting Haaland behind the scenes – and it was a huge blow to his pride. But he was also galvanised. He went on to break the 40-goal barrier for the seventh successive season, topping the Bundesliga goal charts for the seventh time with 35 to equal the record of Bayern legend Gerd Müller.

Lewandowski was not interested in taking the record for himself. Just a few days after it was confirmed that Haaland would be going to Manchester, the Pole took his revenge by telling Bayern his time at the club was over, 'After what has happened, I cannot imagine a good cooperation between me and the club in the future.' Barcelona wanted to take him to the Camp Nou – and he departed in a €50m deal to score

23 La Liga goals to help the Catalan club become Spanish champions in 2022/23.

Erling Haaland understood what had transpired, 'Inside Lewandowski's head, I don't know how many goals and titles he has, but you start to feel sorry for him. Seriously. I think it's disrespectful. But at the same time, it's actually also another opportunity for him.'

* * *

Mino Raiola

Mino Raiola was instrumental in brokering an agreement with Manchester City during negotiations with the club's chief executive Ferran Soriano, director of football Txiki Begiristain and Omar Berrada, the chief football operations officer. But he was also fighting a losing battle against cancer.

The former pizza restaurant owner who was born in Italy and raised in the Netherlands passed away in April 2022 at Milan's San Raffaele Hospital, aged 54, less than a month before the transfer was confirmed. Two days before he died, Raiola had taken to his Twitter account to assure the world that reports of his demise were premature.

City would trigger Haaland's £51m release clause – and even though the Premier League champions also agreed to pay a further £34m in agency fees, it was still regarded as value for money just a year after they had made it clear they would pay Tottenham Hotspur in excess of £100m for England captain Harry Kane, seven years Haaland's senior.

Rafaela Pimenta, the 49-year-old Brazilian lawyer who worked at Raiola's side, inherited a stable of stellar names that included Haaland, Pogba, Zlatan Ibrahimović, Mario Balotelli, Matthijs de Ligt, Marco Veratti and Gianluigi Donnarumma.

She would split the commission for Haaland's arrival at the Etihad Stadium with Alfie, whose counsel the striker had relied on heavily while deciding his future.

Pimenta spent the first few weeks after Raiola's death fending off enquiries from several agents she later described as 'lowlifes' for the underhand tactics they used trying to take clients away from her. 'One agent called Walter Benitez rang the day that Mino died. His wife picked up the phone and gave him a tongue-lashing, telling him he should be ashamed of himself,' she said.

'Even before Mino died, they called [French goalkeeper] Alphonse Areola. Thousands of people called Erling. Thousands of people called Paul [Pogba]. They also called me and said, "If you need help, I can run the business for you."'

Pimenta needed no assistance. Haaland was one of the first to call to offer his sympathies before telling her it was business as usual. A signed shirt from the player, originally presented to Raiola by Haaland, went up on the wall of her office. The inscription read 'From a Viking to a Viking'. Haaland assured Pimenta she wouldn't have been out of place in a long ship and told her to keep the shirt.

Haaland said, 'In the last period [before signing for City], Rafaela, who is in many ways the female version of Mino, knew what she was doing.

'I don't like to talk about Mino's death. It is a very sad story since he was such a good man. It is tough and such a shame. He did a lot for me, of course. When I went to Salzburg he managed to get the clause and I also got the clause in Dortmund. That's why I am where I am today, because of him.

'A big part of what I have worked with his team for many years is that they are very good and skilled people who have helped my dad a lot – both with and without Mino.'

Raiola did the groundwork for Haaland's agreement to join City, and Pimenta completed the deal. It was done with the same efficiency with which Kevin De Bruyne would load the bullets for Haaland to fire in a sky blue shirt. But the role that Alfie Haaland played in plotting his son's future can't be underestimated.

City portrayed the transfer as a homecoming. Team Haaland furnished the club's social media team with numerous photographs of their new signing as a toddler and teenager, wearing a sky blue City shirt in the days when a successful season meant securing 40 points and Premier League safety.

Haaland was born in Leeds in July 2000, just a month after his father completed a £2.5m move from the Yorkshire club to Manchester City following the Blues' promotion to the Premier League under Joe Royle. Just 12 months earlier, City had played a season in the third tier of English football for the only time in their history and had only been promoted thanks to an incredible comeback in the play-off final against Gillingham at Wembley, when they scored twice in injury time to take the game into extra time before winning a penalty shoot-out. That was the club's first appearance in front of the Twin Towers since they had lost to Chelsea in the Full Members' Cup Final 13 years earlier.

City's return to the top flight lasted for just a single season. Haaland senior made 35 Premier League appearances and was made captain ahead of a 2-1 City victory at Elland Road in September. But he was injured in a 1-0 win over West Ham United at Maine Road and missed the final two games. A 2-1 defeat at Ipswich Town in the penultimate match of the season confirmed City's relegation.

The midfielder underwent knee surgery at the end of the season, but only made three substitute appearances as City won promotion under Kevin Keegan a year later. He was eventually forced to retire in the summer of 2003 after City opted to trigger a clause in his contract, stipulating that they could terminate his employment on medical advice.

His young son was already developing his skills wearing a replica kit with 'DAD' on the back. Erling retained faded memories of being taken to Maine Road – but was unable to recall whether he was there when City played their final game at the 80-year-old stadium against Southampton in May 2003. 'I don't remember,' Haaland admitted after being asked if he had been at Maine Road's last stand in his first interview with the City website after joining the club. 'But I was at a lot of games with my mum, sister and brother, watching my father.'

Haaland also told reporters, 'I like City and Leeds because my dad played for both clubs. Earlier in his career, he played for Nottingham [Forest], so my brother and sister support them a bit more. But I have followed City and Leeds all of my life.'

Leeds had actually turned down an invitation to bid for the striker when he was leaving Molde in 2018. They opted to spend their money on Patrick Bamford instead.

Erling had briefly accepted an invitation to join a Norwegian Manchester City fan page on Facebook the year before he signed for the club, so the Blues made the most of his old loyalties.

But Alfie insisted, 'I have always said that it is one thing supporting a club and another to be a professional footballer. You must put your feelings aside when choosing where to play. You have to choose what is right for you, not the club the family supports.

'I couldn't have played for any club, since some of the family supported Tottenham, some Arsenal, some Liverpool, some Man U, some City and others Leeds. We have to put that aside and choose what is right for Erling.'

One UK newspaper report in April 2021 claimed Raiola was demanding a £1m-a-week wage for Haaland. German publication *Bild* pitched his asking price at £820,000 a week.

The player insisted, 'When I was a young boy, like everyone else, I dreamed about becoming the best footballer in the world and making a living out of it. I think money is important for everyone in the world. To make the most money is not my main focus, but if you can get 5,000 Norwegian Krone to do a job and get 10,000 Norwegian Krone to do the same job, then you take the 10,000. Everyone would do that.

'Money has never been my main motivation, but I have dreamed about making a living from football and living on that money for the rest of my life.'

Haaland was on holiday in Marbella when news leaked out on 20 May 2022 that he would be joining City at the start of July. 'It was a lot of relief and a lot of joy,' he said. 'It was not easy because it has been a difficult few months. But it was a good choice in the end and I am happy about it.

'The reason I chose City is that I think I can develop best at that club. And, yes, I think it's the best sporting project in the world right now. It's where I think I will do best. It's the best league and a cool club.'

Find out how much the wage agreement was in chapter 25.

2

Reach for the Stars

IT WAS fitting that a season that would see City reach for the stars should start with a visit to Houston's Lyndon B. Johnson Space Center as Pep Guardiola prepared his players for lift-off. The Premier League champions travelled to the United States on 16 July 2022 for two friendlies against Mexico's Club América and German giants Bayern Munich. When they checked in at Manchester Airport, they were met by comedian Troy Hawke, the self-styled 'President of the Greeters' Guild'. City's players were left in hysterics when Hawke told Erling Haaland, 'You are a tremendous Nordic meat shield.' The City striker was suitably confused.

First stop was Texas – and City took the opportunity to launch their new away kit at NASA's iconic Mission Control, with Haaland one of four players, along with Jack Grealish, Kyle Walker and Ederson, designated to model a red and black shirt that was first made famous when City under Joe Mercer's leadership won the FA Cup in 1969 – just three months before Neil Armstrong and Buzz Aldrin, supported by Michael Collins, landed their Apollo 11 module on the moon.

The City quartet posed in front of the Little Joe II rocket that was once used for unmanned test flights.

Later that evening at a team dinner, Haaland and fellow new-boys Kalvin Phillips and Julián Álvarez were informed that they had to go through an initiation ceremony in which all three players had to sing a song in front of their teammates. Haaland's rendition of Enrique Inglesias's hit single 'Hero' was well received, as was Álvarez's cover version of a South American hit by Luis Fonsi called 'Despacito'. But it was agreed that Phillips was top of the pops that evening for his version of George Ezra's 'Budapest'.

Haaland had been dropped off by his father, driving a grey Land Rover, at the City Football Academy for the first day of pre-season on 11 July, but was soon complaining of muscle soreness. Given his injury problems the previous season, City's medics advised he should be put on a fitness programme tailored for his needs. He was still feeling the strain when Guardiola put his players through their paces at a training session opened up for any Texas-based City supporters at the Houston Sports Park. Guardiola later revealed at a press conference that it was unlikely that his new number nine would be facing Club América at the magnificent 72,000-capacity NRG Stadium, the home to NFL franchise Houston Texans.

More than 61,000 fans still turned up, many of them wearing sky blue shirts despite the huge enclave of Mexican expats who call the city home. The stadium's retractable roof was closed as two Kevin De Bruyne goals ensured City won 2-1 to take the Copa de Lone Star trophy back to Manchester. Haaland, wearing a navy blue hoodie, was cheered every time the big screen showed him sat on the bench.

Guardiola promised afterwards that Haaland would feature against Bayern Munich two days later at one of American football's most famous stadiums, Lambeau Field in Wisconsin, home of the much-revered Green Bay Packers. 'Erling will be ready for the next game,' he said. 'He had niggles and we don't want to take risks. Maybe against Bayern we will see. Erling had problems last season at Dortmund, but we will try to handle that. It's not a big issue, but we want to take care of him.'

Haaland had gravitated towards academy graduates James McAtee and Cole Palmer during his first few days at the Etihad, but it quickly became clear that his closest mate would be the effervescent Jack Grealish. The England midfielder joked during the US tour that his £100m price tag had eased the level of expectation on City's new striker, 'Erling actually said to me, "I'm only half the price of you so I haven't got the pressure!" Obviously there's always going to be big expectations, but nowadays you have to deal with it.

'But Erling is a great guy, a brilliant guy. The first day I met him we took a car together and after that ride I thought, "What a guy." He's so down to earth and quite up front with the way he is.'

Wisconsin has a big German population, but there was still a sizeable contingent of City supporters in the 78,128 crowd that had paid to witness the first 'soccer' game to be played at Lambeau – including the Packers' veteran Super Bowl-winning quarterback Aaron Rodgers, who visited the Blues in their locker room at the final whistle to swap signed shirts with De Bruyne.

Supporters from all 50 US states and 19 foreign countries bought tickets for the showpiece occasion. There was a pre-game weather warning suggesting that Thor, the Norse god of thunder, would also be in attendance to see City's Viking make his debut – and before a ball had been kicked fans were evacuated from the stands to take shelter in the stadium concourses as a spectacular electrical storm battered the area. Kick-off was delayed by ten minutes – and both teams then agreed that the game could be reduced to 80 minutes because they had return flights to catch later that night.

The stadium's playing area measured 120 yards x 53.5 yards – too small according to FIFA regulations – but both clubs were happy for the game to go ahead with so much local interest guaranteeing a virtual sell-out. All eyes were on Haaland. Much of the pre-match hype centred on the fact he had scored five goals in seven games against Bayern during his time in Germany – but had still finished on the losing side every time. This was the year he would change the record in spectacular style.

Haaland managed just three touches in the opening 11 minutes – but his fourth brought him a goal to open his City account. It would be a feature of his season. De Bruyne's smart pass enabled Grealish to cross low from the left and the striker slid into Manuel Neuer's six-yard box to guide the ball home. That was the cue for another spectacular lightning show that sent players and fans scurrying for cover and prompted a further break in play. Haaland was substituted at half-time and there were no further goals as City won 1-0.

Haaland very rarely speaks to the media unless it's a sponsorship event or an interview that his club have granted to rights holders. He wasn't impressed when City's head of football communications Alex Rowan suggested he should take questions from a posse of journalists waiting outside the dressing room. 'How long will this take?' he asked. 'Only five minutes,' replied Rowan, who looking at the frown on the striker's face, then added, 'We can make it ten minutes if you want?' At least that brought a smile. 'It was a good feeling to get started again after six weeks without football,' said Haaland. 'I've been watching a lot of City games over the last years and they've been without a striker so, of course, I've been seeing myself in these situations. I'm not surprised I scored. It's good. I have to say the first time winning against Bayern, it was about time after seven losses in a row. Guardiola is a bit crazy – and I like that. I've been training well and I'm ready for what is next.'

Next was Liverpool in the Community Shield, with the showpiece curtain-raiser scheduled to be played at Leicester City's King Power Stadium on 30 July because Wembley was being used the following day for the final of the Women's European Championship. Jürgen Klopp's FA Cup and EFL Cup winners had missed out on a historic Quadruple on the final six days of the previous season, losing out to City in a Premier League title race by just a point after the Blues had come back from 2-0 down to beat Aston Villa on the final day, before being edged out 1-0 by Real Madrid in the Champions League Final in Paris. It was the third time in nine seasons that they had ended runners-up to City. The Community Shield was seen as a genuine marker for the coming campaign.

Klopp had been interested in taking Haaland to Anfield ever since the Norwegian had capped an impressive performance by scoring for RB Salzburg against his team in a 4-3 Champions League defeat on Merseyside in October 2019. But the Norwegian assured City that he was Manchester-bound when he met with Txiki Begiristain in Monaco in February 2022. When City immediately informed Dortmund that they would be triggering the £51m clause in Haaland's contract, it didn't take long for news of City's scoop to leak out.

On 24 May, it became official. Haaland took a private jet to Barcelona to undergo a medical with Guardiola's favourite physician, Dr Ramon Cugat, a Spanish surgeon specialising in orthopaedic surgery and sports medicine. Dr Cugat has been Guardiola's go-to guy throughout his managerial career, despite the fact that City spent millions building a cutting-edge medical centre at their training ground. After passing all the necessary tests, Haaland was whisked back to Manchester for an evening in Tast restaurant, the city-centre eatery specialising in Catalan tapas opened by Guardiola,

Begiristain and Ferran Soriano in 2018. Haaland, again accompanied by his father and Ivar Eggja, arrived through a rear entrance to throw any lurking photographers off the scent. They met with City's three restaurateurs as well as club operations officer Omar Berrada and Guardiola's confidante Manuel Estiarte, a former world-champion water polo player who won a gold medal at the 1996 Olympics. Haaland's entourage were then secreted back to the nearby Dakota Hotel.

The following day, Haaland met with Begiristain and Berrada again for brunch at the training ground, along with former City striker Paul Dickov. After ordering a cheese and ham omelette, Haaland asked to be introduced to the chefs who prepared the players' meals. 'You will be my favourite people,' he told them.

Haaland consumes 6,000 calories a day. His Norway team-mate Josh King once said, 'Erling eats like a bear.' Soon after his arrival, a club nutritionist ordered cooks to give the striker 200g more food than his team-mates so he could fully refuel his massive frame. City take regular deliveries of the finest Norwegian salmon to keep their striker's belly full – although Haaland insists that his favourite delicacy is his father's lasagne. 'I have eaten it before every home game,' he said after becoming the first City player in almost 52 years to score a hat-trick in the Manchester derby in October 2022. 'It has turned out fairly well, so there has to be something special to it.' He later told Gary Neville in an interview with Sky Sports, 'I absolutely love eating kebabs. It is one of the best things but I can never eat them. Sometimes I sit at home and I'm like, "Oh, that would be so good." But then I go to the fridge and make something else.'

But Haaland is ultra-disciplined when it comes to looking after his body and mind. He felt the injury problems he suffered in his final Dortmund year were linked to the stress of deciding on his next move – despite his strict adherence to a diet that includes such large amounts of offal that one tabloid newspaper felt it was able to compare him to fictional serial killer and cannibal Dr Hannibal Lecter. The sensationalist headline prompted a complaint being made by Team Haaland.

'When I go to bed I think about where I am moving to,' admitted Haaland as he agonised over his future. 'Sometimes I struggle to sleep because I am thinking about it. Eventually, I said to myself, "OK, now you have to stop thinking about it."

'Muscle strains then became a factor because I was not taking enough care of my body – but injuries can also be caused by stress.

'In my subconscious, maybe [the transfer] affected me. I think a lot of factors played a part. Maybe if I felt something, I would try to forget it and think I was fine. I am a footballer. If I feel something, so fucking what? Just go out and play. Playing is the only thing on my mind. I am concerned with looking after my body and I think eating quality food that is as local as possible is very important. A lot of things influence your health. For example, people talk about meat not being very healthy. But which meat? The meat you get at McDonald's or the local cow eating grass just over there? I think having good routines is important. Even if it is the first thing you do in the morning. When I get up the first thing I do is get some daylight into my eyes because it is good for my circadian rhythm. I also filtrate my water because I think it can have great benefits for my body.'

Yet when Haaland took a trip into enemy territory to shop for groceries on his arrival in Manchester, the items in his trolley prompted a fellow customer to compare him to a student grabbing some cheap essentials before starting a university course. It also raised a few eyebrows that he had chosen a Sainsbury's store on Regent Road in Salford – an area that is staunchly wedded to Manchester United. His father and Ivar Eggja accompanied him as he purchased a pack of toilet rolls, two pedal bins, wine glasses, a coffee cafetière, a 50p jar of English mustard and an oversized bottle of tomato ketchup costing £3.50.

When Haaland's first game for City in England ended in a 3-1 Community Shield defeat, it was his critics who were licking their lips. After losing out to City in the race for one highly rated young striker, Klopp had identified another in the form of Benfica's 23-year-old Uruguayan centre-forward Darwin Núñez – and a deal worth £85m was done.

Núñez only needed a 31-minute cameo as a substitute to win the Shield and claim the man of the match award, while Haaland toiled against Virgil van Dijk and appeared rusty in front of goal. He missed two chances inside five first-half seconds, shooting straight at Liverpool keeper Adrián and then failing to get proper contact on Bernardo Silva's cross after the Portuguese midfielder had returned the loose ball into the heart of the box.

Trent Alexander-Arnold gave Liverpool the lead with a 21st-minute shot that took a deflection off Nathan Aké only for Julián Álvarez to scramble home an equaliser with 20 minutes left.

But Núñez turned the contest back towards the Merseysiders, winning the 83rd-minute penalty that enabled Mohamed Salah to put Liverpool back in front after referee Craig Pawson had decided Rúben Dias had handled the Uruguayan's header after a VAR check. Núñez's close-range header sealed the contest in the fourth minute of injury time, although there was still time for Haaland to blast a shot against the top off the crossbar from eight yards with the goal gaping.

Pep Guardiola recalled at the end of the season the vow Haaland made to him after the medals had been handed out,

'I think Erling handled the pressure really well. At 22 years, handling the expectation. When he hears people with no respect he laughs. I remember the Community Shield, we lost 3-1. He missed one clear chance. I remember. All the memes, all the people talked about that. We didn't know each other then as we had just one month working together but he said, "Don't worry, I'll score goals."'

The player himself also later reflected on the missed King Power chances, 'I was the biggest flop after missing an open goal against Liverpool. I have shown since that I'm not. It was good I missed chances in that game. It gave me a reminder that I couldn't be 99 per cent. You have to be 100 per cent and completely focused on your game. When I missed those chances, it meant I was 100 per cent focused for the next week.

'When I was 16 years old, I would bury myself if I missed a chance in training. Now I move on. I think of all the things I've done well. I know I will score some chances and I know I will miss some chances. But I try to look forward.

'I don't watch games back. What is the point? If you think too much it is stressful. I look to the future because that is something you can do something about.'

3

Bright Start

THE EYES of the football world were on Erling Haaland when he exited the tunnel at the London Stadium for his official debut for Manchester City against David Moyes's West Ham.

The East Londoners had done well in 2021/22 by qualifying for Europe and drawing 2-2 in their final home game against Pep Guardiola's team, a result that set up Manchester City to beat – thanks to three late goals in a sensational five-minute spell – Aston Villa the following weekend and take the Premier League title for a second consecutive season.

Yet even from the start the Hammers looked uncertain, allowing Haaland time to familiarise himself with his surroundings before going on to score twice and begin to establish a partnership with Kevin De Bruyne just behind him in a relatively comfortable win.

His performance delighted his manager and already had Manchester City fans convinced they were going to be thrilled watching the big Norwegian over the following months and years.

Success also gave Pep Guardiola an opportunity to round on Haaland's critics after the Community Shield at Wembley with defeat. In a sarcastic way of highlighting their comments he said, 'He was a failure, he will not adapt in the Premier

League,' before stating, 'Numbers, you can analyse it but it is numbers – exceptional. I cannot teach him to score goals. He is an incredible threat in the box ... it is a question of time; he is adapting in the locker room ... the team played well and when we have the ball he can score [but] ... he can improve.' The City manager felt his forwards were 'brilliant' and his players had 'made a lot of passes such that apart from the last five minutes it had been the perfect performance'. He stressed the need to retain the ball.

West Ham's capital rivals Tottenham Hotspur had beaten Manchester City in their magnificent new stadium on the opening day of the 2021/22 season. It proved to be City's only away defeat in the season. There was never any possibility of the Hammers, watched by an all-time record home crowd of 62,443, hitting City for a second opening-day defeat in consecutive seasons.

Haaland at number nine was flanked by Jack Grealish and Phil Foden and once the game settled down it was clear that Moyes's back four of Ben Johnson, Aaron Cresswell, Kurt Zouma and Vladimír Coufal were in for a difficult Sunday afternoon.

Haaland gave City the lead with a perfect left-footed penalty that went into the goal off the inside of the post nine minutes before half-time. He had been brought down by West Ham's substitute goalkeeper Alphonse Areola, on for the injured Łukasz Fabiański. It was the perfect start.

It got even better. Haaland had already combined well in some initial moves with De Bruyne. On 65 minutes the Belgian international's superb pass was knocked home with Haaland's left foot from the centre of the box to the bottom-left corner. It was greeted with massive cheers by the travelling fans and moans from home supporters left frustrated by their side's unwillingness to push forward after the first 15 minutes.

Assisted by captain İlkay Gündoğan, there was another left-footed shot by Haaland from the left side of the box on 76 minutes but this was blocked to prevent him repeating his feat of scoring a Bundesliga hat-trick on his debut for Dortmund in January 2020. Two minutes later he was replaced by Argentinian international Julián Álvarez, also making his Premier League debut, who was immediately into the action and towards the end had a right-footed shot from outside the box blocked. With many home fans having left before the end, when referee Michael Oliver blew the final whistle the away faithful's cheers echoed round a largely empty stadium.

* * *

'Proud moment for me and my family'

Afterwards, Moyes admitted his side were well beaten while a smiling Haaland expressed his joy at his dad having made it to the match before half-time. 'It was a proud moment for me and my family,' he said. He then remarked that he was playing with some 'amazing players' who had given him 'some good balls, that will become even more' due to practice.

On the pass that made his second goal, the debutant was effusive with his praise, 'The pass was the best pass I have ever seen or ever got because I only had to run around the ball and put it in the back of the net. I really didn't have to do anything because the pace is so perfect. When Rodri passed to Kevin I knew I was going to get it. But I didn't expect it to be so good. Passing the ball like that is in Kevin's blood. So we don't speak about it, I just know it's going to happen.'

Although he had been under pressure, Haaland had worked to enjoy the occasion. He admitted to the BBC, 'I tried to go out and enjoy the beautiful game. It is my dream when I was young to live for this and play for this every single week.'

* * *

Number 74

Haaland's debut made him the 74th Norwegian to play in the Premier League. The first was goalkeeper Erik Thorstvedt, whose debut for Tottenham Hotspur was in the pre-Premier League days in 1989, leading to him winning a trophy when the London side won the 1991 FA Cup. Thorstvedt, who was at his best at the 1994 World Cup, later played regularly in the Premier League before a back injury forced him into retirement.

Other Norwegians who followed included Morten Gamst Pedersen, Steffen Iversen, Henning Berg, John Carew, Tore André Flo, John Arne Riise, Ole Gunnar Solskjær, Alfie Haaland and his Nottingham Forest teammate Lars Bohinen, who described the Norwegian influx when the Premier League kicked off in 1992 as the result of the players 'just constantly being professional and producing performances'.

Bohinen said, 'We were a decent generation ... able to adapt quickly. When one succeeded then so did the next and third. It became a sort of snowball effect.' Bohinen and Alfie Haaland were part of a Forest team that finished third in the 1994/95 Premier League. Bohinen described himself and Haaland senior as 'hardworking' and compared this to English players at the time among whom there was 'a bit of a different mentality'.

This attitude has been passed on down the generations. Bohinen's son Emil, who at the time of publication played for Salernitana in Serie A, was born in Derby in March 1999. The midfielder played regularly with Erling at youth levels for Norway including in the 2019 FIFA U-20 World Cup where the forward remarkably scored nine goals in one match, a 12-0 victory over Honduras.

Lars said, 'Just like most of the guys in my generation he's been self-driven and only needed guidance here and there ... the benefit we have as fathers in the game is that we know the pitfalls and challenges that can occur ... we can help them maybe more than a regular father can, but they have to have that inner drive.'

Lars Bohinen, manager of Norwegian top-flight side Stabek as of the summer of 2023, could see in Erling a mix of his mother's Gry Marita Braut's heptathlete skills and dad Alfie's football abilities, 'He has his father's speed and running style and a mixture of physicality from his father and mother. As a package he's got the whole package, he's something out on his own.' Lars saw the finishing technique of Solskjær, some of the skills of Jan Åge Fjørtoft and Tore André Flo plus Jostein Flo's physical presence in Erling whose career he has followed keenly by retaining a deep friendship with Alfie.

If Erling had picked an opponent to kick off his career at the Etihad Stadium then newly promoted Bournemouth would have been ideal as he must have been very confident that he could, at least, grab one goal.

Things though did not quite work out as despite making the opening goal he failed to net and was often a peripheral player during an impressive team performance that confirmed the Premier League champions would again be a tough side to overcome.

When these sides had played at Maine Road early in the 1998/99 season it was in an English third-tier match and Bournemouth did well before Paul Dickov scored the winner. In the return game at Dean Court it ended goalless as City battled to win automatic promotion.

The teams had last faced off in 2020 when City secured a 2-1 victory. Bournemouth were relegated when the season finished but had bounced back immediately and had pulled off quite an upset in the first game of the season by beating Steven Gerrard's Aston Villa 2-1. This was despite being on the back foot for most of that game with only 34 per cent possession. But against the different animal that was City, Bournemouth's defence knew they were certain to come under a severe examination.

The omens were not good as only once in the last 22 years had City lost their first home match of the season. Unsurprisingly, the bookies' odds on a Bournemouth victory were long, at 28/1.

The bookies were to be right. The only goal that the visitors scored was an own goal by Jefferson Lerma, who was attempting to prevent João Cancelo's low cross from reaching substitute Bernardo Silva. That completed the scoring after Gündoğan, De Bruyne and Foden had all scored between 18 and 37 minutes.

Haaland had not even touched the ball but when he did he was deadly using it to set up Gündoğan's opening goal.

De Bruyne made it 2-0 with a dazzling solo strike before Foden ran on to the Belgian's pass to let fly with a shot that Cherries keeper Mark Travers got his body behind, but could not keep out. De Bruyne had scored 15 goals and made eight assists from 30 Premier League appearances in 2021/22 and now had one goal and two assists from his first two games of 2022/23.

In defence, City were never threatened with Ederson called into action once.

Such had been the high expectations surrounding Haaland that it was a surprise to see Guardiola's side score four without their new striker getting any of them. Victory was thus a reminder of the goal threat pulsing right through City's team, and not just from their number nine.

The manager was unconcerned that Haaland had not hit the high peaks of the previous weekend. 'Erling plays the most difficult job in the world', said Guardiola, 'when you are a striker against a team defending like Bournemouth with three central defenders and two players in front of them. So, it is difficult, we know. And we will find many of these situations, but it is just a little bit of a question of time.

'With the right movement and the right tempo, and with the quality of the players that we have behind him to assist him, we will find him – I don't have any doubts about that.'

Before making the trip to Newcastle, Guardiola's current side went off to play a former one, Barcelona, in what proved to be a highly entertaining charity match friendly at the Camp Nou. The teams tied 3-3 with City avoiding defeat after Mahrez scored from the penalty spot following a foul on Haaland, a 73rd-minute replacement for Álvarez who had opened the scoring on 21 minutes only for Pierre-Emerick Aubameyang to equalise eight minutes later.

Frenkie de Jong's 66th-minute goal was levelled soon after by teenager Cole Palmer before Memphis Depay scored the fifth goal of a match that was watched by 92,062 fans. Gate receipts meant a huge amount was raised for the Luzon Foundation and research into amyotrophic lateral sclerosis, highlighted by former Barça goalkeeper Juan Carlos Unzué who was diagnosed with the neurodegenerative disease in 2020.

The game at St James' Park was an opportunity for the Premier League holders to lay down an early marker in the race for the title by making it three wins in a row.

It was an encounter that Haaland must have dreamed of playing in when he watched English football on his TV as a youngster in Norway: his team going a goal up, then 3-1 down, and he scores a real predator's goal to bring them back into the game before they equalise and almost go on to win in front of a raucous crowd.

The fixture has a long history. When the sides had first played each other competitively at St James' Park on 6 January 1894 it was Newcastle United v Ardwick, who, in a bid to overcome financial difficulties, a few short months later became Manchester City, who have twice faced the Geordies in a Wembley cup final, losing 3-1 in 1955 in the FA Cup and winning 2-1 in 1976 in the League Cup.

That FA Cup remained the last domestic trophy captured by Newcastle as of publication but following their takeover, concluded October 2021, by a consortium headed by the Saudi Public Investment Fund, a fresh wave of optimism had swept across Tyneside. Manager Steve Bruce was sacked, Eddie Howe appointed and money was spent in the January transfer window on Kieran Trippier, Chris Wood, Bruno Guimarães and Dan Burn. Further big money moves had followed in the summer of 2022. Newcastle had started the new season by taking four points from their opening two games.

That looked almost certain to rise to seven points when on 54 minutes Trippier, rejected by City early in his career, sent a curling out-swinging free kick, awarded for a foul on Allan Saint-Maximin, beyond Ederson's reach. This was despite Gündoğan giving his side the lead from the spot on five minutes only for Newcastle to equalise through Miguel Almirón on 28 minutes and Callum Wilson to put them ahead on 39. Both goals had been made by Saint-Maximin who rivalled Haaland as the best forward on the pitch.

But Guardiola's men showed their determination and talent to ensure no game is ever lost. On the hour Haaland scored his third Premier League goal and four minutes later millions of worldwide TV viewers witnessed Bernardo Silva equalise to show the new pretenders they still had a lot to learn from the Premier League champions.

* * *

Fast as lightning

Haaland's goal followed a short corner to De Bruyne, who then curled the ball towards the far post. As fast as lightning, Haaland made his way to the front post and superbly turned Rodri's pull-back in on the volley beyond Nick Pope, who did his England chances no harm by making several fine saves.

One of these came as City, searching for an equaliser, had De Bruyne send Haaland through only for Pope to get out quickly to capitalise on a slightly heavy touch, saving the rushed finish with his feet.

The visitors though did draw level soon after when Newcastle gave De Bruyne too much time and space allowing the Belgian to slide a lovely ball between Joe Willock's ankles and as Sven Botman dallied Silva took it well before guiding a smart finish past Pope. With 25 minutes remaining an away victory looked the more likely result, and Haaland might have been the hero but his left-footed shot from the left side of the six-yard box was too high on 78 minutes.

This was two minutes after Trippier had been shown a red card by referee Jarred Gillett for a high challenge on De Bruyne, only for VAR to step in and downgrade it to a booking.

'It was an incredible game, a rollercoaster of emotions through the match,' said Howe afterwards. 'We go 1-0 down and it's the worst possible start against this team because then you have to chase the game and potentially leave open spaces, but the players responded brilliantly to that.'

Guardiola said of Howe, 'He is one of the top managers. He took over the team last season in difficult position [and] circumstances, and [he's] made an incredible effort … they [Newcastle] have everything.' He also praised Saint-Maximin.

* * *

'More passes'

Of his own team, Guardiola remarked that it was a 'proper football game … at 3-1 it was difficult but the team showed who we are'.

But he also offered a word of caution when stating, 'We need to show a little bit more time in the final third, we want to finish the action too early … we need more passes, more passes.'

He felt that De Bruyne, Foden and Haaland were trying to finish things too quickly and of the latter he commented that he was 'more involved than the last game and he had a brilliant goal and had another two or three man-to-man [chances] with the keeper and he made a good assist'.

It had been an afternoon to remember for all concerned.

4

Six Goals in Five Days

WHEN MANCHESTER City returned home for a double-header against Crystal Palace and Nottingham Forest it was time for their new number nine to blast his way to the top of the Premier League scoring charts with hat-tricks in both matches to take his total to nine in five appearances.

Against Palace Erling Haaland's goals helped rescue City from a two-goal interval deficit and against Forest he bagged the first three before being taken off to a standing ovation at 4-0 in a 6-0 victory.

It was little wonder that after the Palace match Pep Guardiola was full of praise for his new striker. But he noted, 'We did not do anything special that he has not done before, Salzburg, Dortmund … he has the sensibility to score goals,' and the Catalan manager singled out the third goal when the big striker had shimmed his body before getting 'in front of the two defenders and [having] the quality to not rush and put it inside'.

Palace had looked on course to win at the Etihad for the second consecutive season when they led 2-0 at the break through John Stones's own goal and Joachim Andersen's driving header.

City had toiled to find any rhythm but on 53 minutes Bernardo Silva cut in from the right and when his low shot took a slight deflection it left Vicente Guaita helpless.

The goal failed to prevent Guardiola then shaking things up by making a double substitution and shifting Phil Foden to left-back and immediately afterwards he had delivered a pinpoint cross which Haaland met with a fine glancing header.

And with the hosts in complete command Haaland, who in the opening period had been well marshalled by Marc Guéhi and Andersen, then took centre stage by prodding in Stones's wayward shot to complete the turnaround.

With Palace chasing the game, Haaland rounded off the scoring by racing on to İlkay Gündoğan's pass before holding off Joel Ward to cap a fine performance with a powerful finish that he celebrated by running towards the City fans.

Little wonder he was given a standing ovation – with Guardiola joining in – when he was substituted on 84 minutes.

These same fans celebrated at full time while Palace boss and former City player Patrick Vieira and his players were left to reflect on what might have been after a gutsy first-half display of stout defending and some excellent counterattacking.

The hat-trick hero was pleased to tell the media afterwards, 'It was a proud moment for me and my family and I'm so happy. Amazing feeling to score a hat-trick. It's about trying to continue what we are doing. It was about small adjustments and we did that and got results. We had to listen to the manager.'

The Norwegian felt it was important that City remained calm and composed after Palace's early goals, 'It's a mentality that we trust each other and we know the chances will come. It's about keeping going. In the end we scored four goals and that's a really good thing. It's a warning that we have to become better, training hard and develop. When we play at home we shouldn't concede early goals. It's about working harder.'

Haaland's return of three goals was a rich reward for a player showing few indications of needing to adapt to the demands of a new manager or country.

Only Diego Costa, with seven goals in his early Chelsea career in 2014, had produced a better goalscoring return in his first four Premier League games than the former Salzburg striker.

Despite their victory, Guardiola felt his side needed 'to improve'. The result put City into second place, two points behind Arsenal who were slowly emerging as the likely title rivals.

Four days later the two-time European champions Nottingham Forest made the trip from the East Midlands to face the Premier League champions for the first time in the top flight since 1999. It was sure to present a difficult challenge.

So it proved with Haaland scoring all three first-half goals before being replaced at 4-0 by De Bruyne on 69 minutes and following which Julián Álvarez, making his full Premier League debut, added two to João Cancelo's wonderful earlier effort.

Haaland thus became the first player to score nine goals in his first five Premier League games and the first player to score nine times in the month of August.

* * *

Doesn't get much better than this! #mancity

'He's brilliant. He's got the lot,' said Forest manager Steve Cooper, while Dion Dublin remarked, 'Man City have the best striker in the world right now. If he stays in the Premier League, every record will be broken.'

With Forest looking to contain City by defending deep, the home side dominated the game from the start. It was a risky approach considering Haaland, up against his father's former team, was bigger, quicker and stronger than any opposition defender.

The opener came when Haaland met Foden's cross. Then Forest goalkeeper Dean Henderson could only find Silva with his pass and when the midfielder sought out Haaland he fed Foden only for the ball to break back to him for a simple tap-in.

The third was similarly straightforward; latching on to a nodded centre from Stones, Haaland headed home his second consecutive hat-trick. After that it was simply a case of could Forest, whose fans stuck with them to the end, keep the scoreline respectable.

After the game the Premier League top scorer was ecstatic, posting, 'Doesn't get much better than this! #mancity' on his Twitter account.

Cooper was rueful afterwards but declared the result would not define Forest, 'First and foremost, they are an incredible team. You have to be more than perfect to succeed against them. But at the same time, I thought we were naive with the goals we gave away in the first half. We made it an even tougher task than it was at the start.

'We didn't give up. We kept going. The massive learning curve in the game is just how ruthless the league is and particularly these teams right at the top. They are brilliant.'

Guardiola spoke of having two strikers who 'are both incredible finishers and in games like today that is so important. Against teams that will defend deep, having the two guys there who have that incredible smell to score goals will help.'

Although he did not directly criticise the three top-class players – Raheem Sterling, Gabriel Jesus and Oleksandr Zinchenko – who had left in the summer for London, Guardiola indicated he was happy to replace them with other players of high quality, which in addition to Haaland and

Álvarez also included Kalvin Phillips and Manuel Akanji, by stating 'They are nice people, nice guys, but sometimes a team has to shake it up a little.'

On his two frontmen specifically, he said, 'I have that feeling that they want to prove themselves to the world in the toughest league in the world. They have that ambition. This is an extra energy for all of us.' Even him? 'A little bit. They change me. They improve me. I have to improve myself in front of them.'

Guardiola, though, believed that his team could improve by dealing better with set pieces and transitions.

5

'Haaland Has Scored More Than You'

SEPTEMBER 2022 was to be a month in which by scoring in all four games Haaland helped his side return from the West Midlands with four points from games at Aston Villa and Wolves while also ensuring that City made a great start in the Champions League with victories over Sevilla and his former club, Borussia Dortmund.

The game at Aston Villa was, however, a frustrating afternoon for the player and his side who failed to build on an early second-half lead.

Despite two goals against Forest, Julián Álvarez was on the bench. Meanwhile, under-pressure Villa boss Steven Gerrard had decided to pack out his midfield and defence and play only Ollie Watkins up front. It was a move that eventually paid off in the 74th minute when Leon Bailey equalised Haaland's goal on 50 minutes to earn Villa a point they possibly deserved in a fixture with a history which dates back to 21 October 1899 when Manchester City, playing in the top flight for the first time, lost 2-1 with local man Fred Williams scoring.

Haaland's tenth goal of the season in his opening six games, which tied him up with a record set by the slightly portlier figure of Micky Quinn of Coventry City, came after Kevin De Bruyne strode down the right to collect a precise forward ball by Silva. The Belgian then delivered a long, looping, swerving cross over Argentinian goalkeeper Emi Martínez and towards Haaland, who, taking to the sky, high-kicked the ball into the net from a couple of yards. A broad smile covered the Norwegian's face when he landed on earth.

Fourteen minutes later he won the ball off Tyrone Mings before laying it off to Bernardo Silva, who on entering the box let Haaland take over again. Haaland spun and shot, forcing Martínez to kick clear. De Bruyne soon after crossed from the right to force Ezri Konsa to head clear under pressure from Haaland as he sought his second to finish off the match.

Soon afterwards, a De Bruyne free kick hit the bar with Martínez beaten before the keeper kept out a shot towards the top corner of the net by Haaland who had been found by his regular midfield supplier. It was surely a matter of time before a second goal. But when it did come it was Villa.

Bailey had missed a sitter earlier. But when Jacob Ramsey picked up a loose ball, drove down the left, looked up and rolled the ball inside for Bailey, the Jamaican opened his body and side-footed powerfully past Ederson, into the top corner.

With four minutes remaining, Haaland had one last attempt to win the game when he played a one-two with Phil Foden down the inside-left channel, but Konsa held his position.

When the final whistle sounded Villa, European champions in 1982 and seven times top-flight champions, had become the second side in 2022/23 to have taken a point off Pep Guardiola's side. The manager told Sky Sports afterwards, 'It was a good game, we conceded just one goal to one shot on target. We were not precise enough on our final touches. The game was in our hands. They defended really well, so we drew. We were better after our goal. They were well organised, but for the way they defended, we created enough chances to score goals. Every game is difficult.'

His opposition counterpart Gerrard remarked, 'I am very proud. The players have come together and put an incredible amount of effort and application into the game. They've followed instructions for the majority of the game. City are always going to have moments, and we had to ride our luck, but this is what we wanted out of the game.' Gerrard was to be sacked in late October.

The fixture at Sevilla three days later, in the opening match of the Champions League group stage, was to prove a much easier affair for City. Haaland accepted the opportunity in full to score twice for the third time against the Spaniards to take his Champions League total to an incredible 25 goals in 20 matches in Europe's number-one competition.

On paper the game looked a tricky fixture, especially as City had won just three of their last 13 visits to Spain. Buoyed though by a strong Premier League start and an emerging almost telepathic partnership between De Bruyne and Haaland, it was immediately apparent that their Andalusian opponents, who had made their worst start in 41 years, were in for a very difficult evening on a night when Guardiola handed new signing Manuel Akanji a full debut at the heart of the defence. He partnered Rúben Dias with John Stones out injured.

The last time Sevilla had tried to stop Haaland he had scored four – two at home and away – of Dortmund's five in a 5-4 aggregate victory in the last 16 of the 2021 Europa League.

Keen to continue his success, he might have opened the scoring on eight minutes but his flick from a De Bruyne cross drifted just wide. It did not take long for the first to arrive with De Bruyne drifting into space on the edge of the box and being found by Foden to sweep a precise cross into the box that, as expected, found Haaland who stretched out to poke home the ball past Moroccan goalkeeper Bono for his 11th City goal. It was just reward for his patience and determination as before Foden found the big man, Haaland made three separate runs into pockets of space in the box and demanded the cross from João Cancelo. There was no disappointment or berating his team-mates – he just continued to seek space for the ball.

It was a surprise that no more City goals arrived in a first half where Sevilla never seriously threatened such that at the interval the home side, who had started with just Isco up front, brought on two attackers in Joan Jordán and Rafa Mir and they were later joined by former Manchester United player Adnan Januzaj. None had any impact on matters, with Mir later substituted.

In comparison Foden was everywhere after the break and got the goal his play deserved on 58 minutes when he was found by Cancelo, Foden shifted one way and back before neatly burying the ball after moving beyond Nemanja Gudelj.

The number 47 then produced some nifty footwork for a shot that Bono should have saved and could only despairingly watch as Haaland snapped up the rebound.

However, any hopes that Haaland, who had made just 19 touches, entertained of starting his City European journey with a hat-trick were to be dashed when he, Foden and De Bruyne were substituted soon after.

Little good this did Sevilla who conceded a fourth when Dias was on hand to power home a Riyad Mahrez cross.

De Bruyne was certain that Haaland was going to continue to be a success, 'I try to do my job, make the right movements and create as many chances as I can. I know one way or the other Erling is going to be there. For the moment, he's scoring the goals and that helps us win games. It's a perfect start for him.

'I think the way he has adapted to us is really good. Outside the goalscoring, there is still another part of the game and I think that part is maybe more tough to adapt to. But it makes it more exciting. If he can adjust to the way we play there, then the level is going to go up. That's what we demand from him. He knows and we know we can still do better but that's only positive.'

Guardiola was also full of praise for the man who had caused him to abandon the false nine that the Catalan manager favoured, 'We make not a good first half, we wanted to attack too quick. When they were playing better, we scored the second one with a brilliant action from Phil. After that, it was easy.

'I think his [Haaland] numbers across his career, not just here, is quite similar. He has an incredible sense of goal. We have incredible numbers in scoring goals, so we want to continue like that.'

* * *

Cruyff v Atlético Madrid; Haaland v Borussia Dortmund

Having thrashed Sevilla, Pep Guardiola's side knew they could put one foot firmly into the Champions League last 16 by beating Haaland's former employers Borussia Dortmund at home in their second group-stage game.

The visitors had beaten Copenhagen 3-0 in their opening match with goals from Marco Reus, Raphaël Guerreiro and Jude Bellingham and had started their domestic competition with four wins and a single defeat, against Werder Bremen at home.

Monies from the departure of Erling Haaland to England had been reinvested in the squad with £25m each on two strikers, German international Karim Adeyemi from RB Salzburg and Ivorian international Sébastien Haller from Ajax, while central defender Nico Schlotterbeck cost around £17m on his arrival from Freiburg.

Funds from the recent £15m sale of Manuel Akanji to Manchester City were to be later invested in Julian Reyerson and Julien Duranville.

The game was to prove a frustrating affair for Dortmund as for the third time in 18 months City came from a goal down to beat them with two late goals. And it was to be that man Haaland who proved to be the difference with a sensational acrobatic winner that sparked off Guardiola's comparisons to two great goalscorers, Johan Cruyff and Zlatan Ibrahimović.

The first half was lacking in any real quality but the match came alive 11 minutes after the restart when Bellingham, who had until then pulled the strings in midfield, nodded home a Reus cross into an empty net. With Mats Hummels thereafter marshalling his defence superbly, such that City had not even registered an effort on goal, it looked like the visitors were going to record a famous victory especially when fortune smiled on them when the outside of the post was hit from a tight angle by Haaland.

Dortmund might still have won if they had possessed a better backup goalkeeper than Alexander Meyer who was slow to react when Stones hit a far from powerful long-range shot on 80 minutes to draw the scores level.

Even a point was then swept away from the German side when João Cancelo produced a stunning cross with the outside of his right foot. Moving away from his markers Haaland, rising high, found the back of the net with an acrobatic left-footed finish on 83 minutes. The joy on the scorer's face at his remarkable finish was matched by the great cheers of the crowd who nine minutes later again rose to applaud their new hero when, in an attempt by Guardiola to run down the clock, he was replaced by Kalvin Phillips.

The manager was quick to draw comparisons with a goal that Cruyff had scored in 1973 against Atlético Madrid and which is rated the best goal the Netherlands genius ever scored for Barcelona. The number nine rose high to meet a cross with the outside of his right foot, followed by wild celebrations. It can be viewed on YouTube. 'It is quite similar to the goal Erling Haaland scored, a really good one,' said the former Barcelona player and manager. Then clearly enjoying himself by combining the past and the present Guardiola went on to bring Ibrahimović, who played under him at the Camp Nou in 2009/10, into the conversation, stating, 'I remember my friend Ibrahimović really having this ability,' before pointing high up into the sky, 'to the roof and Erling is quite similar to that.'

Haaland attempted to downplay his goal, 'In the end we showed what we are. This is what we are and this is how we have to play. I'm proud of the last 20, 25 minutes ... we scored two wonderful goals today – mine was a bit better, honestly. It was a nice cross from Cancelo.'

On another night, Bellingham would have run off with the man of the match award in a winning team. The English midfielder could only reflect on the predictability of the match-winner, 'It wasn't a game to get on the ball and loads of possession. We knew we would spend most of the game without the ball – which we did brilliantly for 75 minutes

'Yeah, I knew it [would be him] to be honest. Not many people know how to stop him. We did a really good job tonight and then he did what he does – unfortunately for us.

'That's Erling, it shows his quality. He doesn't do anything but you just know that if you give him a sniff then he'll score a goal – and that's exactly what he's done. I'm gutted, but that's football against the top teams.'

Being told that when City scored it was their first shot on target, Bellingham said, 'You're kidding me. That's what great teams can do to you. You don't give them a sniff and they score out of nothing and tilt the game in their favour.'

The man who clinched the points had been warmly greeted by his ex-colleagues when he returned to the pitch to shake their hands at the final whistle, and as Haaland and Bellingham left the pitch a TV microphone picked up Bellingham saying, 'For fuck's sake, mate.' They then embraced.

Bellingham was to score for Dortmund against Sevilla in the next group match. He thus became the second teenager to score in three successive Champions League games. When he was informed that Haaland had been the first to do it, Bellingham said, 'Erling – of course. I can't get anything over that geezer at the minute, I swear to God. That sums him up.'

With Queen Elizabeth II dying on 8 September the home match against Tottenham Hotspur was postponed and when City returned to Premier League action 14 days after the Villa game then Wolverhampton Wanderers had set out determined not to give Haaland the sort of space he had enjoyed in Spain.

He thus found it a difficult afternoon, being routinely blocked at set pieces and harried on every occasion he had the ball at his feet. There was, though, never any chance of a surprise defeat as with Jack Grealish showing his true talent and João Cancelo shining at both ends the result was a routine win for Guardiola's side.

When City had first travelled to play at Molineux in the top flight on 3 February 1900 they returned home with a point in a 1-1 draw in which one of the greatest players in their history scored the goal – wide man Billy Meredith, who later went on to score the winning goal against Bolton Wanderers at the 1904 FA Cup Final and thus help City win their first major trophy. The Welsh international's scoring record was a good one and his pace, dribbling, passing and ability to deliver a precise pass and dead ball would have had Erling Haaland purring.

Only 2,000 were present in 1900, some 1,000 fewer than City's travelling support to the Black Country in September 2022; the visiting supporters were soon cheering when Grealish, coming in from a wide position, pushed their favourites ahead after 55 seconds, converting De Bruyne's accurate cross from close range for his first goal of the season. Meredith would have approved.

Haaland, with his 11th Premier League goal, made it two with his right foot on 16 minutes and it was his first from outside the box for City. His shot appeared to be a slight mishit but it was still too powerful for José Sa.

* * *

100 goals in 99 games

He thus became the first player in Premier League history to score in each of his first four away games in the competition. It meant he had scored 100 goals in his last 99 appearances in all competitions since leaving RB Salzburg in January 2020.

Any remote hopes of a Wolves comeback disappeared on 33 minutes when Nathan Collins, a £20m summer signing from Burnley, made a wild, dangerously high challenge on man of the match Grealish that left Bruno Lage's side with the impossible task of facing the Premier League champions for an hour with ten men.

Haaland was to help create the final goal in the second half, feeding De Bruyne whose low right-wing cross was turned in by Foden.

Having scored eight more goals so far in the season than the Wolves team combined, Haaland's feat was lauded by the travelling supporters who taunted those in Old Gold by singing, 'Erling Haaland has scored more than you.'

Guardiola felt that considering his team had played in the Champions League in midweek and were up against a tough team in an early Saturday kick-off he was 'pleased to have taken an early lead' and hoped that Grealish's 'confidence' would be boosted as a result.

'He played really good and strong, a good goal arriving there,' said Guardiola. 'He doesn't lose the ball and a good performance for me. Hopefully he can continue in the national team and come back fit.'

'I did enjoy it,' said Grealish afterwards, speaking to BT Sport.

With most of his squad now set to be on international duty, Guardiola told reporters that many of his backroom staff would be taking a break after a promising start that had left his side with 17 from a possible 21 Premier League points.

6

Six More as City Score 15
in Triple Home Slaughters

AFTER WATCHING Erling Haaland score another two goals against Copenhagen, Guardiola moved as swiftly off the pitch as his new superstar on it to deny that Haaland's contract contained a special €200m release clause for him to join Real Madrid in 2024, saying, 'It's not true ... he has not got a release clause for Real Madrid, or any other team. Am I annoyed by the rumours? No, absolutely not. Rumours, and people talking, you cannot control it – so always we have to worry about what we can control. The important thing is that he has adapted [since joining City] really well. I have the feeling he is incredibly happy here, and this is the most important thing.'

The Norwegian ace had every reason to be happy after another night of plunder. And if it had not been for a magnificent display by Copenhagen keeper Kamil Grabara he would have been even happier with, at least, another hat-trick.

Having been unable to prevent Haaland's first touch from opening the scoring, Grabara then pulled off two magnificent saves from a header and a stunning drive by the number nine. The Pole, though, was left helpless when following his fine save from Sergio Gómez's long-range drive he was let down by his defence among whom no one was quick enough to get to the rebound before Haaland made it 2-0 before the break. At which point Guardiola was good enough to give Grabara, who had just also unluckily conceded a Davit Khocholava own goal, a glimmer of hope by taking his star striker off. The substitution was made with the upcoming Premier League match against Southampton in mind. 'I've got to be honest with you, with Erling what he wants is the same as all of us, which is to win games,' Guardiola said. 'When he made those hat-tricks, it was to win the games. Of course, if he played 45 more minutes, he would get more chances but he has played a lot of minutes, it was 3-0 and the game was under control.

'If the game was tight then Erling would continue to play but it was better to rest and think of Southampton, a team we were not able to beat last season. Hopefully this season we can do it.'

City continued to show that any accusations of them being a one-man team were false and as Copenhagen toiled, they rammed home a further two second-half goals through a penalty from Mahrez who later turned provider for Álvarez, his first in Europe for his new club.

The decision to take Haaland off at half-time was to prove a good decision as while never at his best, his ruthless finish for the fourth goal against Southampton at home meant he became just the second player to score in seven consecutive Premier League games for Manchester City, after Sergio Agüero.

In addition, in a highly one-sided match City became the first team to score at least four goals in five consecutive top flight home games since Tottenham Hotspur in September 1963.

It was all a far cry from the previous occasion when the Saints had last visited the Etihad Stadium when a shot-shy City had been forced to accept a point in a goalless draw in September 2021.

In truth, Southampton were fortunate not to concede many more goals and looked in for a difficult season after losing their fourth consecutive league fixture to put mounting pressure on boss Ralph Hasenhüttl.

City opened the scoring on 20 minutes when João Cancelo weaved through the Southampton defence, evaded James Ward-Prowse's challenge and fired through the legs of keeper Gavin Bazunu.

The lead was doubled when Foden advanced on to De Bruyne's pass and deftly dinked the ball over Bazunu into the far corner after 32 minutes. With so little attacking threat from Southampton that all but ended the visitors' hopes.

On 49 minutes the scoreline became a more accurate reflection when from a tight angle Riyad Mahrez met Rodri's cross with a clinical volley. Under pressure from Mohammed Salisu, Haaland, who had earlier missed several half chances, was unable to get on the end of De Bruyne's cross and then soon afterwards he was brilliantly blocked by Bazunu's dive at his feet as he charged through on goal.

Haaland wasn't going to be denied and he finished off Cancelo's pass with a typically ruthless close-range effort in the 65th minute for his 15th Premier League goal of 2022/23.

There was now no chance of a comeback by Southampton who managed only one touch in the City area and a total of two off-target shots.

Having set such a blistering start, it was something of a surprise that Haaland did not score more than once against the south coast side. Guardiola made fun of this afterwards by stating, 'I am so upset with him. He did not score three goals.' The manager then added more seriously, 'He helped us again, he keeps the ball and fights. I think Erling played really good today.'

When Haaland was unveiled as a City player outside the Etihad Stadium in July 2022, he was asked which team he was most looking forward to. 'I don't like to say the words – but it is Manchester United,' was the reply which delighted the thousands of fans enjoying the Mancunian sunshine and the sight of the world's most coveted centre-forward wearing a sky blue club T-shirt.

Haaland was exactly eight months old when dad Alfie had been poleaxed by a controversial Roy Keane tackle that took him out at his right knee in a Manchester derby at Old Trafford in April 2001. Keane was sent off and hit with a three-match ban and a £5,000 fine, but United had already clinched a third successive title the previous week – while his former Nottingham Forest team-mate would only feature in one more City game that season, lasting 68 minutes of a 1-0 home win over West Ham as the Sky Blues were relegated after just one year back in the Premier League. The midfielder retired the following season after failing to get through another 90 minutes – and although it was an injury to Haaland's left knee that eventually forced him to quit the game, the Norwegian felt Keane's challenge had still played a part. 'If you're in the ground and someone hits you in the right leg, you can still twist your other leg,' claimed Haaland. 'It can get injured and that's what probably happened.'

When Keane admitted in his autobiography the following year that his tackle was an act of revenge for Haaland's reaction to an incident in a game between United and Leeds at Elland Road in 1997 in which the Irishman ruptured his cruciate ligament, he was banned for another five games by the FA and hit with a £150,000 fine. Keane wrote, 'I'd waited long enough. I fucking hit him hard. The ball was there (I think). Take that you cunt and don't ever stand over me again sneering about fake injuries.' Keane is now an accomplished pundit for Sky Sports.

Perhaps it is a coincidence that during Erling Haaland's first season in England, he didn't speak to Keane once on camera. The former United captain was at the Etihad when the striker took a sledgehammer to the team being built by Erik ten Hag by becoming the first City player since Francis Lee in December 1970 to score a Manchester derby hat-trick. In doing so, he became the first player to score hat-tricks in three consecutive Premier League home games. Eleven minutes later, Phil Foden became the second City player in 52 years to score a derby treble as City thrashed the Reds 6-3. Two boyhood City fans with Manchester derby hat-tricks in the same game – and the scoreline flattered the visitors.

Haaland was interviewed by Keane's former United colleague Gary Neville in the build up to the 188th meeting of the two Manchester teams. He warned, 'If we play our game properly, it doesn't matter who stands in United's defence or what the team is. It's against Manchester United, it's a derby, and it means a lot so you have to be focused. It means a lot to our people so you have to be ready.'

There was then a more light-hearted moment when Haaland was asked about some of his favourite things. Favourite band, 'I have to say Oasis.' Favourite drink, 'I like wine a lot, I cannot lie.' Favourite player growing up, 'Zlatan Ibrahimović.' Best goal, 'The one against Dortmund was nice, so was the one against PSG on my Dortmund debut. I think the PSG one.' One player to take a penalty for your life, 'I'd have to say me because I trust myself – or Mario Balotelli. He scored some good ones.' Three people you would take to a desert island, 'Kevin De Bruyne – and also my mum and dad to look after me to cook some good Norwegian food.'

* * *

Hat-trick history

Alfie was there to see his son make a meal of Manchester United. So was Keane – as was former Old Trafford boss Sir

Alex Ferguson. Cristiano Ronaldo started the game on the bench – and stayed there as his team-mates folded. Foden started the rout with a close-range finish before Haaland outjumped Scott McTominay in the 34th minute to score with a header that had crossed the line before defender Tyrell Malacia could hack the ball clear. Haaland's second goal was a thing of beauty, De Bruyne serving up a delicious bouncing cross to the far post for the striker to time his lunge to perfection to divert the ball home on the half-volley. The Norwegian then turned provider, crossing low for Foden to score after De Bruyne had led a counterattack. When Haaland fired a fierce first-time finish past David de Gea from Sergio Gómez's cross in the 64th minute, he became the first City player to score a derby hat-trick in 18,923 days. The last Sky Blues man to score a home treble was Horace Barnes in a 4-1 win at Hyde Road in October 1921, with Welsh legend Billy Meredith alongside him in attack. When Foden scored his third after collecting Haaland's poked pass, City were 6-1 ahead with 17 minutes still remaining.

Guardiola called off the dogs by making four substitutions a minute later – and when United substitute Anthony Martial scored two late goals to add to Antony's long-range strike at the start of the second half, there was a feeling that the visitors had got off the hook. When United manager Ten Hag was asked why he didn't send on Ronaldo, he explained, 'I didn't bring him on out of respect for Cristiano and his big career.' The Portuguese had spent the summer trying to engineer his departure from Old Trafford and would eventually have his contract cancelled while he was playing in the World Cup before taking up a bank-busting £173m-a-year offer from Saudi club Al Nassr. Ronaldo may have found himself making more money than at any time of his career, but with long-time Ballon d'Or rival Lionel Messi later joining MLS side Inter Miami after helping Argentina become world champions in Qatar, it was clear that a new age was dawning – and that Haaland was a big part of it.

'It felt amazing,' said Haaland after he had laid waste to the Red Devils. 'The atmosphere was insane and hat-tricks for me and Phil means it doesn't get any better than that. We only came back from playing for our national teams on Thursday and by Friday I could really feel it. When I got to the training ground, I knew that something special was going to happen. It's hard to explain. You have to experience the feeling to understand the feeling, the aura and the energy around it. It was special. We always want to attack. That is what I love so much about this team.' Asked who would be taking home the match ball, Haaland added, 'Both me and Phil have one – there's one for each half.' Sky Sports were also unable to split the pair, awarding them both a share of the man of the match award.

Former England striker and Ballon d'Or winner Michael Owen had been the fastest player to score three Premier League hat-tricks, in 48 games for Liverpool. Haaland had matched his feat in just eight appearances. Owen paid tribute to the Norwegian in a live TV link-up after the game. 'I said a few weeks ago that you could score 50 goals in all competitions this season and a lot of people laughed,' said Owen. 'Now I am thinking that I was stupid – and that you could get 60 or 70.'

7

Stuttering City Fail to Shine in Front of Goal

HAVING BASHED home goals for fun against Manchester United, Copenhagen and Southampton it was perhaps never to be expected that even a side as good as Pep Guardiola's team could maintain such prolific pace in front of goal. Even the best of teams have periods when scoring can be difficult and so it proved as City failed over the following four games to net against Liverpool, Copenhagen and Dortmund, although in that period they beat Brighton & Hove Albion 3-1 with Erling Haaland scoring twice. Fortunately, having already taken nine points in the Champions League, the goalless draws in Denmark and Germany were sufficient to put City into the knockout stages of the competition they were desperate to win. However, by failing to score at Anfield, Haaland tasted defeat for the first time in a sky blue shirt as City slipped behind Arsenal in the Premier League title race.

Haaland failed to appear for the game in Scandinavia with Guardiola telling reporters afterwards, 'He finished the game against Southampton so tired and didn't recover well. Yesterday was not good, today a little better but not perfect so we decide not to take the risk.'

There was little doubt Copenhagen keeper Kamil Grabara must have been delighted when he heard that the number nine was taking a rest.

Although they should have won the game the Norwegian's absence meant City, who had Sergio Gómez sent off on 30 minutes, were not at their fluent best and they failed to score for the first time in the season but nevertheless qualified for the Champions League last 16.

Technology dominated the opening half with a thunderbolt from Rodri chalked off after referee Artur Soares Dias was invited to consult VAR before ruling that Riyad Mahrez, to the consternation of the City contingent, had handled in the build-up.

Mahrez was then the beneficiary of VAR when the referee awarded City a penalty following another review in which he concluded that Nicolai Boilesen had handled Manuel Akanji's header at goal. Mahrez failed to take advantage as Grabara saved his poor spot-kick.

There was then further controversy when Gómez tangled with Hákon Arnar Haraldsson on the edge of the area. Dias initially allowed play to go on but, after later studying replays, decided to dismiss the left-back. It looked a harsh decision but at the same time the foul that led to a free kick being subsequently awarded may well have been in the box.

Facing ten men, Copenhagen were able to push forward more but they were rarely able to trouble Ederson and with 15 minutes to go both sides seemed content with a point.

Guardiola told reporters that Haaland was not the only player to be feeling the effects of their recent exertions, 'I thought about energy levels. Many players didn't start because they are really exhausted with fatigue and some niggles. Phil [Foden] has also some problems and Bernardo [Silva] was so tired yesterday, he told us. The players I played felt better.'

There was certainly no lack of energy five days later at Anfield. Yet despite an impressive performance it proved not to be Haaland's day in a hot-tempered encounter when a simmering rivalry boiled over once again at the end of which Manchester City lost for the first time in 2022/23.

A single goal from Mo Salah ended Liverpool's recent poor form but only after Foden was convinced he had put his side ahead.

Off the pitch, some City fans embarrassed the club with songs about the Hillsborough tragedy while there were coins thrown at Guardiola by home supporters and Jürgen Klopp was later dismissed for claiming a foul on Salah, who in midweek had returned to form by scoring three in a 7-1 away Champions League drubbing of Rangers.

The only goal, with 14 minutes left, had come from a slight mistake when Alisson's long clearance from a poor City free kick was misjudged by João Cancelo allowing Salah to sprint clear from 40 yards out to beat Ederson, who had earlier defied the Egyptian in a similar situation, to send the Kop behind the goal into ecstasy with a composed finish.

There was though naturally a strong sense of injustice felt by the away side at falling behind because earlier in the half it looked like Foden had scored with a shot that took a slight deflection off Joe Gomez to put his side ahead. The effort was to be disallowed when referee Anthony Taylor was advised to check by the video assistant referee and duly chalked the goal off for a foul by Haaland on Fabinho earlier in the move. On another day the decision might have gone the other way.

With Haaland alongside him, Foden's wild celebrations in front of the City fans had been matched by those he had as a youngster belonged to. Not for the first time, Guardiola was infuriated about a decision that had gone against his side at Anfield and he said so after the game ended, 'We played a really good game but this is a game where there are really fine margins and the mistakes are punished ... We made a mistake and we cannot concede and that's why we lost the game. We played to beat Liverpool today, definitely we played for that. After 1-0 the crowd shouted but we shouted more on the pitch.

'The referee spoke with my assistant and Jürgen and said he was not going to make fouls unless it was clear ... all the game it was "play on" and "play on", except the goal we scored. But we didn't lose the game for that. Nobody knows what would have happened, but it was a moment when we had momentum and control.'

The chalking-off of Haaland's assist confirmed it was not going to be his day as twice in the first half he had been denied by smart saves from Allison, also seeing one shot go narrowly wide and another blocked.

Yet the Norwegian international never gave up trying and later forced Allison into action, when assisted by İlkay Gündoğan – his left-footed shot from the centre of the box was saved in the bottom-left corner.

He was still persisting in his efforts right to the end and in the 96th minute he met Kevin De Bruyne's cross from a central position to force the Liverpool goalkeeper to make a top-right corner save.

Four minutes later, when Taylor sounded the final whistle, Liverpool had beaten City for the second time in the season and Haaland had not scored in an away game in the Premier League for the first time.

City got back on track when Brighton arrived in Manchester and were struck down by a Haaland double that took him on to 17 Premier League goals already. Small wonder therefore that Pep Guardiola was purring about his number nine and praised his hard work in training.

City made three changes from their loss to Liverpool with Nathan Aké, Phil Foden and İlkay Gündoğan dropped to the bench, with Aymeric Laporte, Jack Grealish and Riyad Mahrez returning to the side.

In a fierce first 45 minutes there were so many decisions made at the side of the pitch by referee Craig Pawson that it was easy to imagine the game was back to pre-1891 when the referee actually sat there and was only asked to intervene if the two on-field umpires – one for each side – had, but only if players appealed, failed to agree on a decision.

Robert Sánchez's trip on Haaland was not deemed to have had enough contact by VAR just minutes before Haaland fired his team ahead following a sensational Ederson goal kick that picked him out. Then after muscling Adam Webster aside Haaland rounded Sánchez before netting. VAR did check the goal for a foul, but Haaland was simply too strong for the Brighton defender.

Grealish then had a penalty appeal checked by VAR before Pawson, alerted to a possible foul by VAR, was forced to spend some minutes looking at the pitchside monitor before deciding that Bernardo Silva had been tripped by Lewis Dunk. It was a decision hotly disputed by the Seagulls. Haaland showed no mercy to make it 2-0 with his 17th Premier League goal.

The Seagulls finally broke their three-match dry spell when, soon after Mahrez had passed up a glorious chance, Leandro Trossard on 53 minutes rocketed home following some lovely link-up play with Solly March down the left.

The visitors were good enough to then take control and sensed an equaliser as the game became an end-to-end affair. But with 15 minutes remaining, De Bruyne made sure of the three points with a stunning long-range strike after Silva slipped the ball across the area to the midfielder who, offered acres of space, used it to power home a sumptuous effort.

It meant that since his Premier League debut in September 2015, De Bruyne had scored more goals from outside the box than any other player in the competition in this period.

Guardiola recognised how good it was to have taken all three points against a Brighton side still seeking to get over the departure of manager Graham Potter to Chelsea, 'It was a really tough game, one of the toughest games we can face right now. An incredible compliment to my team, but of course to Brighton for the bravery to play, to come here ... With the ball, they are really good but in the first half, they played with a high press and intensity and we were playing on their terms.

'In the second half, the turning point was when we could've scored three goals with Riyad Mahrez, who normally doesn't miss because he's so clinical and one minute later, we concede. After, the emotions are there and with the quality they have to play. We suffered, but the quality from Kevin made the difference. I didn't see it [the penalty that was given]. I don't know the rules [on timings for VAR]. It's so annoying talking about VAR and things, I'm sorry.'

The City manager praised his number nine, 'His numbers are incredible, unbelievable ... There's no doubt about his quality. He's one of the best I've ever [coached], that's for sure. He's an ambitious player, there's no doubt about that, but most importantly, he helped us win the game.'

According to Brighton manager Roberto De Zerbi his side had 'played one of the most important teams in the Premier League, but the lessons are the same. In the other games, maybe we deserved more points ... but City is a very good team'.

City played their next match three days later when Haaland returned to face Dortmund in Germany. He enjoyed a great reception from both sets of supporters but that was as good as it got in a largely forgettable Champions League match where chances were at a premium.

The exception was another penalty miss. On 57 minutes, Mahrez was felled by Emre Can's reckless challenge, but the winger's subsequent spot-kick was, to the home fans' delight, comfortably saved by Swiss international Gregor Kobel, who later saved Julián Álvarez's first-time volley.

On another occasion, Haaland would have taken the penalty but he had been replaced at the interval. It was revealed later that he was suffering from a fever and had a slight knock. The forward had touched the ball on just 13 occasions and had one shot blocked.

Guardiola had handed goalkeeper Stefan Ortega his club debut while England defender John Stones returned to action for the first time in seven matches after recovering from a hamstring injury. Ortega went on to make several good saves from Karim Adeyemi, Giovanni Reyna and teenager Youssoufa Moukoko in the opening half.

Meanwhile, despite City having 66 per cent of the first-half possession they never seriously troubled Kobel, with Aké's towering header from a Foden free kick that flew just over the crossbar as half-time loomed their best attempt.

Following the penalty miss and with both teams knowing they would go through if no goals were scored, there was little real urgency and neither side created any further chances.

Having seen his side miss 25 of their 80 penalties in regular play since he had arrived in Manchester in 2016, Guardiola admitted there was a 'problem' from the spot.

* * *

Injury concern

When asked if Haaland's knock was serious, Guardiola said 'I don't know right now ... [There were] three things. I saw him so tired. Second one, he had a little bit of influenza in his body. Like João – João had a fever.

'Then the third, he had a knock in his foot. That's why he was not able to play the second half. I spoke with [the medical staff] at half-time and they were a little bit concerned, but I saw him walking more or less normally. We will see.'

8

Bees Take Sting Out of Title Charge Before World Cup Break

HAVING BEEN taken off in Germany, Erling Haaland missed City's next two games away to Leicester City in the Premier League at the weekend and at home to Sevilla in the Champions League in midweek.

Prior to the match against the Foxes, Pep Guardiola told BT Sport, 'I don't know [when he will return from injury]. He has ligament damage. He feels better, we have one more week.'

Even with Haaland out, Leicester boss Brendan Rodgers took no chances, playing five men at the back to combat the Sky Blues' attackers. It was a tactic that against most sides might have been sufficient for the East Midlands strugglers to grab a precious point. However, the silence in the stands when City were awarded a free kick around 25 yards out just after the interval meant Leicester fans rightly feared what might come next. Kevin De Bruyne, who had been the outstanding player on the pitch, lined it up and his stunning shot beat Danny Ward for the only goal.

De Bruyne had now contributed to 12 goals – three goals and nine assists – in as many Premier League appearances this season.

Guardiola felt De Bruyne had under-performed recently, but added, 'He's back. He was not playing good in the last games. [Today] he was amazing. He knows it, he knows it. We need his dynamic, when he can move in different pockets. What can I say about Kevin? Everyone knows him.'

City's victory saw them climb to the top of the table, one point clear of Arsenal who had a game in hand.

As a spectator, Haaland must have been impressed by the performance against Sevilla of 17-year-old Rico Lewis who scored the equalising goal on his full Manchester City debut as Guardiola's side came from behind to beat the six-times Europa League champions in their final Champions League group game.

Trailing to a first-half header from former Wolves and Nottingham Forest striker Rafa Mir, Lewis strode on to Julián Álvarez's 50th-minute pass before driving a powerful shot past Bono.

It was a moment that Bury-born Lewis would, as he became the youngest scorer on a first start in a Champions League match and City's youngest-ever Champions League scorer, remember for the rest of his life. It was such a shame that he subsequently received racist abuse from some Sevilla fans, among whom two arrests were made for the incident.

The home side took the lead when substitute De Bruyne sent a precision pass around the back of the Sevilla defence for Álvarez to run clear and finish. Riyad Mahrez wrapped up the scoring on 83 minutes for a City side who not only finished top of the group but were now unbeaten in 23 Champions League games at the Etihad Stadium.

After learning about how good Lewis was from City's youth coaches, Guardiola had taken the youngster on the pre-season USA tour where he made an immediate impact, 'The players didn't know him before. But you know good players in two minutes. They knew they could rely on him 100 per cent.'

With just two Premier League matches to play before the break in play for the Qatar World Cup, there was the prospect of taking six points at the Etihad from two west London clubs, Fulham and Brentford. In the event two late goals in both matches were to produce dramatic swings in the final outcomes.

In the first against Fulham, substitute Haaland's last-minute penalty was to prove enough to give City victory against a battling Fulham side.

These two teams had faced one another in the third tier in 1998/99 when in a reversal of the away fixture Fulham lost 3-0 at Maine Road. The Cottagers had earlier fallen as far as the fourth tier before being promoted in 1996/97 and then being taken over that summer by the Harrods owner Mohamed Al-Fayed, who had the foresight to persuade former Newcastle United manager Kevin Keegan to take on the chief operating officer role at Craven Cottage later that year, before becoming manager in May 1998. Keegan, one of the few English players good enough to go overseas and enjoy success, winning the Bundesliga and Ballon d'Or with Hamburg, later became the England manager, combining the role with his Fulham role before leaving the west London club to lead the national team full time at the end of the 1998/99 season. After quitting the England post in October 2000, Keegan became Manchester City manager for four years and returned the Citizens to the top flight in 2001/02.

Relegated from the Premier League in 2020/21, Fulham had immediately bounced back and arrived at the Etihad Stadium after an impressive opening to the season. Unbeaten in four games, the Londoners started confidently before falling behind when Álvarez scored on 17 minutes only for City to suffer a double blow ten minutes later. First, Cancelo was dismissed by referee Darren England, for barging down Harry Wilson as the last man. The Citizens had gone 40 league games without having a player dismissed before that. From the resulting penalty, Andreas Pereira equalised for a side missing their top striker, Serbian Aleksandar Mitrović.

With the scores tied at 1-1 and City desperately needing all three points, Guardiola was forced to send Haaland on in an attempt to win the game early in the second half. He seemed to have done that by scoring after getting to the ball in front of Issa Diop only for VAR Stuart Attwell to advise England to chalk off the goal with Haaland deemed to be just the wrong side of Diop's back leg.

Having enjoyed a degree of good fortune and despite their one-man advantage, Fulham boss Marco Silva was still content to try and see out the match in which his side had under 30 per cent possession. This proved to be a mistake because just as the game entered added time American international Antonee Robinson – nicknamed 'Jedi' and set to face England at the World Cup – dangled a leg at De Bruyne and City were rightly awarded a penalty.

Haaland duly stepped forward to mark 5 November by rocketing the ball underneath Bernd Leno with virtually the last kick, on 94 minutes and 33 seconds, to ensure that City won their tenth consecutive match against Fulham. The two extra points meant they rose temporarily above Arsenal, and afterwards the scorer said, 'It's fantastic. I was nervous [for the penalty]. It was one of the most nervous moments of my life, but fantastic. A penalty in the last minute, of course I would be nervous. But it's an amazing feeling. I love it. I have been injured for a week and it is really important to win.

'I want to play every game. It was difficult [to be on the sidelines] but in the end we needed three points and that is what we got. I am so tired, but so happy. You have no idea.'

Pep Guardiola was also delighted, 'My heart is still alive. It was like two games as 11 vs 11 we played really well but we played 65 minutes 10 vs 11 and against Fulham it's not easy.

'With and without the ball then we had to play at the right tempo and in the right moments. It was really good and one of the best experiences we've ever had here.

'You saw how we came together at the end and so it was a great afternoon for us. They missed Mitrović who is really important for them, but the way we played for 65 minutes was amazing.

'We had more chances, more control and showed personality. We played with the right amount of anger and disappointment for many reasons.'

Over the years, Chelsea – who, watching Fulham's success, were set up in 1905 – have proved a much better side than their neighbours at Craven Cottage. Not so in 2022/23 and that was demonstrated clearly when they followed Fulham in midweek at the Etihad in the EFL Cup third round, which Guardiola had never lost in. With Haaland rested there was another opportunity for Julián Álvarez to show his skills in front of goal. As eight-time winners, the first in 1970, City were keen to make it nine and after an even first period in which Christian Pulisic was twice denied by Ortega the home side took advantage when Mahrez drove home an early second-half free kick. Soon afterwards, Álvarez made it 2-0 with a close-range finish before former City favourite Raheem Sterling ran on to make his first appearance against his previous employers.

The England international was, though, unable to trouble a home side that thus extended their winning Etihad run to 16 games in all competitions. The defeat left new Chelsea manager Graham Potter under increased pressure following a poor start to the season.

Football is a results-driven business but City's performance against Fulham had convinced near neighbours Brentford that they could win their game at the Etihad by adopting the exact opposite of Silva's tactics and attacking the home side. It was to bring about a famous victory, arguably the greatest in the Bees' history, which began in 1889.

Not that it meant abandoning their defence or seeking to prevent the ball reaching Haaland.

It was a point highlighted after the match by an ecstatic Brentford head coach Thomas Frank, 'We spoke a lot about how do we eliminate Haaland? We stopped the source into him and when it got into the box, we defended brilliantly.' The result was a fantastic 2-1 away win.

You had to go back to Christmas Day 1937 for the last time City, then the reigning league champions, had lost at home to Brentford. Scottish international Duncan McKenzie and Bob 'The Flying Scotsman' Reid had stung City in a 2-1 win at Maine Road.

With just one win in their last eight and having failed to score in both meetings with City in 2021/22 the signs for the visitors looked ominous before the lunchtime kick-off. Yet with Ivan Toney back after suspension, the Bees were sure to present problems up front.

Having remained on the bench with a slight ankle concern in the midweek EFL Cup victory against Chelsea, Haaland returned to the starting XI.

City went into the match with Guardiola branding the upcoming World Cup as 'crazy' and, with Kyle Walker and Kalvin Phillips injured and worried they may miss the tournament, fearing for his players' wellbeing prior to the 21st game of the season, 'The players have one eye on the World Cup. If you get an injury against Brentford, it's not going to change anything in terms of winning the Premier League or not, but you're going to miss the World Cup.

'I had to tell the guys to be focused a month ago, but now it's around the corner. We play Saturday, and on Sunday they have to be with the national team. I'm pretty sure that will be in the players' minds. I would be the same.'

With Norway not having qualified for the World Cup, Haaland, no doubt to his intense disappointment, had no such fears and was set to watch the early action from a Marbella beach.

Toney, too, was not going to Qatar having been left out of Gareth Southgate's squad. The centre-forward showed what England might be missing in a man-of-the-match performance in which he scored a last-minute winner.

Noting the vulnerability that saw City just scrape victory over Fulham, Brentford went at them from the off and after the visitors had created several chances, Ederson was finally beaten when Toney headed home. Brentford had never previously lost a Premier League match when they had taken the lead on 15 occasions but this was surely their biggest challenge yet.

It was one they rejoiced in with Haaland tightly marshalled in the box and City's wide men blocked from getting the ball towards him.

It was only when four VAR checks – Rico Henry's handball might have been inside the box, Haaland appeared to be hauled down in the area, Gündoğan's cross struck an arm and De Bruyne went down under a challenge – all went against them that the home side sprang into action. They tied the game up when De Bruyne's corner found its way to Foden at the back post who lashed an unstoppable half-volley into the top corner. It was a rare moment of home quality.

Brentford, though, were not overawed and continued to look forward only to be consistently denied by Ederson. The Brazilian was only finally beaten deep in added time when following a swift break Toney swept home Josh Dasilva's cross. There was even time for the striker to almost complete a hat-trick seconds later only for De Bruyne to clear off the line.

Following the game, which ended City's run of 20 unbeaten home matches, Thomas Frank contended, 'This is probably the single biggest ever result, against one of the richest clubs in the world and we have one of the lowest budgets in the division. We're just a bus stop in Hounslow.'

In contradiction to his pre-match remarks, Guardiola was insistent that the upcoming World Cup had no bearing on the result and it was the tactics instead, 'I don't think so … I saw how good they trained, how focused they are, but tactically we had problems to control, we struggled to win the long balls from [goalkeeper David] Raya to Toney. You have to be brilliant in smaller spaces and we weren't able to do it.

'The better team won. We had a lot of problems, we couldn't high press because of the balls [from] keeper to striker. In this process we could not win any ball because when Toney flicked the ball he created problems, when Toney kept the ball and played with the three players in the middle he created problems. And we could not regain the ball in the end.'

Guardiola also offered an injury update on Haaland, 'I don't know. He made a good effort but he feels it a little bit. We thought the game would be similar and we needed a target man there for the crosses.'

Defeat in the final match before 16 of City's players headed out to the Middle East was a big blow to hopes of a third consecutive Premier League title, with Arsenal sitting five points clear.

The next match looked a long time away at 47 days. Still, it was a lot better than in 1937/38 because, despite finishing the season as the top scorers in the First Division, the 1936/37 league champions were relegated. It is certainly Manchester City's most unique, unwelcome record.

* * *

Guardiola extends contract

Eleven days into the World Cup break City made their most important signing of the season when Pep Guardiola, the second-longest serving Premier League manager behind Jürgen Klopp, signed a new two-year contract extension.

According to the former Barcelona and Bayern Munich boss his decision to put pen to paper was 'just the confirmation of how comfortable we are, the club and myself, again, like signing at the beginning. I cannot say thank you enough to all the club to trust me, to give me the opportunity to do my job as best as possible, but that is just papers. We have to be comfortable with the team, with the club, otherwise it makes no sense. The incredible, beautiful memories we had together and still have the dream to achieve more. I know what the club wants. I will fight for that with our players and staff to do our club as best as possible.'

9

Who is Erling Haaland and How Did he Become a Striking Viking?

FOOTBALL IN Norway has a long history and in 1902 the Norwegian Football Federation (NFF) was founded and established the Norwegian Football Cup as the main knockout competition nationally. Today's winners qualify for the UEFA Europa Conference League.

In 1908 Norway played Sweden in Gothenburg in their first international. Despite taking an early lead the visitors lost 11-3. Four years later they entered the Olympic Games but were eliminated following defeats against Denmark and Austria. Two years later the NFF established a national league with six clubs.

At the 1936 Olympics, Norway took the bronze medal in the football after beating Poland 3-2 in the third-place play-off match.

A year later, the League of Norway, then known as Norgesserien and divided into 11 groups from eight regions, was formed with a championship play-off final deciding the national champions.

Norway's top flight is known as the Eliteserien and contains 16 clubs nationally with a subsequent pyramid structure stretching down to the Tenth Division.

In 1981 Norway's team of part-time professionals shocked the world by beating England 2-1 in a World Cup qualifier in Oslo. When Bryan Robson gave England a 14th-minute lead a comfortable victory looked certain, but the Norwegians battled back to snatch a 34th-minute Roger Albertsen equaliser that gave them the momentum to go on to what was considered the greatest triumph in a football history that had mostly been about taking part. Hallvar Thoresen took advantage of dithering in the England defence in the 40th minute to force home what proved the match-winning goal. It was a humiliating defeat to rank with the 1950 World Cup loss to the United States.

The game lives on through the delirious words of Norwegian television commentator Bjørge Lillelien, who switched to English as the final whistle blew, 'Lord Nelson! Lord Beaverbrook! Sir Winston Churchill! Sir Anthony Eden! Clement Attlee! Henry Cooper! Lady Diana! Maggie Thatcher – can you hear me, Maggie Thatcher! Your boys took one hell of a beating! Your boys took one hell of a beating!'

Thoresen needed to leave Norway aged 19 to play professionally for FC Twente, where he won the KNVB Cup in 1977, and later three titles with PSV Eindhoven. He played 50 times for his country but never played professionally in it as professionalism only really began in Norway in 1992.

* * *

Bryne FK

Alf-Inge (known as Alfie) Haaland was born in 1972 in Stavanger, Norway's oil capital, but was brought up in nearby Bryne, a town with a population of around 7,000, with many great nearby beaches on the west coast of Norway and surrounded by rich, productive farming areas. Schools were within walking distance. Bryne FK, formed in 1926, was known for its youth football and Alfie joined when he was still in primary school. He played football outside in the summer months from April to October before being forced indoors between October and March, when daylight can be as little as five hours, to play handball and some tennis.

He recalled, 'Bryne were an amateur club but, like a lot of other clubs in the Norwegian Premier League, they were gradually becoming more professional ... At school, I combined my studies with playing football, and then, after school, I'd go along to the club to train. Erik Mykland, the former Norwegian international, went to the same school as me. I stayed at school until I was 16, then went to college for three years, studying the equivalent of A-levels in order to get a good education behind me.'

Alfie progressed through the various youth teams, spending two years at each level, before making his senior debut in 1989 aged 17, the year after the club had been relegated from the top flight. Bryne had won their solitary Norwegian Football Cup in 1987 and finished as league runners-up in 1980 and 1982.

'I came on for the last ten minutes of the game [to make his debut] but I don't remember being particularly nervous; when you've grown up with a club like that and trained with them nearly all your life it means you're well prepared when you make your first appearance for them. It was the club I'd always wanted to play for,' Alfie said.

Alfie was a regular first-teamer between 1990 and 1993 and in those four years Bryne made the play-offs three times but lost out on each occasion.

Over 100 years of Football League history in England was to be overturned in the summer of 1992 when, in an ongoing argument over TV money, the 'Big Five' – Manchester United, Liverpool, Everton, Arsenal and Tottenham Hotspur – had, by threatening to quit the Football League, forced the FA to back the new breakaway Premier League.

Determined to win the battle for exclusive coverage, Rupert Murdoch's offer of £304m was accepted. Sixty live games – on Sunday afternoons and Monday evenings – a season of Premier League football were to be shown on Sky Sports from 1992 to 1997. The monies were to be exclusively shared among clubs in the new competition and, meanwhile, the BBC came back as a junior partner within the deal allowing the return of *Match of the Day* and *Football Focus*.

Armed with a large wedge of cash the richer clubs could afford to recruit some of the world's best players by paying them large salaries.

The number of foreign players in English football has rocketed since 1992 when there were just 13 players from outside the British Isles and Ireland involved in the Premier League's opening fixtures. The promotional advertisement for the revised top league, which featured one player from each of the 22 clubs, included only one foreigner – Wimbledon's Dutch goalkeeper Hans Segers. Today, well over 100 different nations have been represented on the pitch in the Premier League era.

Scandinavians have, of course, always had a soft spot for English football. As early as the 1920s the Norwegian daily press was providing coverage of the English game and as most people live in the countryside, they have tended to support whoever they see on TV. English football first began to be broadcast live to Norway in 1969 when viewers saw Wolves take on Sunderland at Molineux in a First Division match. Nowadays a lot of people support their local clubs too.

Alfie Haaland was set to be one of the first pioneers when Brian Clough tried to sign him in October 1992 for Nottingham Forest. By the time protracted negotiations were completed in December 1993 and he arrived at the City Ground the legendary manager had left Forest following relegation and had been replaced by Frank Clark. Forest, European Cup winners in 1979 and 1980, made an instant return to the Premier League, where they remained for three seasons.

After Forest's relegation, Haaland then stayed in the top flight and signed for Leeds United. He was employed over three seasons as a utility player at the back and in midfield in a side that reached the UEFA Cup semi-final in 1999/2000 and also qualified for the Champions League. One of the highlights was scoring in a 3-1 defeat at Liverpool, a feat later achieved by Erling, born in Leeds on 21 July 2000.

At the time of Erling's birth his dad was a Manchester City player as in early June 2000 he had been signed for £2.5m by Joe Royle who had been chasing him for almost two years and during which time City had risen from the third tier to the top flight, a remarkable feat.

'I've been a big admirer ... he's a versatile player who can play anywhere in midfield or defence and he will be an important part of our Premier League campaign,' said Royle. This was to prove tricky for City who were to be immediately relegated. Haaland was not around for the final match as he had been left crippled by a horrendous tackle on his right knee by Manchester United midfielder Roy Keane in the derby match in April 2001. Keane was nursing a grievance for a tackle on him in 1997 during Haaland's time in West Yorkshire which left the Irishman out of action for a year with an injury to his anterior cruciate ligament. The only difference was that the Norwegian international, a member of the 1994 World Cup squad in the USA, had not set out to crock his opponent. Haaland was only able to make four more City appearances – one in the FA Cup and three in the First Division from which promotion was won with a then-record 99 points.

Haaland's five-year contract expired at the end of the 2003/04 season, when he retired from top-class football. He considered following the example of England under-21 international Ian Knight who had won an out of court settlement against Chester City following a Gary Bennett tackle on him that ultimately ended his career.

These plans were abandoned because the Norwegian had previously revealed that he had been playing with an injury to his left knee and that Keane had not caused his long-term medical problem.

Even so, this showed that Alfie would stand up for his rights and knew the pitfalls that might arise from a professional football career. This would assist his son as he grew up.

Alfie, though, was not finished as a footballer. Having returned home in 2003, he came out of retirement to play once in 2011 for Bryne's third team in the Norwegian Fifth Division. He was booked in the game.

He then made six appearances, scoring once for Rosseland in the Fourth Division in 2012. He played twice in 2013 by which time Erling, aged 13, had been demonstrating he had the talents to follow in his dad's footsteps. But did he also have Alfie's dedication and determination?

Alfie had encouraged Erling to play the sport he loved and at more or less the same age as his dad, the youngster joined Bryne. Facilities had improved dramatically in the intervening 30 years especially as a result of the construction in 2005 of an indoor grass-covered pitch. Local youngsters could now play throughout the harsh winters.

From the age of five onwards, Erling could be found every weekend playing hours of football for fun with 20 of his friends, all with mixed abilities.

Even before England had taken up the academy system where boys as young as eight could be attached to a club from 1998 onwards, Norway had been doing so. In 2000 and with British football again going through one of its many crises about being unable to develop young talent, Scotland manager Craig Brown had remarked, 'Which countries should we take our lead from in terms of youth development? France have got the model system. Norway is also very good. Both these countries have invested heavily in facilities – almost every town there now has a beautiful playing field.'

Even today, Norway remains in the forefront of the revolution in youth football. For nearly half a century, Oslo has hosted the Norway Cup. Billed as the largest youth competition in the world, over 2,000 teams compete.

From the start Erling had caught the attention of Alf Inge Berntsen, one of many local coaches to give an outlet to Norwegian youth. Norwegian clubs had taken the care to invest in good coaches who could instil a sound training regime with the emphasis on developing players with both skill and attitude.

'He was five when he joined indoor training with a group one year older,' Berntsen told Goal.com. 'His first two touches led to goals. He was very, very good from the first moment, even though he hadn't played in the club before. He started playing in his own year group, but because he was so much better than the others, we immediately pulled him up to under-six.'

According to Berntsen, 'Erling was a little smaller than his opponents because he was a year younger. But even if his opponent was significantly taller, he kept scoring goals. When he was 11 or 12, we knew he would go far. We already knew back then that he had what it takes to be a youth international.'

Berntsen provided a constant variation of training so that all his trainees could learn many different body movements. He recognised that Erling was fast and had good body control from an early age.

The youngster was also very hardworking and a pleasure for coaches to work with as he was constantly smiling, loved playing football and scoring goals and while he always respected his opponents he refused to be intimidated by them even if they were bigger and stronger.

What also must have helped was the attitude of Alfie who according to Berntsen, 'Always let Erling train with us, without any pressure. He never told us what to do, he simply let his son grow up alone, with a large group. Later they made smart choices with the chosen clubs.'

A YouTube compilation of some of Haaland's matches in his early teenage years shows him constantly taking control of the ball with both feet before creating the space to find a team-mate or more generally hitting a shot from all angles towards goal. Some of the opposing young goalkeepers are seen wondering just where the ball has gone as it whistles past them. There is an ongoing debate that artificial pitches produce a faster-paced, more technical game and it could be that the coverage of Haaland at this time confirms that.

Haaland was given the chance to put himself up against senior footballers when at age 15 during the 2016 season he was selected in the first-team squad by under-fire coach Gaute Larsen for Bryne in a Norwegian First Division (the second tier) match at Ranheim, an alliance sports club from Trondheim with sections for football, handball and track and field athletics, on 12 May 2016.

On an astroturf pitch, he came on as a substitute wearing number nine and immediately ran into space down the right before beating his man on the outside and crossing the ball with his right foot towards the six-yard box. With no one coming in it was cleared by a defender.

Soon afterwards, a similar movement down the right sees the teenager play the ball into an empty space directly in front of goal six yards out but with no Bryne forward to be seen the ball was again booted to safety.

Then followed a high ball over his head and when he chased it down a defender hit it long before Haaland used his chest well to bring the ball down to move it on to the man outside him on the left wing. The youngster was clearly not intimidated by the older men he was competing against. A handful of spectators were watching on.

Just before the finish the ball was pushed into him down the right and as he slipped, he somehow managed, whether deliberately or not, to push it backwards around 30 yards out. It was picked up by the defender who moved forward to find an attacker who then found Haaland who from 25 yards turned and shot but it was easily blocked. When the final whistle sounded the new man must have been looking forward to the future.

That was not going to include Larsen, now in his fourth season as Bryne manager, as after winning just one and drawing three of the opening seven First Division games he was dismissed.

Youth coach Berntsen was promoted to caretaker boss and the interim manager handed the teenager his home first team debut.

The new appointment did not make a massively significant improvement. Unable to score goals, Berntsen's side took five points from nine games. He resigned and, in the aftermath, Bryne sought to bolster their attack with new signings Bajram Ajeti and Marius Helle, but come the end of the season they were outside of the top two levels of Norwegian football for the first time since 1973. In Haaland's first campaign, during which time he turned 16, his team had been relegated. Furthermore, he had played – initially out wide before being moved inside to his favoured striker's role – 16 games and failed to score.

Yet Bryne's struggles had benefitted the school student as it meant he played first-team football earlier than would have, otherwise, been the case. 'It was a great experience for him to understand his best movements and prepare his body physically for what was coming. It was a good education for him,' stated Berntsen.

It was much easier when the teenager played for Bryne's reserves. In 14 appearances he averaged more than a goal a game at 18. He was also scoring a lot of goals for Norway under-15s and under-16s.

At around this time Alfie asked Erling, 'what he wanted – and it was clear he wanted to be a professional. I told him a lot of people his age wanted to become a pro – but not everyone wants to pay the price you pay for following your dreams. It's a lot of hard work. That's the only way to reach your goal.

'When Molde showed their interest, it became quite exciting. In retrospect, that was definitely the right step to take.'

Being picked for Norway's under-15s was a big break as with the nation being vast, it is difficult for the top-level sides to keep track of the promising youngsters.

There he met Gunnar Halle, a team-mate of his father at Leeds. Halle was impressed but uncertain that Erling could make it to the very top because of his gangly physique.

'He was without a doubt a good player who scored many goals, but was by no means outstanding. His physique and coordination still had to develop at that time. That he would one day become a superstar was still a long way off,' Halle said later.

The point was made clear by Astor, Erling's older brother, who made it apparent that it was only later that Haaland developed physically, 'It was during the Molde era that he started to grow. Suddenly, he grew about 20cm in one year and put on 20kg. He was now the same size as me.

'No one could have imagined what he would one day be capable of. Today he benefits from the fact that he had to learn to read a game back then because he was not as assertive as he is today.'

Haaland's form was good enough to see him be offered a trial by Hoffenheim 1899 of Germany's Bundesliga. To have signed for such a club would have required waiting for a first-team opportunity.

* * *

Molde FK and Ole Gunnar Solskjær

After discussing the matter with his dad, Erling looked to find a team where he would get a swifter opportunity to play in a better league. He chose to move 400 miles north to play for Norwegian top-flight side Molde, one of the most successful clubs in Norwegian football, under Manchester United legend Ole Gunnar Solskjær.

Berntsen was not surprised by the transfer in February 2017, 'He just didn't care who was watching. He didn't care whether he played against his friends just for fun or for the national team. He was never afraid. He always had respect for his opponents, he just never cared who they were.

'Switching to Molde was not a big deal, it was a normal process. He was just too good for the team. The next logical step was Molde.'

Known because of its lush rose gardens as The City of Roses, Molde, which is framed by mountains on the shore of the Romsdalsfjord, has over 30,000 residents. The football club was formed in 1911. By 2017 it had won the Eliteserien three times including in 2012 and 2014 to earn a place in the Champions League qualifying rounds.

Most of Haaland's new team-mates were Norwegian including Ruben Gabrielsen, Petter Strand and Eirik Hestad. Overseas players included Sweden's Andreas Linde. The new man made his debut on 26 April 2017 in a Norwegian Football Cup match against Volda TI, scoring in a 3-2 win.

On his league debut as a 71st-minute substitute on 4 June against Sarpsborg 08, Haaland was yellow-carded almost immediately. He notched his first league goal and later added a 77th-minute winner against Tromsø.

There was then a touch of controversy after he bagged the winner in a 3-2 victory against Viking FK and celebrated in front of the opposing fans with his team-mate Björn Bergmann Sigurðarson criticising him for doing so.

Haaland finished his first season at Molde with four goals in 20 appearances.

When the following campaign kicked off against Sandefjord, he scored on 63 minutes in a 5-0 home win, the biggest home league win during the season. The visitors had made a 383-mile trip north and it must have been a long journey home. Away games for Norwegian fans are lengthy with Molde's game at Tromsø involving a 1,672-mile round trip.

There was a heavy 4-0 defeat for Molde at Rosenborg, the most successful club in Norwegian football, before the youngster scored a penalty in a 2-1 defeat of Lillestrøm before a crowd of 7,411 at the Aker Stadion.

Then on 1 July 2018 his side won 4-0 at Brann in Bergen. Showing pace, strength, one-on-one finishing and composure, he scored all the goals, including a penalty, in the first 21 minutes before later being taken off on 60 minutes by Solskjær who gave him a huge pat on his back.

His success came as a bit of a shock. 'Training the week before the game was so poor. Every pass was a bad pass. I lost the ball every time I got it,' Haaland admitted.

'But two days before the match, Ole Gunnar said, "I think this match will suit you so you're starting." I just thought, "What the fuck is wrong with him? Now I have to deliver."

'It was a pivotal moment for me. I realised that even if you are absolutely miserable in training, it can turn with a click of your fingers.'

Watching the game were scouts from top European clubs including Manchester United's Tommy Møller Nielsen.

Haaland was unaffected by the attention, saying, 'It's nice that they are here. I'm a Molde player, so I need to focus on performing here. It's that simple.'

Solskjær was reminded of a Manchester United number nine, 'He can become a top striker for sure ... He reminds me of the type of striker [Romelu] Lukaku is. There is a lot of interest in him. We have had offers from good clubs this year but we rejected them.'

The young player continued scoring with two in a 5-1 win over Vålerenga, a penalty as Brann were beaten by the same score, one in a 3-1 defeat to Stabaek and another in a 3-2 home defeat against Ranheim. His two goals against Strømsgodset saw Molde win 2-1.

He then scored the only goal at Bodø/Glimt and scored the last goal in a 2-2 draw against Sarpsborg at home. Molde ended the league campaign in great form, winning eight and drawing once, but their indifferent results in April and into May, when just five points from six games were taken, meant they ultimately ended in second place, five points behind Rosenborg.

* * *

European debut

In the 2018/19 Europa League qualifying rounds Molde first overcame Northern Ireland's Glenavon 6-2 on aggregate.

Haaland's best moment came early on in his European debut in the first leg on 11 July 2018 when his clever pass put Eirik Hested, who scored Molde's goal in a 2-1 defeat, through only for the striker to shoot tamely at Jonny Tuffey. Eight days later Haaland was left out as Hested scored three in a 5-1 win.

Haaland scored from the spot on six minutes in a 3-0 home-leg success against Albanian side Laçi. He was replaced by Petter Strand on 74 minutes. Molde then won the away leg 2-0 with Strand scoring. Haaland was not in the squad.

After a 0-0 draw at Easter Road in which Haaland did not play, Molde beat Neil Lennon's Hibernian, the first British side to play in Europe in 1955/56, 3-0 at home with Haaland grabbing two, one a penalty. Having been fortunate to remain level after a few scares the Scottish team gifted Haaland the opening goal on 35 minutes when they allowed Ruben Gabrielsen to lose his markers from a deep free kick to head across goal where Haaland had the simple task of nodding home at the far post.

The watching scouts from Salzburg who had made an £8m bid for Haaland must have been slightly anxious that if he continued in such a fashion, bigger clubs might come calling.

Haaland then turned provider. It was again not pretty from Hibs' perspective. Hestad galloped into the box from near the halfway line and his strike partner was able to outmuscle his marker to prod the ball into the path of Fredrik Aursnes for an easy tap-in. With nine minutes remaining it was all over as a deflected effort fell to Haaland, who after netting was replaced by Leke James two minutes later and was met by a beaming, hand-slapping Solksjaer.

On 23 August, Molde travelled to Russia to face Zenit Saint Petersburg, winners of the UEFA Cup when they beat Rangers at the City of Manchester Stadium in 2007/08, at the 67,800 capacity Krestovsky Stadium. A crowd of 40,677 turned up to watch Molde.

Having taken the lead through Hestad in the opening half, Molde faded in the second, during which Haaland was replaced by Stian Rode Gregersen on 78 minutes, to concede three in the final 20 minutes.

The contest appeared over when Daler Kuzyayev opened the scoring on 21 minutes in the second leg to make it 4-1 on aggregate. But after Hestad netted on 65 minutes the Russians were left hanging on when Haaland, who had just been booked 90 seconds earlier, composed himself before scoring from the spot on 77 minutes. A crowd of 5,414 watched what was a thrilling match.

The season ended with Haaland having made 17 league starts and eight substitute appearances, scoring 12 goals, four more than Hestad. His strike partner netted seven in seven games in Europe to take his season's total to 15, one fewer than Haaland whose four goals in Europe took him to 16 overall. Just turned 18, the young man was not hanging around and his decision to play for Molde had proved justified. He was awarded the Eliteserien Breakthrough of the Year Award.

10

Striking a Strong Note
in Mozart's Birthplace

AGED 18, Haaland's form at club and international level meant it was inevitable he would leave Norway to play for a bigger club abroad.

Formed 1933, SV Austria Salzburg, three times Austrian Bundesliga champions, had been bought out by Austrian energy drinks company Red Bull GmbH in 2005 who renamed the club to FC Red Bull Salzburg and changed its colours from violet and white to red and white. The changes resulted in some fans forming a new club, SV Austria Salzburg.

The new RB Salzburg owners immediately pumped considerable resources into the club and hired veteran Italian coach Giovanni Trapattoni, together with his former player at Inter Milan, German World Cup winner Lothar Matthäus, as co-trainers. The 2006/07 title was won by a considerable margin. It was the first of eight championships in 12 seasons with five consecutive successes from 2013/14 onwards.

In 2017/18, RB Salzburg had been eliminated in the Champions League qualifying rounds. Although they then reached the Europa League semi-final the ambition was to reach, at least, the Champions League group stage.

In August 2018 it was announced that Erling Haaland had agreed to move to RB Salzburg who on New Year's Day

2019 paid £8m to sign the striker on a five-year contract from Molde. The Austrian giants had first spotted Haaland in a Norwegian under-16 fixture and because there were few recordings of his matches at home, they had the game recorded and later analysis confirmed he was just the sort of young player they wanted.

Salzburg's philosophy had changed in 2012 when Ralf Rangnick arrived as director of football, the first of several roles the German held with Red Bull, who had set up a club in the former East German city of Leipzig in 2009.

Salzburg's focus switched to buying and developing youth by rarely signing players over the age of 23. The system's effectiveness has been highlighted by the players who later moved on for substantial fees. Salzburg say they first search for local young talent before extending the pool to European players over the age of 16 – those that top clubs might be hesitant to take on. From the age of 18, Salzburg then seek to sign players internationally.

In 2017, Salzburg signed teenager Patson Daka and he helped them win the UEFA Youth League before becoming the first Zambian player to score in the Champions League group stage.

In June 2017, Enock Mwepu, aged 18, joined the club and during the 2019/20 season he established himself among Salzburg's starting 11. He made his debut in the Champions League at Liverpool. Mwepu later joined Brighton & Hove Albion.

On the pitch, RB Salzburg adopted a counter-pressing legacy. From 2017 to 2019 they were managed by Marco Rose who never lost a home game.

Certain that Haaland would suit their style of play, RB Salzburg began a long-winded pursuit of the young Norwegian forward. According to the club's sporting director Christopher Freund, 'Our scout contacted him and his father. It is a great advantage to be in personal contact with a talent and their guardians before any other potentially interested club. It also helps that we have a very good reputation for developing talents.

'That was in 2018. He seemed very focused, intelligent and self-confident to me. He knew exactly what he wanted,' which no doubt included the knowledge, explained Freund, that Salzburg aim to facilitate 'as much playing time as possible in the professional game very early on', 'They come into a system that is perfect for young talents and helps them to develop and show their qualities as best as possible.'

'They come to Red Bull Salzburg as they know they will get the opportunity at some time to move to a big club, if they perform. That's why we are already looking for the next generation.'

Prior to Haaland's arrival the Austrian club had signed earlier in the season Zlatko Junuzović, Jasper van der Werff, Jérôme Onguéné, Phillip Kohn, Darko Todorović and Ousmana Yeleen, all for undisclosed fees.

Following the huge media interest in Haaland's signing there were great expectations. But, despite doing well in his preparations over the winter break and in friendly games, he had to bide his time as he was a spectator for most of his initial six months.

'The club were determined to sign me. Christoph [Freund] and Johannes [Jahns, the club's players relation manager] gave me this feeling in every conversation and pointed out to me the way things are done and the opportunities here in Salzburg. It was clearly communicated to me that the first half of a year would be difficult for me and I would need the time to settle in, but from the summer I should be able to take a leading role in the team. The club bosses kept their word, and that impressed me – as it's not always the case in football. I was happy to accept their plan, and it has paid off completely,' said Haaland.

Prior to the 2018 Winter Break, RB Salzburg had won 15 and drawn three of their 18 league fixtures, qualified for the Austrian Cup quarter-finals and also reached the knockout phase of the Europa League after earlier failing to make it beyond the Champions League group stage.

Haaland's transfer to Salzburg, Mozart's birthplace, saw him move to a compact and comfortably well-off city with lakes, parks and easy access to the surrounding mountainous countryside. Two city parks are featured in *The Sound of Music*.

For Haaland, Salzburg was a perfect place to go sightseeing and relaxing off the pitch. On it he was all action, scoring in consecutive victories in friendlies against USK Anif, Blau-Weiß Linz and Chinese Super League side Beijing Sinobo Guoan.

His first competitive outing came on 17 February 2019 when he replaced Israeli international Mu'nas Dabbur on 71 minutes in a 2-1 Austrian Cup win at Wiener Neustadt and later in the season he also replaced Dabbur in a 6-0 semi-final success in the competition against Grazer AK. Salzburg were to take the trophy by beating Rapid Vienna 2-0 in the final but Haaland was not part of the matchday squad.

Seven days after his first competitive outing and listed at number 30, Haaland made his league debut as a substitute by coming on for Japanese international Takumi Minamino on 76 minutes against Rapid Vienna. Salzburg eventually lost their first league fixture of the season 2-0. The defeated side remained 11 points clear of second placed LASK.

The young player did get on the field against Napoli in the second leg of the Europa League last 32 match. Trailing 4-2 on aggregate he again replaced Minamino with four minutes remaining. Despite helping his side score a third they were eliminated.

He was then either an unused substitute or not selected over the following months as Salzburg closed in on the title, which they had won when he played at home against LASK on 12 May 2019 for his full debut and in which he, assisted by Austrian under-21 international Patrick Farkas, scored within 13 minutes of the start in a 2-1 victory.

The season ended with Haaland having made just one start and four substitute appearances. He had scored once but he was confident that the 2019/20 campaign would be a great one.

Interviewed in late October 2019, Haaland was quite frank when stating, 'I was sure that this season would be my season. I'm aware that I am very important for the team and I can help them. So far, I have been able to do that. We have a hungry team, we are highly focused in our play, and we are all proud and appreciative of what we have here in Salzburg. We can really achieve a lot together in Europe and Austria this year and make a big statement.'

* * *

Amazing leap

Alfie had helped a lot. Erling said, 'The combination of what he offers is ideal. He covers all important areas and helps me in every situation … It's good that he really likes Salzburg and often comes here. I really have the feeling that I have a lot of people with great character around me.' Erling also revealed, 'For many years I was the record holder for under-fives in the standing long jump. I have no clue how the idea came about to keep a record of that kind of thing, but I was apparently much better than all the others. It has carried on like that through my life and I am trying to carry that into football now.'

The 19-year-old remarked that aside from golf he was good at most sports.

Despite admiring his dad, he never entertained any thoughts of being a defender or midfielder, 'That was pretty boring for me. I wanted to go forward all the time and score goals. It was soon clear I was going to be a striker.'

In June 2019, Jesse Marsch was appointed as Haaland's new manager. In the friendly games Haaland scored against SV Kirchanschöring, Russian side Arsenal Tula and Feyenoord of the Netherlands.

Haaland played in the opening fixture of the 2019/20 season away to Rapid Vienna, Austria's most successful club historically and the backbone of a brilliant national team before and after the Second World War. Although he did not score in a 2-0 win, he did make three successful dribbles and 15 tackles before being replaced.

He was soon on the scoresheet with three in a 5-2 home win against Wolfsberger AC, two in a 6-0 win at SKN St. Pölten, one in a 5-0 defeat of Admira Wacker, one in a 5-1 win at Wattens and another three in a 7-2 defeat of Hartberg. Ten goals in five league games.

He later scored a second hat-trick against Wolfsberger in a 3-0 win. He had earlier scored three in the 7-1 Austrian Cup victory at SC-ESV Parndorf 1919.

By the time of the midwinter break, after 18 league games he had 15 league goals and his side remained unbeaten with 13 victories and five draws. Haaland was on his way to bagging his second league title medal.

Following the qualifying rounds there were 32 teams competing in the Champions League group stages to decide the 16 places in the knockout phase.

* * *

Three goals on his Champions League debut

RB Salzburg found themselves facing Genk, holders Liverpool and Italian giants Napoli. When the Belgian champions travelled to the 30,000 capacity Red Bull Arena they were blown away and were 5-1 down at the break with Haaland having scored three on two, 34 and 45 minutes. His first saw him played in around the penalty area and he finished with his right foot; his second saw him put clear and he finished with his left and for his third he side-footed home a cross with his right foot from six yards out. The home side won 6-2.

Among his Genk opponents was his international midfield team-mate Sander Berge. He said, '[I] went into the game having talked him down to my team-mates because I remembered he couldn't even keep the ball in the box with the national team.

'Erling had scored a lot in the Austrian league, but I thought that league was mediocre and I did not think he would score against us in the Champions League.

'When he ran around celebrating, I could see why other players get annoyed with him. It is not a mild celebration. He makes a great show of it. It suits him – but when he scored his third, he stood up on top of the advertising boards.

'After the match, I was sat with him in the doping room and he had the match ball. He was holding it like he had won three or four Ballon d'Ors, like it was the most natural thing in the world. He wasn't being rude on purpose, but it was particularly provocative. If I had been someone who didn't know him, I would have thought it was so annoying.'

Salzburg then travelled to Liverpool and played marvellously. Illness reduced Haaland to a place on the bench and it was not until the 56th minute when he ran out aiming to emulate his dad's scoring achievement at Anfield.

Liverpool had lost their Group E opener to Napoli but got off to the ideal start when former Salzburg player Sadio Mané struck inside ten minutes, sweeping home at the near post.

Andrew Robertson then turned in a cross from Trent Alexander-Arnold before Mohamed Salah poked a third under keeper Cican Stanković to make it 3-0.

Having scored 40 goals in their nine league games, Salzburg then struck back with a treble of their own to stun their hosts. First, South Korean international Hwang Hee-chan got the better of Virgil van Dijk before scoring with a powerful strike. It was one of three goals by the energetic striker in the tournament and he also made three assists and won two penalties.

The deficit was reduced further when Takumi Minamino volleyed home. When the same player found space to square the ball across the box substitute Haaland tapped in an equaliser with his left foot – his 18th goal of the season – sparking wild celebrations among away fans behind the goal.

Liverpool had won their last 12 Anfield games and they were to make it 13 when Salah latched on to Roberto Firmino's header and scored with a fierce strike.

In the end, Salzburg just fell short but the away fans were cheering and singing long after the final whistle.

There then followed a 3-2 home defeat against Napoli in which Lorenzo Insigne scored the winner just a minute after Haaland, watched by his proud father, had scored his second of the game when left unmarked six yards out he headed home. His first had come from the spot after Hwang had been hauled down. The problem was that while Salzburg could score for fun, they were leaky at the back.

Haaland's two goals meant he became the first player to score six times in their first three Champions League games. He also became the second teenager to score in his first three matches in the competition after Karim Benzema.

His success delighted him, 'Champions League matches have always fascinated me, and the anthem has been a real part of my life since my childhood. Now I am a part of it, of course, and I listen to it as a player in the stadium. It's just incredible. Some people think I'm a bit crazy for listening to the anthem in the car or at home. It drives me on and has the potential to be my favourite song for the rest of my life. We have shown that our team belongs in this competition, and that we can compete with any set of opponents and take something from them.'

As he was by now well-known for his admiration of fellow Scandinavian Zlatan Ibrahimović the Norwegian remarked, 'You can take a lot of things from Zlatan, especially in the mental area. He has shown at every club that he is the best. That really impresses me. That is also my aim!'

When Salzburg then made the trip to southern Italy, they drew 1-1 with Napoli as Haaland scored from the spot on 11 minutes before Hirving Lozano equalised.

Haaland thus became the first player to score more than six goals in the opening four group games in a Champions League campaign since Lionel Messi did so for Barcelona in 2016/17. He also became just the second teenager to score in four Champions League appearances in a row, following in the footsteps of French World Cup winner Kylian Mbappé.

Haaland scored in the fifth group game as Salzburg recorded the double over Genk with a 4-1 win at the multi-purpose Cegeka Arena. He had been a surprise absence from the starting XI and he certainly made up for lost time after his introduction at 2-1. He created a goal with a low cross for Hwang, then bizarrely had a goal ruled out for a perceived foul before striking late on to become just the third player to score in his first five Champions League appearances, joining Alessandro Del Piero and Diego Costa in that illustrious group.

It was a tribute to Jesse Marsch's management skills that it meant that if Salzburg could beat Liverpool at home, they would leapfrog Jürgen Klopp's side and go through at the

Merseysiders' expense into the knockout stages of the world's biggest club tournament.

Liverpool at times were on the ropes with goalkeeper Allison forced to make six first-half saves but eventually they won through after two quickfire goals just before the hour when first Naby Keïta headed in Mané's cross and then Salah clinched victory with an excellent tight-angle finish.

'It was a bit like a heavyweight boxing contest,' said Marsch afterwards. 'We fought really hard, but they fought back. In the end they got two more punches in. That's how close the margin is between victory and defeat in the Champions League. We are very disappointed, as we played really good football, and we probably couldn't have played any better than in the first half.'

Playing up front with Hwang, Haaland was replaced on 75 minutes after having three shots and 23 touches.

The loss was set to be the Europa League's gain, with the Austrian champions moving into that tournament.

Whether Haaland would be playing in Europe's second tournament was in some doubt. This was due to considerable speculation that he was set to join one of the Champions League clubs, and he was missing when Salzburg played their final game of 2019.

On 18 December, RB Salzburg extended the contracts of Enock Mwepu, Sékou Koïta and Patson Daka and 24 hours later the club announced they were selling Takumi Minamino to Liverpool.

Haaland had made 22 appearances – six of which had been as substitute – for Salzburg in the season and scored 28 goals, made up of 16 in the league, four in the Austrian Cup and eight in the Champions League.

Despite being a reported target of Manchester United, Juventus and Barcelona, it was Borussia Dortmund who confirmed the signing of Haaland on 29 December 2019 for a fee reported to be in the region of €20m, the player signing a four-and-a-half-year contract.

United were said to be one of the frontrunners to sign him with his former boss Ole Gunnar Solskjær, now manager at Old Trafford, reportedly even meeting him in an attempt to seal the deal for his number one target, who he hoped to partner with Dortmund's Jadon Sancho.

According to ESPN, United's executive vice-chairman Ed Woodward had pulled out of the deal because of agent fees and the insistence of Haaland's camp that a release clause be inserted in the contract.

Pundit Trevor Sinclair was convinced United's arrogance had cost them the opportunity to sign Europe's hottest star for just £18m, 'They would have loved to have taken him ... but they didn't want to put in the clause that Haaland wanted in the contract from RB Salzburg ... they chose not to because they didn't want him to have that option.

'I would have taken him, sold the club to him, make sure he understands the project ... I think that was a bit of arrogance by Manchester United because they're a big club. They've said, "We're not accepting that."'

Haaland himself said on moving to Germany, 'I had extensive talks with the Dortmund club's management team, in particular with Dortmund CEO Hans-Joachim Watzke, [sporting director] Michael Zorc and coach Lucien Favre.

'Right from the very start, I knew I wanted to move here. I can't wait to get started and play in front of over 80,000 fans in the incredible Dortmund atmosphere.'

Zorc said on Haaland's credentials, 'We can expect an ambitious, athletic and physical centre-forward with a proven nose for goal. At 19 Erling is still at the start of what will hopefully be a massive career.'

Salzburg were pleased for Haaland, insisting that his departure would not have a detrimental effect on the Salzburg squad, as selling on high-quality younger players was central to the club's policy for growth.

Salzburg chief Christoph Freund added, 'Erling was not only a special story in this respect. That doesn't hurt at all, it makes us proud because it's part of our concept ... The player can take the next step, we get income through a transfer, which we can invest in scouting and new talent, among other things.

'In addition, there is again a free place in the squad that the next talent can take. It is a confirmation for us that we are on the right path.'

Daka and midfielder Mwepu were to later bring in just shy of another £50m for the Austrian club when they joined Leicester and Brighton respectively.

Haaland was to link up with his new Dortmund teammates at their winter training camp in Marbella, Spain. He was set to make his competitive debut against Augsburg on 18 January 2020.

11

Breaking Down Defences in
Germany's Industrial Heartland

Borussia Dortmund

Manchester United's unwillingness to sign Erling Haaland from RB Salzburg was to be Borussia Dortmund's gain as he was to score with remarkable regularity for the Black and Yellows over the following two and a half seasons before they sold on the Norwegian international for around three times what they paid for him.

He was signed because the German side had been playing without a number nine, a goalscorer, for several seasons since Pierre-Emerick Aubameyang, top scorer with 31 in the Bundesliga in 2016/17, had left for Arsenal in January 2018 for a £56m fee.

Dortmund had won Germany's national cup, known as the DFB-Pokal, in 2016/17 but had failed to win the Bundesliga since 2011/12. The hope was that Haaland would change the dynamic by giving the team someone making the runs into the box and going into the channels. There would be no more false nines around the box.

Formed in 1909, Dortmund waited until 1956 before winning their first Bundesliga title. In the European Cup they were eliminated in the first round by Manchester United when following a 0-0 draw at home they lost 3-2 at Maine Road, where Matt Busby's side played their

European home games due to Old Trafford being without floodlights.

Dortmund won the title for a second consecutive season and won it for a third time in 1966 when they also won the European Cup Winners' Cup by beating Liverpool 2-1 in the final at Hampden Park.

The club then suffered severe financial problems and were relegated in 1972. Under Ottmar Hitzfeld's leadership, Dortmund reached the 1993 UEFA Cup Final. From the prize money earned they were able to sign better players. Back-to-back titles were secured in 1995 and 1996 and in 1997 they reached the Champions League Final where they beat hot favourites Juventus, whose side included Zinedine Zidane, 3-1 in Munich.

Despite winning the 2001/02 title, Dortmund were facing bankruptcy before new chief executive Hans-Joachim Watzke streamlined the publicly listed company. Then in 2008, Jürgen Klopp became manager and set about developing a pressing game. A younger fitter team won the title in 2011 and 2012, when they also won the DFB-Pokal.

In 2013 Dortmund again reached the Champions League Final but in a great game they lost to Bayern Munich 2-1 at Wembley. Klopp departed to Liverpool in 2015 and Dortmund subsequently continued to rival but not beat Bayern Munich for the German title. They finished second in 2015/16 and 2018/19 and won the DFB-Pokal in 2016/17.

Key to the club's success was the building in 1974 of the Westfalenstadion, the seventh-largest ground in Europe, which could accommodate 81,359 spectators for league matches and 65,829 for European games when the massive southern terraces were re-equipped with seats.

On his signing, Haaland remarked how he was looking forward to playing in front of the 'Yellow Wall' who had one thing in common with Manchester City fans as at the start of the 21st century they had followed Citizens by taking up the craze of taking plastic yellow bananas to games.

Dortmund had spent big at the start of the 2019/20 season, spending over €100m on Julian Brandt, Thorgan Hazard, Nico Shulz and Mats Hummels while Mateu Morey arrived on a free from Barcelona's under-19s and Achraf Hakimi and Emre Can were on loan.

Although the season had started well with Jadon Sancho scoring in the 5-1 and 3-1 wins against Augsburg and Köln, Dortmund had faltered and by the winter break they had a relatively modest 30 points from 17 games. Thankfully, Bayern had also stuttered and had 32 points. The title race was very much alive.

* * *

Debut hat-trick

On their return in January 2020, Dortmund again notched five against Augsburg. However, after 55 minutes they had fallen 3-1 behind before head coach Lucien Favre replaced defender Łukasz Piszczek with their new signing.

Three minutes later Haaland reduced the arrears when Axel Witsel played the ball into the striker's feet and despite the angle, he fired a first-time, left-footed effort across goal and in off the post.

Sancho then equalised with his second goal and Haaland put Dortmund ahead for the first time with 18 minutes left when he tapped home after Hazard got in behind the Augsburg defence. The offside flag had gone up but after VAR inspection, the goal was allowed to stand.

Nine minutes later, Haaland marked his incredible Bundesliga debut with a hat-trick. Once again, Augsburg's defence was high up the pitch, allowing Marco Reus to slide Haaland in on goal. He produced a composed finish to make it 5-3 and put the game out of sight.

After the game the new star told reporters that he was 'pretty relaxed' about his success, 'I don't really know why … I'm at a fantastic club with great team-mates and good people around me. I came here to score goals and it was a good debut for me.'

Few in the 30,660 crowd could have any doubt that they were watching a player set to be a major star in German football.

Haaland was again a substitute at home to Köln. He replaced Hazard on 65 minutes and knocked home two in a 5-1 win before a sold-out ground. The Norwegian was to start for the first time in the next game and after Sancho, who he had already formed an effective partnership with as the central striker in a 3-4-3 formation, had put his side ahead against Union Berlin the 19-year-old scored twice in a 5-0 win with Reus also scoring from the spot after Haaland was brought down.

Despite his success, Haaland reported that he still needed to get fit after a knee injury in the previous month had restricted his training. He told Sky, 'It was pretty tough today, but it was also nice to play from the start. I have to get even fitter; I am still not 100 per cent.'

There was then disappointment, though, as despite scoring at Werder Bremen, Dortmund were eliminated from the DFB-Pokal 3-2 at the Weserstadion.

Haaland remained in the side as the lone up-front striker for the Bundesliga trip to Bayer Leverkusen, Champions League finalists in 2002, and at 3-2 up with ten minutes remaining a fourth consecutive league success was within touching distance before Leon Bailey and Lars Bender smashed home two goals for the home side, for whom Moussa Diaby featured.

After then scoring in the 4-0 home win against Eintracht Frankfurt it was time for Haaland's favourite tournament, the

Champions League. Dortmund had qualified for the knockout stages after finishing in second place in their group behind Barcelona with Inter Milan and Slavia Prague below them.

* * *

Buddha celebrations not viewed calmly

Dortmund faced big-spending Paris Saint-Germain in the last 16. Before a home crowd of 66,098 it was PSG who initially took the game to their opponents. Neymar fizzed a free kick just wide and after the interval, Roman Bürki twice saved from Kylian Mbappé before Haaland, who in the first half had been restricted to a couple of half-chances, fired in the opening goal after the ball ran loose. Neymar then levelled following Mbappé's mazy run before the home side's man of the moment took on substitute Giovanni Reyna's astute pass to hammer home with his left foot past Keylor Navas for his 11th goal in seven games since his transfer.

The double scorer had taken to celebrating some of his goals at Salzburg with a Buddha-like meditation after hitting the net. He had felt considerable benefits from making meditation part of his pre-match routine and that's why he chose to highlight it with his goal celebration. It was a nod to his spiritual practice.

'I really enjoy meditation,' Haaland said in 2020. 'It makes me feel calm and gives me tranquillity. This is why I sometimes celebrate like that when I score. I train a lot, and I meditate a lot. Before a game, I always listen to a song called "Keep Dreaming" – and I also meditate.' Haaland performed his trademark celebration after netting the opener against PSG.

Dortmund journeyed to Paris for the second leg a goal ahead. Wearing number 17 with Hazard and Sancho supporting him from just behind, Haaland had to largely watch as Dortmund soaked up constant first-half pressure and were unable to hit the French side on the break. The away defence conceded a goal when Neymar escaped the attentions of Achraf Hakimi in the 28th minute to head home a corner. Juan Bernat applied a deft touch to make it 2-0, which was how the game ended to put PSG through 3-2 on aggregate.

It was a fair result which PSG chose to 'celebrate' by attempting to scorn the opposition centre-forward.

During the game, Neymar had mocked Haaland's celebration after having scored the opener. Afterwards he then went a step further by posting a self-image of imitating the Haaland celebration on his Instagram account, writing the caption, 'PARIS our city, not yours 🥱.'

When the game ended some of the PSG squad also sat down together on the pitch to mockingly perform the Haaland celebration following their victory. Following the final whistle, defender Presnel Kimpembe also defended his team-mates' actions. 'They are great players but now I will say they lost their humility,' he told RMC Sport. 'Because after their victory at home they put out a lot of tweets, a lot of Instagrams, a lot of words, a lot of this and that.'

When Haaland was asked if the PSG players' antics had upset him, he told ESPN, 'No, not really. I think they helped me a lot to get meditation out in the world and to show the whole world that meditation is an important thing so I'm thankful that they helped me with that.'

Out of Europe, Haaland scored in a 2-0 win at Werder Bremen and in a 2-1 success at Borussia Mönchengladbach before the season was brought to a sudden halt with Dortmund on 51 points, three behind Bayern with nine league games remaining.

Since the start of the year, Covid-19 had swept across the globe forcing football authorities everywhere to suspend matches with even talk of seasons not being completed.

FIFA established a working group to tackle the issues facing football as a result of the pandemic, and UEFA announced they would postpone Euro 2020 for a year.

'We are at the helm of a sport that vast numbers of people live and breathe that has been laid low by this invisible and fast-moving opponent,' said UEFA president Aleksander Čeferin.

'The health of fans, staff and players has to be our number one priority and, in that spirit, UEFA tabled a range of options so that competitions can finish this season safely and I am proud of the response of my colleagues across European football.'

The German Bundesliga, suspended on Friday, 13 March 2020, was the first European League to restart games behind closed doors. There was a police presence at every stadium to ensure fans did not enter and to prevent disturbances.

Dortmund returned at home to fierce local rivals Schalke 04, nicknamed The Miners, a reference to the industry that along with steel manufacturing provided the backbone of the Ruhr area.

For decades, Schalke had dominated their rivals with six title wins in the 1930s and '40s before winning a seventh in 1958.

That was a long time ago and the visitors were heavily beaten 4-0 with Haaland showing great energy and scoring once.

With seven games remaining, Dortmund could go top by beating Bayern Munich. It would have aided Haaland's side if they had had the backing of the largest terrace in the world, the Yellow Wall. Joshua Kimmich opened the scoring for Bayern on 43 minutes following which Favre threw on substitutes Can and Sancho at the start of the second half. It proved to be of no avail and the coach then replaced Haaland with Giovanni Reyna on 72 minutes. The reigning champions saw out the match to take a six-point lead in the table with four games remaining.

Hansi Flick's side won every one of their remaining fixtures to end the season on 82 points from 34 games. Key to the success was the goalscoring record of former Dortmund favourite Robert Lewandowski, with 34 league goals as part of an overall total of 55 that included 15 in the Champions League, which Bayern won by beating PSG 1-0 in the final.

Dortmund ended second in the Bundesliga, 13 points behind Bayern. Sancho was their top scorer in the league and overall, with 17 and 20 goals respectively in 44 games. Haaland had scored 16, 13 of which came in the league, in 18 games to take his overall club record in 2019/20 with Salzburg (where in 22 appearances he had scored 28 goals) and Dortmund up to 44 goals, including ten in the Champions League, in 40 appearances.

Convinced by Dortmund's record of including young players as regular first-teamers, 17-year-old Jude Bellingham had made the move from Birmingham City at a cost of over £20m over the shortened summer break and was joined by Thomas Meunier on a free from PSG and Reinier Jesus on loan from Real Madrid.

All games during the 2020/21 season were to be played in front of reduced crowds and Haaland started it well by banging home two goals, one a penalty, in the 3-0 opening-day 3-0 defeat of Borussia Mönchengladbach. However Augsburg, by beating them 2-0 next up, showed that Dortmund still had work to do. The defeated side rallied to win the next four without conceding a goal and scoring eight with Haaland netting three.

He also scored in the home game against Bayern, which with Covid now back in full flow was played without spectators present, but it proved a late consolation goal in a 3-2 defeat as Leroy Sané scored the visitors' third.

Haaland then hammered home four in a 5-2 win at Hertha Berlin but Dortmund subsequently fell away badly with three defeats, two at home, including a 5-1 beating by Stuttgart, in five matches before the winter break.

A torn muscle fibre meant Haaland was absent against Stuttgart, following which Lucien Favre was relieved of his post and replaced by Edin Terzić. Haaland missed seven games in all competitions at this time. He was to also miss one with a knee problem, one with a minor knock and another with muscular problems before the season ended.

He returned to first-team action by scoring in a 2-0 success at home to Wolfsburg on 3 January 2021 and followed this by scoring two in a 3-1 win in Leipzig, but any title hopes were being destroyed when Dortmund were beaten at Bayer Leverkusen, Mönchengladbach and SC Freiburg. They had just 32 points from 20 games.

Haaland, playing up front with Thorgan Hazard and Marco Reus, scored twice at Bayern Munich to put his side 2-0 ahead after nine minutes. His opener had taken a slight nick off Jérôme Boateng but was always heading beyond Manuel Neuer and his second ended a classy move when he swept home Hazard's pass.

However, once again Robert Lewandowski showed what Dortmund were missing as the Polish international scored twice, one a penalty, before the break. Then, after Leon Goretzka made it 3-2 on 88 minutes, Lewandowski scored his third.

The result thus took the shine off Haaland's achievement of making it 100 senior goals in all competitions at the tender age of 20. He had played only 145 matches – by comparison, Kylian Mbappé took 180 matches to rack up a century, Lionel Messi 210 and Cristiano Ronaldo 301.

A 2-1 home defeat to Eintracht Frankfurt even raised the prospect that Dortmund might not qualify for the

Champions League. As featured in chapter one this was to raise considerable speculation that Haaland would be moving on when the season ended.

There was better news in the DFB-Pokal where Dortmund had beaten four sides to reach the last four, and they would then face – without Haaland – and beat Holstein Kiel 5-0. That victory followed four consecutive Bundesliga successes in the league in which Haaland scored doubles against Werder Bremen and Wolfsburg, the latter seeing Bellingham dismissed following two bookings. A 2021/22 Champions League spot was now back on.

* * *

DFB-Pokal win

A sixth consecutive victory followed in a 3-2 defeat of RB Leipzig. Five days later, when the sides met again in the DFB-Pokal Final in Berlin, Sancho's superb right-footed curled finish put his side ahead early on. After outmuscling Leipzig's French defender Dayot Upamecano, Haaland then showed great composure to stretch the lead before Sancho as good as wrapped things up before the break. Although Dani Olmo reduced the arrears with 19 minutes remaining the game ended 4-1 after Haaland scored – his 39th goal in 39 games at club level so far in the season – with a miskick that deceived Péter Gulácsi on 87 minutes. Dortmund won the national cup competition for the fifth time.

Haaland also scored twice in the final league fixture against Bayer Leverkusen and this put Dortmund on to 64 points, well behind Bayern Munich with 77, but good enough to finish in third place a point behind runners-up RB Leipzig. In the Bundesliga. Haaland had made 27 starts and one substitute appearance and scored 27 goals. No one else at Dortmund came anywhere near with Reus and Sancho both on eight and Portuguese defender Raphaël Guerreiro on five. Haaland still, though, had some catching up with Robert Lewandowski who ended up scoring 41 league goals, overtaking previous 40-goal record holder Gerd Müller, also of Bayern Munich.

Nevertheless, a goal a game in the Bundesliga was a healthy return for a first full season for a player not yet given his 21st-birthday key of the door, and it was beaten in eight appearances in the Champions League where Haaland played in eight of 12 games and scored ten times.

His first, a powerful left-footed finish from a square pass from American substitute Giovanni Reyna on 71 minutes, ultimately proved a mere consolation in a 3-1 group-stage defeat at Lazio whose defence struggled to contain him in the second period.

However, his second, where he ran on to a Bellingham pass to beat Mikhail Kerzhakov in the last minute against Zenit Saint Petersburg saw an under-performing Dortmund win 2-0 at home after Sancho had scored a penalty.

Haaland then put two into the Club Brugge net as visitors Dortmund rushed into a 3-0 lead by 32 minutes and thereafter were rarely troubled. After Thorgan Hazard had put his side ahead, Haaland turned in the rebound after Simon Mignolet had parried his header. His second came as a result of a fine run and pass beyond a retreating defence by former Brugge right-back Thomas Meunier that left the striker with a simple tap-in.

He now had 14 goals in the Champions League in 11 games, six less than it had taken Harry Kane to record.

In the return fixture, Haaland ran on to score from a pass from Sancho, who then scored himself with a curling 20-yard free kick to make it 2-0 at the interval and following which the Norwegian made it 16 goals in 12 career Champions League appearances as the Belgian side again lost 3-0.

When Dortmund then drew without Haaland 1-1 at home to Lazio it meant they had already qualified for the knockout stages even before they beat Zenit 2-1, another game Haaland missed. Dortmund ended in top place three points ahead of Lazio.

Twenty-four hours after Mbappé had announced himself as Europe's potential top goalscorer by scoring three for Paris Saint-Germain in the Camp Nou, Haaland showed he presented real opposition when he scored twice in a 3-2 win in Sevilla in the first leg of the last-16 tie. He followed Mbappé's display by terrorising Sevilla's defence with pace and power. After Mahmoud Dahoud had drawn the scores level, Haaland played a one-two with Sancho and beat Bono who in the second half was again beaten when Haaland's intelligent run was completed with a perfectly placed low side-foot shot. He had scored against all eight of his Champions League opponents.

Haaland repeated his two-goal feat in the return occasion in which the Spanish side scored their equalising goal in a 2-2 draw with virtually the last kick of the match.

This was despite Haaland only touching the ball once in the opposition box in the first half when he pushed Reus's pull-back home and he made it 2-0. His earlier effort on goal was chalked off after a VAR check ruled that he had been fouled himself earlier in the action. When he took the spot kick and it and the subsequent follow-up shot were saved by Bono he was rescued when it was ruled that the goalkeeper had moved too early. From the retaken kick, Haaland made it 5-2 on aggregate. He had now scored twice in each of his last four Champions League matches. Victory put Dortmund through to face Premier League champions Manchester City in the quarter-final.

Haaland was to be kept relatively quiet at the Etihad Stadium but then he found Reus with six minutes to go who made it 1-1. The celebrations of Dortmund players and staff were joyous, prematurely so. Kevin De Bruyne had put City ahead on 19 minutes with a crisp finish and when his cross was then touched back by İlkay Gündoğan for Phil Foden it was dispatched beyond Marwin Hitz for a precious late winner. Despite his disappointment Haaland shook hands warmly with the match winner on the final whistle and Foden began, as featured in the opening chapter, what proved to be a coordinated charm offensive by City's players that would last for a year.

There had been moments of controversy with Jude Bellingham, after netting, being harshly penalised for a foul on Ederson when, if anything, the English player had been fouled. The hosts had also had a first-half penalty award harshly overruled by VAR.

In the return match Dortmund struck first when Bellingham, making a bid to be included in Gareth Southgate's squad for the summer European Championship, curled in a beauty from the edge of the box on 15 minutes. De Bruyne smashed a shot off the bar as City stepped up the pressure with Bellingham somehow forcing a Riyad Mahrez shot off the line.

The visitors, though, couldn't be denied after the break when Can was penalised for handling the ball and Mahrez scored from the spot on 55 minutes, before 20 minutes later Foden scored his second of the tie to make it 4-2 on aggregate – which was how it finished. Haaland never stopped trying but couldn't get clear of John Stones and Rúben Dias and had just a late wayward shot to show for his efforts. With Dortmund outside of the Champions League spots in the Bundesliga the speculation that both Sancho and Haaland would depart in the summer heightened.

The second full season was to prove a frustrating one as despite some fine performances Dortmund again finished second well behind Bayern Munich, were eliminated in the cup by second-tier FC St. Pauli and following their Champions League failure they were put out of Europe when Rangers beat them over two legs in the Europa Cup.

For Haaland himself there was a series of injuries that kept him on the touchline for around three months. When he was fit, he continued to regularly ruffle the opposition net to demonstrate he was now one of the finest centre-forwards globally.

In February 2021, Dortmund had announced that the former RB Salzburg boss Marco Rose would be leaving Borussia Mönchengladbach to join them as coach for the 2021/22 season. The new man helped bring in Gregor Kobel, Soumaïla Coulibaly, Adboulaye Kamara, Donyell Malen and Marin Pongračić for a combined total of £35m. This was a figure dwarfed by the departures of Jeremy Toljan, Łukasz Piszczek, Sergio Gómez, Leonardo Balerdi, Thomas Delaney, Ansgar Knauff, Tobias Raschl and Jadon Sancho for over £85m, of which the latter's move to Manchester United comprised 80 per cent. Sancho and Haaland had formed a tight bond during their brief time together. The loss of the partnership was bound to weaken Dortmund.

The 2021/22 pre-season friendly results were not inspiring with two defeats and two victories, and this indifferent form continued in the Bundesliga. Haaland scored twice in an opening-day 5-2 defeat of Eintracht Frankfurt but he failed to score in a 2-1 defeat to SC Freiburg-1. A last-minute winner in a 3-2 defeat of 1899 Hoffenheim in which Bellingham also scored was followed by two goals, including the winner, in a 4-3 win away to Leverkusen. Two more were knocked home in a 4-2 defeat of Union Berlin before Rose, missing the injured Haaland, traveled home from his previous club beaten 1-0 with Mahmoud Dahoud also sent off. Returning to the first team two games later

Haaland scored twice as Mainz 05 were beaten 3-1 before 63,812 spectators.

Haaland missed the next three games and in the third Dortmund were beaten more easily by RB Leipzig than the 2-1 scoreline suggested with Reus, who scored, and Donyell Malen struggling to make space up front in a 3-3-2-2 formation. With three defeats in 11 games, it was already looking like Dortmund couldn't win the Bundesliga.

With Covid-19 remaining highly contagious only 15,000 spectators were allowed into the must-win home game with Bayern Munich but after Haaland, with a curled shot into the corner from Bellingham's lay-off, made it 2-2 on 48 minutes it was again Lewandowski who scored the vital fifth goal, his second of a competitive match that lacked some flair, with a penalty. That was now four defeats in 14 league fixtures and murmurs were starting to blossom among the fans that Rose, who had been sent to the stands for arguing that his side should have been awarded a spot-kick, was not good enough. Sancho's departure was undoubtedly a big loss.

Dortmund had 34 points from 51 going into the new year which they knew would bring with it a tie in February with Rangers in the knockout stage of the Europa League.

This was because, despite a last-gasp 5-0 hammering of Turkish side Beşiktaş in the sixth game of the Champions League group stage, Dortmund had been eliminated after finishing third, on equal points with Sporting but the Portuguese side had a superior goal difference. Both clubs had been beaten home and away by Ajax who finished with maximum points.

The Germans had started with a 2-1 victory in Turkey with Haaland maintaining his remarkable record of scoring in the Champions League with his side's second after 18-year-old man of the match Bellingham, who had teed up Haaland's goal, had opened the scoring. The Norwegian now had 21 goals in 17 Champions League matches with Salzburg and Dortmund, plus his four goals in five Europa League games for Molde.

He missed the home meeting against Sporting and watched as Malen scored the only goal. On his return, Ajax hammered Dortmund 4-0 with Reus's own goal opening the scoring at the Johan Cruyff Arena in a game where Daley Blind was outstanding and scored the second.

Despite the heavy reverse, Haaland played well and had three of Dortmund's four shots on target in the game, with one of them tipped on to the bar by Remko Pasveer.

Reus scored in the correct goal when the sides met again in Germany but eight minutes earlier, in the 29th minute, his side had lost Mats Hummels after he was shown a straight red card by Michael Oliver. With Haaland out injured, Rose had switched to a single player up front in Steffen Tigges and the ten men battled to keep out Erik ten Hag's side featuring Dušan Tadić, Sébastien Haller and Antony as a front three. Eventually the constant pressure paid off and when Tadić scored on 72 minutes there was only going to be one winner and towards the end both Haller and Davy Klaassen netted.

The key match was going to be in Portugal and missing Haaland this went badly for Dortmund, who again lost their discipline with substitute Can dismissed with 16 minutes remaining. By that time they were two down and the game ended 3-1. Dortmund needed to win big against Beşiktaş, which they did with 63rd-minute substitute Haaland scoring the fourth and fifth goals from close-range headers, and hope Ajax hammered Sporting, who in the event by only losing 4-2 in Amsterdam moved forward on goal difference.

On Haaland's return to competitive action in January 2022 he was booked at Eintracht Frankfurt who at one point led 2-0 only for the visitors to show great spirit by scoring three in the last 20 minutes with Hazard scoring on 71, Bellingham on 87 and Dahoud on 89.

Haaland was missing for the home game against Leverkusen, watching helplessly as his team-mates were ripped apart and lost 5-2 with Tigges's late goal failing to still the discontent among the 10,000 crowd. It was now 43 points from 63 available.

With Haaland absent, Dortmund were also easily beaten as Rangers struck three before Bellingham reduced the arrears in a game the Scottish side won 4-2.

In the return, with Malen playing as a lone striker, Dortmund did at one point lead 2-1 but when James Tavernier, with his second, levelled the game up with just over half an hour to go the away side were unable to exert pressure and Rangers progressed 6-4 on aggregate.

After missing four league games Haaland returned against Arminia Bielefeld and also played at Mainz and at Köln and in the 4-1 defeat at home to RB Leipzig. He failed to score in the four games.

A 2-0 success in Stuttgart was a welcome result with substitute Julian Brandt scoring both goals before Haaland ended his longest run of games without a goal, five, since his move from Norway by scoring twice in a 6-1 beating of Wolfsburg.

Any hopes this would result in a fine finish to the campaign were abruptly ended by a 3-1 defeat at Bayern Munich with Lewandowski scoring the hosts' second. Haaland had thus lost in all five games he had played against Bayern in the Bundesliga.

* * *

Hat-trick hero in another home defeat

Haaland was back to his best in the penultimate home match, scoring three times after Dortmund fell two down to VFL Bochum, who then stunned the 81,365 spectators by scoring late goals from Jürgen Locadia and a penalty by Miloš Pantović to earn a 4-3 victory.

Haaland made what proved to be his final Dortmund appearance in a 2-1 win against Hertha Berlin in which he scored the equalising goal from the spot on 68 minutes, with substitute Youssoufa Moukoko scoring 16 minutes later to put his side on 69 points. This was eight behind Bayern Munich but ahead of Bayer Leverkusen on 64 and RB Leipzig on 58 in fourth. Dortmund would thus line up in the 2022/23 Champions League group stage.

Haaland's 2021/22 statistics saw him score a total of 29 goals – 22 in the Bundesliga, four in the DFB-Pokal and three in the Champions League – in 30 appearances across all competitions, including the DFL-Supercup.

12

Progress Blunted by Saints and Poor Old Trafford Refereeing Decision

ERLING HAALAND would have much preferred to be in Qatar for the 2022 World Cup with Norway, who he had chosen to play for over England. Instead, he was initially on holiday in Marbella and then back with City at their under-23 squad training camp in Abu Dhabi working on an injury with the strength and conditioning coaches.

At the same time, as the player himself explained, the break did give him 'a good opportunity to reset. Every player wants to be at the World Cup. It's my dream to represent my country there and I'll work hard to make sure that I do that one day. I did my best but we couldn't do it. What can I do? That's the situation and I have to try again in four years.

'But the break has been positive. I've had the chance to rest, to take my mind off football for a few weeks and put myself in the best possible place to return. I can't wait for it to start again. I feel mentally really sharp and I am ready for the second half of the season. I am raring to go … against Liverpool [City's first competitive fixture after the break for the World Cup] looking to get a positive result and giving our fans something to be excited about as we head into the second half of the season.'

With his appearances prior to Qatar being limited to a single start in five matches due to an ankle injury against

Dortmund, Haaland's return, much as in pre-season, was, following his Marbella break, managed at the warm-weather camp in Abu Dhabi where the City squad minus those in Qatar were joined by club chairman Khaldoon Al Mubarak at their training sessions where both men spent time chatting to one another.

Film footage showed the number nine training on his own as his team-mates warmed up and took part in passing drills and small-sided games. The striker spoke of how professional footballers are lucky to go to 'travel around the world ... [having] all the facilities we need, the weather is a little warmer than it is in Manchester and we can prepare as a group. OK, not all of our team-mates can be out here but for the ones that are it's a good opportunity to come together in a more relaxed setting and make sure we're ready for when the rest of the group comes back.'

Haaland, Scott Carson and Riyad Mahrez were invited to the five-star Emirates Palace Mandarin Oriental Hotel in Abu Dhabi to take part in a cooking challenge under the gaze of Luigi Stinga, head chef at the one-star Michelin restaurant Talea. The players were given a chef's jacket with their names on the back and asked to cook a farfalle dish – small pieces of pasta shaped like bows or Butterly wings. Haaland was asked by the chef about his lasagne superstition. He replied, 'One day my father made me some lasagne to eat. I ate it and the next day I scored a hat-trick. What can you do then but keep eating it? Next home game, he made lasagne, hat-trick. OK, I have to eat lasagne the day before a home game for the rest of my life.' Haaland won the challenge.

The Norwegian has a particular liking for Italian food and although he doesn't go out drinking he does make late-night jaunts to restaurants. The San Carlo restaurant on Deansgate will open after hours so he can eat without being disturbed. His favourite restaurant is Vero Moderno off Chapel Street in Salford. He also enjoys a curry and his favourite curry house is Dishoom on Bridge Street. He is though no big fan of fish and chips, admitting, 'I haven't eaten fish and chips – and I don't intend to because it isn't good for you.'

Relaxing off the pitch is important. Getting a good night's sleep is vital. To help do so Haaland wears orange-tinted goggles as they block out energy emitted from natural light and digital screens. He schedules his sleep to start between 10pm and 10.30pm most days. He switches his phone on to 'do not disturb' and wears an Oura Ring, a device worn on the finger to measure sleep quality, temperature, stress and heart rate.

When Haaland was deciding which club to join, City pointed out that if he signed for Real Madrid he would be expected to play every game to keep the pressure off the coach and board. He realised this would put him at greater risk of injury.

In September 2022, one of City's masseurs, Mario Pafundi, was sent to work with Norway's medical team during an international break to ensure that Haaland was getting the right treatment and recuperation.

When the World Cup ended and in preparation for the return of domestic football, Manchester City played a friendly before a 4,500 crowd at the Academy Stadium. This was against Spanish side Girona; following the purchase of 44.3 per cent of its shares in 2017 the club are part of the City Football Group, itself a subsidiary of the Abu Dhabi United Group. Another 44.3 per cent is held by Girona Football Group, led by Pere Guardiola, Pep Guardiola's brother.

Kevin De Bruyne netted after five minutes and he later set up Haaland for the second in a game featuring several youth players.

Following on from one of the greatest-ever World Cup tournaments there was the added spice of a pre-Christmas visit to the Etihad of Liverpool in the last 16 of the EFL Cup. With Virgil van Djik missing and Haaland fully rested he might have scored in the first 30 seconds when his pace took him clear only to uncharacteristically send his effort well over the bar.

That was clearly just a sighter. With Joël Matip and Joe Gomez struggling to cope with the City striker's aggression and movement while keeping a high line he was back on the scoresheet on ten minutes when he squeezed in front of Gomez to meet De Bruyne's left-footed cross to prod home the opener. When Fábio Carvalho equalised ten minutes later it was a sign that the 47,000-plus crowd were in for a real thrill.

It was Mahrez who found the goal after 47 minutes with a sublime-first time finish, only for Liverpool to hit back immediately as Núñez set up Mohamed Salah for the equaliser.

Any hopes Liverpool had of progressing to the quarter-finals were thrown away when their defence seemed to lose concentration so when De Bruyne got the ball back from a short corner he picked out an unmarked Nathan Aké at the back post who headed the winner in a tussle of high-level intensity.

Guardiola believed that it was slightly easier for those who had played at the World Cup to re-establish their rhythm once back home, 'It's true that the guys who came back after one week off, they lost a little bit but not much. It's more difficult for the players who were here and had time off like Erling Haaland and Cole Palmer. They were brilliant, intense and really good.'

There was praise for City's opponents, 'Liverpool are so difficult, when they play good, they destroy you. The quality of the transitions they do, they create chances.'

* * *

Hometown success

After his bright start, Haaland made the short trip home and by scoring two goals against Leeds United he helped his side win 3-1. It demonstrated that any hangover from City's defeat to Brentford before the World Cup had long since dissipated.

Haaland's achievement made him the fastest player to reach 20 Premier League goals, doing so in 14 matches. That was seven games quicker than Kevin Phillips, who needed 21 in 1999/2000. The Sunderland forward does though still have the record as the top away scorer in a Premier League season with 16.

Leeds boss Jesse Marsch had coached Haaland at RB Salzburg but could find no way to keep the prolific frontman at bay, who might have scored more against the Peacocks – who the striker had at one time declared he hoped to win the Premier League with. This had prompted Guardiola's tongue-in-cheek pre-match comments, 'Hopefully, Erling won't be contaminated by some kind words from a Leeds opponent.'

Haaland was never going to make an exception for any opponent. While he might have enjoyed a late chant by home fans of 'you're Leeds and you know you are' it certainly did not stop him doing his job of scoring goals.

Yet after dominating the first half it looked like the visitors might fail to take advantage against a Leeds side that had lost 11-0 to City on aggregate over the two games in 2021/22. But Rodri's opener from a sweeping City move in added time atoned for Haaland missing two good chances and a Jack Grealish howler in front of goal.

The two miscreants, almost inevitably, combined on 51 minutes when following a mix-up between Liam Cooper and Robin Koch, Grealish ran unopposed into the penalty area and then drew Ilan Meslier before squaring the ball for Haaland who from five yards put it home.

When asked what made Haaland such a difficult opponent, Cooper later said, 'For one, he doesn't need many chances. You can almost guarantee if he does get a chance, it will go away. He is strong, he is powerful and he is always on your shoulder, always looking to get in behind.'

Haaland's second on 64 minutes came after he again found Grealish inside the penalty area who drew two defenders before making the return pass. With his first touch Haaland drove home from ten yards.

Eleven minutes later and with Haaland in a one-on-one with Meslier his fourth Premier League hat-trick looked certain. The Leeds keeper, who had a decent game, took advantage of a slight mis-control of the ball to plunge down at Haaland's feet and prevent his side conceding a fourth at home for the second consecutive season against Guardiola's side.

The score thus remained 3-1 as Leeds had minutes earlier scored from a Sam Greenwood corner that saw Pascal Struijk rise highest to steer a header past Ederson, who at the end of the match had won 150 of his 197 games in the Premier League, becoming the quickest player to reach 150 victories in the competition.

On the family front, Erling had now had 20 Premier League goals, thus overtaking Alfie.

Great scorers always desire more goals. Thus, it was no surprise to hear Haaland say post-match, 'I could have scored five ... but we win and see Arsenal at the top now so we have to hunt them. I could have got a couple more but what can you do? That's life. I just have to practice more.'

On his World Cup break, he said, 'I was being home, being a little bit mad that I was on the sofa and not at the World Cup. I was a kind of a commentator for the World Cup in my own home. I kind of recharged my batteries and to watch other people score goals to win games in the World Cup, it kind of triggers me and motivates me.'

Haaland was to take his final chance to score in 2022 when he put his side ahead on New Year's Eve at home to Everton. He was, however, perhaps lucky to stay on the field in a game marked out by a marvellous Demarai Gray equalising goal and with the game ending 1-1 it meant City had now failed to win back-to-back home league matches for the first time since May 2021, when they lost against Leeds and Chelsea. And with Arsenal comfortably beating Brighton & Hove Albion 4-2 in an entertaining tussle the Gunners took a clear seven-point lead at the top.

The game had burst to life when Haaland made space for himself to finish off Mahrez's lovely cross on 24 minutes for his 21st Premier League goal in 15 appearances. The scorer, assisted by De Bruyne with a through ball, had earlier been unfortunate with a left-footed shot from a difficult angle that went close. The goal had an extra special meaning as Haaland had been left incensed by an early exchange with Everton's Ben Godfrey for which he required treatment. On his recovery he took revenge on Godfrey by taking him down out on the right wing. Then following the goal Haaland urged the crowd to up the noise and celebrated wildly in Godfrey's direction. He remained though clearly agitated.

With the home side dominating possession with 76 per cent of the ball Everton had to work extremely hard to remain in the contest, but the Toffees were lucky just before the break when following a De Bruyne cross, John Stones hit the post with a header from the centre of the box.

* * *

Booked

A frustrated Haaland was subsequently booked for a nasty two-footed off-the-ground foul on Vitalii Mykolenko, following which he had initially avoided paying for his actions when he fled the scene as James Tarkowski and Jordan Pickford angrily converged on him. He was fortunate to avoid a red but, at least, the yellow finally forced him to calm down.

On the second half return and with the game bogged down in a series of fouls in midfield, Everton's Amadou Onana was shown the yellow card for a bad foul. Then on 64 minutes Gray, an often-frustrating player in front of goal, hit, following a fast break, a powerful right-footed shot from the left of the box to the top-right corner. It sparked wild Everton celebrations.

Tarkowski had been shown the yellow card in the first half but he and Conor Coady in the Everton back five thereafter did a great job to block any hopes that Haaland had of scoring the winning goal.

The visitors' defence should, though, have been breached in the very last minute – the 103rd after a series of second-half injuries plus a six-minute delay on account of the assistant referee's radio being faulty – but Rodri was guilty of a bad miss with a very close-range header from a Mahrez cross following a corner.

A delighted Everton manager Frank Lampard told the press, 'We showed a lot of personality and work ethic. When you play a team of City's level, you understand what's coming. If you open up against them, they put you to bed so we had to have a certain style and the players kept to that and scored a goal. It's very hard but they did it.'

Guardiola was also not that upset about dropping two points, 'We played really well. We played good football in all departments. We won the second balls but we couldn't win. We've dropped five points at home in the last two games which is always tough to take. I would say they had eight at the back. Brentford played in the same shape but we couldn't control their long balls and their second balls. We allowed them one chance and it was a fantastic goal; you have to say "congratulations" but in general what we did was really good.

'The body language of the players against Leeds was amazing and gave me confidence. I saw how they were on the pitch so I kept with most of them. Rico [Lewis] looks like he's the best in every game. He's so smart and helps the way we want to play the game, creating chances and controlling the game.

'The best Everton was for ten minutes in the first half and then they scored a fantastic goal from a counterattack. We needed to score the second goal.'

Despite the manager's comments the points lost failed to prevent several articles on whether City were finding it difficult to win at home.

Five days later City had a chance to strike back at Arsenal following the Gunners' failure to beat Newcastle at home earlier in the week by winning at Stamford Bridge. In a hard-fought tussle against an injury-hit side they did so thanks to a Mahrez goal to go within five points of the top.

With City dominating possession but Haaland quiet the game rarely sparkled in the opening period. The champions might even have gone into the interval a goal down when Carney Chukwuemeka struck a post on 44 minutes for Chelsea, for whom Raheem Sterling and Christian Pulisic had limped off early

Soon after half-time it was City, boosted by the arrival of substitutes Rico Lewis and Manuel Akanji, who hit the frame of the goal through an Aké header before Guardiola's charges upped the pressure. In the 63rd minute they broke Chelsea's resistance when two recently introduced substitutes combined with Mahrez tucking in a low Grealish cross on a night when three points was more important than the less-than-impressive performance.

After the game Pep Guardiola spoke bluntly about the display, 'It was not good first half, it was sloppy, we didn't create much, our pressing was so poor, we were not well organised and in the second half with Manu [Akanji] and Rico, with the quality to not just play good, to help others play better, Rico has the talent to do this. Since we came back, he's playing and he's a key player for us.

'The impact in the second half of all four [substitute] players was so important, they changed the game. In the second half, it was a completely different Man City, a different rhythm. Rico changed his dynamic from minute one.

'There are 63 points still left to play for, we have to continue to improve ourselves. We handle in our mindset that people believe in November we're going to be champions and this is impossible. Arsenal, United don't have this pressure. After four [Premier League titles] in five years it's not easy to push them again, that's why I'm satisfied. We prefer to be closer but the way Arsenal have played they deserve to be there.'

When the teams met again three days later in the FA Cup a rested-up Haaland watched City record a comfortable 4-0 win against a poor Chelsea display. The Norwegian's absence meant another appearance for World Cup winner Julián Álvarez, who scored from the spot. With Chelsea fans singing the name of his predecessor Thomas Tuchel it now seemed unlikely, despite a battling performance in midweek at home to City, that Graham Potter would see out his first year as boss at Stamford Bridge.

City strolled to victory with Mahrez putting them on their way with a brilliant 23rd-minute free kick before Álvarez scored the second following Kai Havertz's handball. Phil Foden scored the third after 38 minutes by turning in Kyle Walker's cross after he had been played in by Mahrez, who got his second from the spot after Kalidou Koulibaly clumsily bundled Foden to the floor.

The draw after the game set up a possible tie with league leaders Arsenal who needed to win at Oxford United on the Monday evening to travel north to the Etihad Stadium at the end of January.

With the weekend derby with Manchester United fast approaching, for the second match running Guardiola chose to leave Haaland out of his line-up, with De Bruyne also rested for the long trip to face Southampton, twice finalists, in the EFL Cup quarter-final.

City were backed by a sold-out away end in a stadium only half full. Home fans who did attend could not believe their good fortune when a side containing Kyle Walker, Aymeric Laporte, Jack Grealish, İlkay Gündoğan, João Cancelo, Phil Foden and Julián Álvarez performed poorly and were beaten 2-0.

There was more than enough quality to beat a struggling Saints side and it was a particularly bad evening for deputy keeper Stefan Ortega and midfielder Kalvin Phillips, who, given his first start since signing from Leeds United in the summer, played so poorly and off the pace that he was substituted.

Nathan Jones's Saints were sent through by Sékou Mara's fine finish after City sloppily squandered possession, and later Moussa Djenepo scored a sublime second with a 30-yard lob that caught Ortega out.

Haaland would have to wait to collect his first medal in the blue of Manchester City with the hope now being that it would come in the Premier League. Collecting, at least, a point at Old Trafford, was thus essential.

Unsurprisingly, Haaland was taunted by the Stretford End on his first appearance on a ground now well past its best – but he was feeling a whole lot worse after the game when a highly controversial decision by referee Stuart Attwell provided Manchester United with the impetus to come from behind and inflict some measure of revenge for their evisceration at the Etihad four months earlier with a 2-1 victory. Chants of 'Haaland, Haaland, how's your dad?', followed immediately by songs paying tribute to Roy Keane, made Erling aware that he had ventured on to enemy territory in search of his first goal of 2023. Haaland's only effort on goal during the game was a first-half shot that was blocked by United midfielder Fred.

It was his only touch inside the opposition's box – and of his paltry 19 touches of the ball over the course of the 90 minutes, three of them came from kick-offs. His contribution sparked more debate over whether his presence made City a less effective team – and the statistics appeared to suggest there was an argument to be made that it did. After 18 games of the season, the champions were eight points behind Premier League leaders Arsenal after dropping eight points in their last five outings. At the same stage of the previous season, Guardiola's team were five points better off having scored just two fewer goals and conceded half as many. Former German international Dietmar Hamann tweeted after the game, 'Man City was a better team last season without Haaland, even if he scores 40 goals this season.'

* * *

Offside?

The argument may have gained less traction had Stuart Attwell done his job properly. United shaded the first 45 minutes, with Marcus Rashford twice failing to find the right finish after breaking clear, but after half-time it was the visitors clearly in the ascendancy. City went ahead on the hour when De Bruyne served up a clipped cross after breaking to the byline and Grealish raced in ahead of Haaland at the far post to score with a header.

United boss Erik ten Hag was about to make defensive changes when the tide of the contest turned in the 78th minute. Rashford was clearly offside when Casemiro threaded a pass forward, and the England man appeared to be setting himself to shoot when Bruno Fernandes called for him to leave the ball before shooting past City keeper Ederson. Both Ederson and his defenders had clearly been affected by Rashford's presence – and assistant referee Darren Cann raised his flag to signal offside. Attwell then sparked red joy and blue misery by awarding the goal. Four minutes later, with City in disarray, United substitute Alejandro Garnacho crossed for Rashford to steer home the decisive goal. It meant that Rashford had become the first United player since Busby Babe and City fan Dennis Viollet in 1959 to score in nine successive home games.

City players confronted the officials in the tunnel at the final whistle. United were now just a point behind their rivals in the Premier League table – although Ten Hag admitted his team had enjoyed some good fortune for their equaliser. 'I can see it from the other side as well,' said the Dutchman. 'It's a confusing moment for the back line of the opponent. The rules say Marcus didn't touch the ball and he wasn't interfering. Bruno came from the back – but I can see it from the other side.' His City counterpart was in no doubt. 'Rashford was offside – and he was distracting our players,' said Guardiola. 'Maybe I don't know what the rule is – but I know where we are playing. In this stadium, with this referee, it can happen. This is Old Trafford. It's like Anfield. You have to play better.'

Guardiola also conceded that he was still trying to come up with a game plan to get the best out of his number nine. Haaland had now gone 280 minutes without a goal and Guardiola said, 'We have to find Erling a little bit more. When teams are sat in their 18-yard box, it is more difficult. But when we are in certain areas, we have to look at him. But we will do it.'

13

Another Hat-Trick and a
North London Double

GIVEN THE chance to watch their fierce rivals Spurs play then every Arsenal fan would want them to lose. It's natural but at 8.50pm on 19 January 2023 every Gunners supporter was up and cheering when the half-time whistle sounded at the Etihad with Tottenham leading 2-0. The Cockerels had taken all six points off Manchester City in 2021/22 and were now set to beat them for a third time in a row. Even a team managed by Pep Guardiola would struggle to recover from such a loss.

This game had been originally due to take place in early September but had been postponed due to the death of Queen Elizabeth II. The sides had been level on points back then but in the intervening period the north Londoners had fallen well behind City and came into the rearranged game seeking points to stay in contention for a top four spot. Spurs, again, looked unlikely to give Harry Kane a winners' medal.

It was therefore a shock when Spurs, twice winners of the top flight in 1950/51 and 1960/61, grabbed two late first half goals from Dejan Kulusevski and Emerson Royal, a header after Ederson could only push out Kane's shot. This sent the away fans leaping into the interval. Could their side really beat City for the fifth time in six matches, including the surprise success in the Champions League semi-final in April 2019?

Having chosen not to make any half-time changes, City benefited when Hugo Lloris, whose form even at the World Cup in Qatar had been well below his normal standards, dropped Riyad Mahrez's cross, permitting Julián Álvarez to reduce the arrears.

Two minutes later Erling Haaland, who had been guilty of spurning two gilt-edged chances in the first half, scored from close range after Mahrez headed Rodri's chipped pass in his direction; it was his 22nd Premier League goal in City's 19th game of the season. It took Haaland to within a goal of Frank Roberts's total of 23 at the same stage of the 1924/25 season.

Surely, City would now go on to win the game and following defeats at Southampton and Manchester United they would return to winning ways?

Spurs though were unfortunate when Ivan Perišić's drive flicked off Rico Lewis and beat Ederson only to hit the woodwork.

If Perišić was unlucky his next intervention was not as he misjudged a long ball that was taken on by Mahrez to beat Lloris at his near post. An opportunity for a fourth goal was then denied even though Richarlison appeared to handle the ball in the area. Spurs' fortune counted for nothing as Clément Lenglet and Lloris left a bouncing ball for each other and the ever-alert Mahrez finally silenced the Cockerels. Little wonder that the City players, booed off at the interval by some supporters, enjoyed a great reception at the finish.

* * *

Guardiola criticism

None of which satisfied Pep Guardiola who criticised his players and fans, 'There's nothing from the stomach, from the guts, and we were lucky but if we don't change, we will drop points.

'We have to prepare better; I cannot deny how happy we are but we are far away from the team that we were. We gave them the first goal, and then the second goal is ridiculous.'

Asked what was missing, the Spaniard said in a remarkable post-match interview, 'Passion, fire and desire to want to win from the first minute. Our fans were silent for 45 minutes – I want my fans back. I want my fans that are here – not my away fans, they are the best – but my fans here to support every corner and every action, because Tottenham are one of the toughest opponents I've ever faced.

'They booed because we were losing but in the second half, we played good, we had more chances. Maybe it's the same with our team, maybe we are so comfortable with winning four Premier Leagues in five years.'

Having kept their title hopes alive, City were inspired by a fourth Premier League hat-trick by Haaland against Wolverhampton Wanderers, following which Guardiola gushingly praised his number nine's character.

Guardiola's questioning of his players' character after their comeback win against Tottenham had set up an extra intrigue to the game with Wolves, whose beating in a friendly of Hungarian side Honvéd in the mid-1950s inspired plans to establish the European Cup. Following a poor start to 2022/23 the Black Country club had sacked head coach Bruno Lage and replaced him with former Real Madrid, Spain and Sevilla manager Julen Lopetegui.

Lopetegui was to be disappointed by his team's first-half performance, during which they had just eight per cent of the possession. Yet at the break they were only a goal down after Haaland, who had earlier forced José Sa into a fine save, headed home from a pinpoint De Bruyne cross in the 40th minute.

The Spaniard's attempt to improve matters by making a half-time triple substitution did not, though, work out too well when Haaland added two more goals before the hour. First, he dispatched a penalty – awarded after Rúben Neves fouled İlkay Gündoğan – before completing his hat-trick with a tap-in after Sa passed the ball directly to Mahrez just outside the box and the Algerian unselfishly squared it to the unmarked Haaland, who shortly after completing his hat-trick was withdrawn to great applause.

If the Norwegian was disappointed at not being given the opportunity to score more, he did not show it, a point his manager took up afterwards, 'He's a fantastic person ... never one bad face, never decisions he doesn't understand, always sad when we can't win, he is that sort of guy.'

Guardiola also spoke out strongly against background claims that City had become a less stylish team since Haaland's arrival from Dortmund, 'When he scores, I don't know how many hat-tricks and goals, [people say] he is the solution in our team and when he does not score a goal, he is a problem in our team. This is a grey vision of this kind of things.

'We know his quality, we know each other. He is not a player to be dropped. We cannot play a false nine with him, we have to adapt with him and I think we are doing quite well.'

Guardiola, though, was not completely satisfied because when he was asked whether City remained, like was the case against Tottenham, a 'happy flowers' team, he said, 'It is getting better but it is just one game. I have to wait.'

Victory set up the following home match against table-topping Arsenal in the FA Cup nicely, especially as the sides had yet to face one another in the Premier League.

Haaland was to win his battle with Rob Holding and while a reshuffled Arsenal team created the better chances they ultimately lost out to a City side who by netting the winning goal scored a psychological punch in the battle for the title race.

The result meant that Arsenal had lost 13 of their last 14 games against Manchester City in all competitions, including the last six.

In a game of few clear chances the main talking points were the team selections. Guardiola left no stone unturned, fielding a fully-fledged first XI with Haaland leading the line. Mikel Arteta, on the other hand, made wholesale changes from Arsenal's nerve-wracking weekend win over Manchester United. Coming into their starting line-up were goalkeeper Matt Turner, Kieran Tierney, Takehiro Tomiyasu and Holding in defence and Fábio Vieira in midfield. Up front Leandro Trossard was earning his full first-team debut following his move from Brighton.

While Manchester City had more possession in the final third it was Arsenal who had the clearer chances and almost sneaked the lead from an unlikely source when Tomiyasu was clear on goal and put his laces through the ball, but Stefan Ortega, who later made a great save from Trossard, was on hand to make a strong save.

At the other end, Turner was called into action on a couple of occasions and needed to be constantly alert as in the battle between Haaland and Holding the attacker constantly got the better of his marker, such that Holding earned himself a booking and needed to be replaced by Arteta at the interval with William Saliba.

When the deadlock was finally broken it was from an unlikely source. Left-back Nathan Aké had been able to quell Bukayo Saka, whose form meant he was one of Haaland's few serious rivals for the prestigious FWA Footballer of the Year award. Following some good work out wide, Grealish fed Aké who used his weaker foot to cushion the ball past Turner in the Arsenal goal.

Even though Arteta then threw on Oleksandr Zinchenko, Gabriel Martinelli and Martin Ødegaard, City held on without any serious concern to see through the game in which the Sky Blues had three shots on target and Arsenal two.

Although afterwards many Arsenal fans consoled themselves that their reshuffled side had played well against a full-strength City team it was still fair to say that round one of three clashes had gone to the Citizens.

Guardiola was full of praise afterwards for both Arsenal and Aké, 'We were definitely better in the second half. Arsenal have taken a step forward. It was a tight game and you realise how good a side they are. I did not expect the approach from them – man-to-man – it was difficult to build up but we beat the team at the top of the league and are in the next round.

'What a season he [Nathan Aké] is playing. He controlled one of the toughest opponents in the Premier League because Saka is in an incredible moment.

'He is really good in the duels in the box, defending the far post and set pieces is an extra bonus. He is an exceptional guy, there was a period where he didn't play and he never complained once.'

14

Off-Pitch Allegations Used to Inspire On-Field Success

WHEN CITY travelled to face Antonio Conte's Spurs only 17 days after beating them at home they must have travelled with high expectations as the north Londoners had lost their previous two matches in front of their own fans, against Aston Villa and Arsenal, and were struggling to stay in touch with the top four. Spurs fans, following the capturing of the Double in 1960/61 – the first club to achieve the feat in the 20th century – were still waiting for a third top-flight title. Surely this was the time for Pep Guardiola to throw off his hoodoo at the Tottenham Hotspur Stadium, which had only been open for three years, where City had lost four in a row.

Yet with Harry Kane still scoring goals, having reached 17 so far in the Premier League, it was Spurs who won 1-0 on a special day that resulted in Kane becoming the club's all-time record scorer, surpassing the great Jimmy Greaves, with his 267th goal. Kane was to be cheered to the rafters at the end.

The last time the teams had faced one another in London, on the opening day of 2021/22 when Kane had failed to appear as he sought to force a move north, City, despite having new £100m signing Jack Grealish starting, had looked blunt without a striker and fell to a 1-0 loss.

City now had a young striker in Haaland and he was set to emulate Kane by finishing a season at the top of the Premier League charts, with the England captain having done so on four occasions.

It was, though, to be the older man who took the glory as Haaland, perhaps missing the unwell Phil Foden, had one of his poorest games for City, who had now lost three away league and cup games in a row, touching the ball on just 27 occasions and none of which were for a shot at goal.

With Kevin De Bruyne and İlkay Gündoğan left on the bench at the start of play and with Haaland quiet the closest City came to striking was a Riyad Mahrez driving effort that smashed against the underside of the crossbar only seconds before the break.

In comparison, Kane reached his landmark with a composed finish from ten yards following a smart Pierre-Emile Højbjerg pass.

Kane's goal – his 200th in the Premier League – was to bring joy across north London as earlier Arsenal, despite having been boosted by the deadline-day signing of Chelsea's Italian midfielder Jorginho, had suffered a first league defeat since September when they lost to a James Tarkowski goal at Everton. A chance to put pressure on the Gunners, who thus stayed five points clear, had been squandered.

In an obvious attempt to take the pressure off his players, Pep Guardiola told Sky Sports after the match, 'We started really well, as usually happens against Tottenham home and away, but after we made a mistake they punished us – 1-0 down it is different, we had chances, and of course when we lose balls in transition with [Dejan] Kulusevski and Son [Heung-min], it is not easy. We dropped three points.' He congratulated Kane on his 'fantastic achievement' before addressing City's poor record at Spurs, 'Sooner or later it is going to change, but it is strange we haven't scored one goal, we have missed penalties in the past. To find an explanation is not easy. We found the positions, made good balls to the channels, but missed the last action up front.

'We are not in the position to think about being champions, just the next game, Aston Villa, we will prepare well and play our game as best as possible.'

Defeat had the media suggesting that Guardiola should start looking over his shoulder at the rejuvenated Manchester United, two points further adrift in third but with one game fewer to play. Newcastle were five points behind the Blues having played the same 21 matches. But City were about to embark on a 25-game unbeaten run that would take them to the brink of immortality, driven by a sense of injustice that Guardiola turned into a siege mentality.

The morning after the defeat in north London, the drama at the Etihad Stadium became a crisis when the Premier League announced they had charged the reigning champions with 115 breaches of their profitability and sustainability rules and a failure to cooperate with an investigation into the finances of the club that had taken four years. City were accused of failing to provide 'accurate financial information that gives a true and fair view of the club's financial position' between the 2009/10 and the 2017/18 seasons, a period in which they had been champions four times.

A Premier League statement read, 'In accordance with Premier League Rule W.82.1, the Premier League confirms that it has today referred a number of alleged breaches of the Premier League Rules by Manchester City Football Club to a Commission under Premier League Rule W.3.4.'

City had only been told of the impending charges minutes before they were laid out in full on the Premier League's website, with league chief executive Richard Masters ringing club CEO Ferran Soriano to deliver the bombshell news. City believed certain sections of the media had already been tipped off and their official response was terse. A club statement read, 'Manchester City FC is surprised by the issuing of these alleged breaches of the Premier League Rules, particularly given the extensive engagement and vast amount of detailed materials that the EPL has been provided with. The club welcomes the review of this matter by an independent Commission, to impartially consider the comprehensive body of irrefutable evidence that exists in support of its position. As such we look forward to this matter being put to rest once and for all.'

City paid a €60m fine in 2014 for failing UEFA's Financial Fair Play Regulations – although it was reduced to €20m when they subsequently showed compliance. Despite accepting the censure, the club refused to accept that they were guilty of any wrongdoing. So when UEFA announced in February 2020 that they were imposing a two-year Champions League ban on the Blues for further irregularities as well as levying a €30m fine, this time City made an appeal to the Court of Arbitration for Sport. UEFA's case was based on claims made in *Der Spiegel* after the German publication had been granted access to a raft of emails stolen by the Portuguese computer hacker Rui Pinto. Five months later, CAS announced that 'most of the alleged breaches were either not established or time-barred' and lifted the punishment, although they did impose a €10m fine over City's failure to cooperate with UEFA's investigation.

The air at the City Football Academy was crackling with anticipation ahead of Guardiola's press conference to preview the home game with Aston Villa on 12 February. Few journalists expected the City manager to address the Premier League charges, believing any questions would be referred to the club's statement four days earlier because of the sensitive legal nature of the issue. Even club officials weren't given a heads up on how the Catalan was going to respond. But his words galvanised the entire club.

Guardiola went on the front foot by turning on City's accusers and sending a passionate rallying call to his players, who were sat 150 yards away in the first-team building watching the live broadcast on Sky Sports News.

'My first thought is that we have already been condemned,' he said. 'The same as we were condemned by UEFA. The club proved we were completely innocent then. Why should this be any different? We are lucky to live in a marvellous country where everyone is innocent until proven guilty. Just in case we are guilty, we will accept the punishment the Premier League decides. But if we are innocent what happens to the damage that has already been done?

'One week after UEFA made the sentence against us nine teams – Burnley, Wolves, Leicester, Newcastle, Spurs, Arsenal [Manchester] United, Liverpool and Chelsea – wanted to take our position in the Champions League. Now we are fighting 19 teams and we are going to defend ourselves.'

Then came a message that resonated with every member of staff at the Etihad, 'In previous seasons, we didn't give up in the toughest moments and I have a feeling we are going to do it again. We are not part of the establishment and it hurts when they try to take away what we have won on the pitch.

'Playing good is not enough for this club. Playing better is not enough. We have to be much, much better because to beat the establishment you have to be perfect because we don't have history and are not part of the hierarchy. I'm not moving from this seat. More than ever I want to stay here because my people told me not to worry with UEFA and they proved it. I trust all of my people. We have to be closer and together than ever.'

City's fans certainly got Guardiola's message, thousands of them turning up outside the stadium 90 minutes before kick-off against Aston Villa to welcome the team bus. One banner read 'Fuck the Premier League' and the traditional pre-game anthem was drowned out by jeers.

The champions had been given a huge lift the previous afternoon when leaders Arsenal were held to a 1-1 draw at the Emirates by Brentford. It meant the Gunners had taken just one point from six including their first defeat in 14 Premier League games at Everton.

Victory over Villa and a midweek win against Mikel Arteta's side in London three days later would take City top of the table on goal difference. City would have still played a game more, but with the Gunners scheduled to travel to the Etihad in April, the title would be back in the hands of the champions.

Haaland failed to get on the scoresheet and was substituted at half-time with a thigh injury as three first-half goals from Rodri, Gündoğan and a Mahrez penalty put them in control on their way to a 3-1 victory. He got a pat on the back from his team-mates for providing Gündoğan with the driven 39th-minute cross from which the City captain fired home from virtually the same spot he was in when he scored the goal against Villa in May 2022 to secure the title. The Norwegian's presence spooked Callum Chambers as the pair chased De Bruyne's pass and the Villa defender could only head the ball wide of Emi Martínez as he raced from his goal. Haaland seized on to the mistake and fired a low cross into Gündoğan's path as he arrived at the far post.

Haaland had been carrying a knock after colliding with Martínez in the 14th minute as they challenged for a bouncing ball. It appeared that both players had made a genuine attempt to gain possession and Gündoğan fired the loose ball into the net only for referee Rob Jones to rule that Martínez had been fouled. The Villa keeper required treatment, while Haaland limped away holding his neck and right thigh.

Perhaps that was why the striker didn't snatch the ball away from Mahrez when Grealish was tripped by his former Villa team-mate Jacob Ramsey in first-half injury time and Jones pointed to the spot. Rodri, who had headed City into a fourth-minute lead, was also interested in stepping up, but Gündoğan stepped in to defuse a potential row before handing the ball to Mahrez.

'I need to talk to them,' said Guardiola after the game. 'Normally Erling is our first taker and Riyad is the second one. Maybe Erling was injured so I will see what they say tomorrow.' It was a situation that would surface again later in the season, but it was clear that Guardiola had other things to concentrate his mind as he admitted that Haaland was a doubt for the showdown at the Emirates. 'Haaland had a big knock and was uncomfortable,' he said. 'At 3-0 we did not want to take any risks. We will see in the next few days how he will do, but at half-time, I spoke to the doctors and they said "don't take risks". I agree. I don't think Erling is injured, but if he is he isn't going to play [at Arsenal].'

Haaland was involved in training the next day, but once again his workload was managed to avoid putting him under excess strain. The injury had been caused by the impact with Martínez rather than any overload, but City were taking no chances for a trip to north London that had been postponed from its original date in October so that Arsenal could fit in a Europa League tie against PSV Eindhoven, which itself had been moved from September due to limited police resources ahead of Queen Elizabeth II's funeral.

On the eve of the game, Guardiola brought his players together over the dinner table to tell them what was on the line – and it wasn't just the opportunity to move to the top of the table for the first time since 5 November. 'We need to be united,' he demanded. 'If you are not together you will not win anything and you will give up an opportunity you will regret for the rest of your lives.'

It was Haaland who sealed a 3-1 victory for the visitors during a second-half performance in which they really flexed their muscles. Rodri and Gündoğan combined to free De Bruyne and when the Belgian dragged a low cross back to Haaland, he controlled instantly with his left foot before finding the bottom corner of Aaron Ramsdale's goal.

But this was more than Erling Haaland, master goalscorer. It was his all-round contribution that caught Guardiola's eye. William Saliba and Gabriel Magalhães had been the central defensive rock on which the Gunners' title bid had been built, but they were beaten up both physically and psychologically by Haaland's classic centre-forward's display.

It was the striker's headed flick that led to Takehiro Tomiyasu trying to find Ramsdale with a back-pass that only allowed De Bruyne to lift City into a 24th-minute lead with a measured finish. And although the Gunners drew level three minutes before the break when referee Anthony Taylor ruled that Ederson's innocuous collision with Eddie Nketiah warranted a penalty that was duly despatched by Bukayo Saka, it prompted Guardiola to alter a game plan that hadn't really worked in the first period with Bernardo Silva operating as a left-back.

City delivered a real statement of intent. Haaland thought he had won a penalty after being dragged back by Gabriel after muscling himself past the Brazilian, but Taylor was forced to rescind his decision and a yellow card when a VAR check showed he was offside before tangling with his marker.

But in the 72nd minute, Silva's pass enabled Haaland to spring Arsenal's offside trap and he squared a pass for Gündoğan to set up Grealish for a side-footed finish that beat Ramsdale with the aid of a deflection off Tomiyasu. When Haaland sealed the deal ten minutes later, Arteta stamped his foot on the ground in frustration. Haaland had put the boot into Arsenal's title pretensions.

It meant City had become the first club to win seven consecutive away games at Arsenal in all competitions. Their previous 61 visits to Highbury or the Emirates had yielded just six victories. Yet this win was secured with only 36 per cent possession of the ball – the lowest percentage of any team managed by Guardiola in a league game. It was clear that Haaland's presence was now adding another dimension to their play. Guardiola said, 'I tried something new and it was horrible. Our shape allowed Arsenal to play, so we adjusted at half-time and we controlled the game more.

'Erling helped us a lot, using his power to keep the ball. He went man-to-man with Gabriel and Saliba and he was so aggressive. He was able to keep the ball and bring the runners into the game. Erling was brilliant. Maybe we have to play more like that to get the best out of him. Not by playing more long balls but by playing more long passes.

'When people complain because he doesn't score a hat-trick every game, it's because of his standards. When your standards are so many goals, they expect you to always score a hat-trick – and that isn't going to happen.'

15

Two-Time European Champions Blunt Title Charge

ERLING HAALAND'S bid to win the Premier League in his first season in England took another twist three days after the landmark win over Arsenal at the Emirates when Manchester City were held to a 1-1 draw at struggling Nottingham Forest, another of his father's former clubs. The striker had claimed his first City hat-trick against Forest at the Etihad back in August – and he could have walked away from the City Ground with another match ball.

Arsenal had served notice that they would not allow their challenge to fade away when they travelled to Aston Villa in the day's early game. Mikel Arteta's side demonstrated their own powers of recovery by twice drawing level through Bukayo Saka and Oleksandr Zinchenko after Ollie Watkins and Philippe Coutinho had twice given Villa the lead. Going into injury time, it appeared the Gunners would drop more precious points until they delivered a blow that was felt all the way across the M42. First midfielder Jorginho saw his first-time blast from 25 yards crash against the underside of the crossbar before bouncing into the net off the head of Villa's World Cup-winning keeper Emi Martínez. Then, in the eighth minute of time added on, with Martínez deciding against following manager Unai Emery's instructions by going forward for a corner, Fábio Vieira led a counterattack that finished with Gabriel Martinelli walking Arsenal's fourth goal into an empty net.

City's players knew of the drama that had unfolded 50 miles away – and that they were back in second place. Guardiola later lauded his team's performance against Forest as 'brilliant'. But the manager knew that this was an opportunity lost as he travelled back to Manchester.

City's first-half dominance was rewarded when Jack Grealish rolled a pass square for Bernardo Silva to bludgeon a rising shot past Forest keeper Keylor Navas from the edge of the box. The visitors should have then gone on to win comfortably, but missed a glut of second-half chances – with Haaland the main culprit.

He would have been left with an empty net had Phil Foden not slipped when trying to play an easy pass, which allowed Forest defender Felipe to clear. Aymeric Laporte then sent a header straight at Navas from a Kevin De Bruyne corner before then poking the follow-up into the arms of the Costa Rican. When Haaland then sent a close-range half-volley against the crossbar before blazing the rebound over from six yards after Navas had spilled Foden's shot, it gave Forest a lifeline which they grasped in the 86th minute when substitute Chris Wood arrived at the far post to squeeze home a finish after Brennan Johnson and Morgan Gibbs-White had carved the visitors open down the right.

It was Forest's only effort on target. During the first half, City enjoyed 84 per cent possession. Guardiola said, 'It was a brilliant performance. We played really good – but just didn't score. That's why we dropped points. But we should have also defended the goal better, with more energy. We conceded one goal from one shot on target.' But Guardiola was also frustrated with his team's lack of ruthlessness in front of goal. He was given a yellow card in the 66th minute by referee Graham Scott for his theatrical touchline reaction when Haaland broke through on goal and then fell to the floor after being impeded by Forest captain Joe Worrall. A VAR check confirmed the officials were right not to award a penalty – and even Guardiola accepted he was wrong to protest with such vehemence after the game. 'I didn't see it,' he admitted. 'It looked like the last man had brought him [Haaland] down and I was asking why Erling would fall down when he was one against one with the keeper. Maybe it was soft, maybe not, I didn't see it. But I complained to the fourth official and asked why Haaland would stop – and so I got a deserved yellow card. But we didn't win in the end because we missed chances that were one metre from the goal – and not just one chance.'

Since his hat-trick against Wolves on 22 January, Haaland had now found the back of the net just once in his last six appearances – and City's season was at a crossroads. But they were starting to head in the right direction in terms of performances. Results would start to follow – and so would goals for their number nine. City would win their next 12 Premier League games to seize the initiative from Arsenal in the run-in and by the time they next dropped points, they had already been crowned champions.

But Haaland's first return to Germany in a City shirt would bring more questions than answers. Guardiola warned that facing RB Leipzig in the last 16 of the Champions League would be a tough task – especially without the injured De Bruyne. Haaland, meanwhile, had faced Leipzig four times for Dortmund – and scored three times on three occasions. That included a brace in a 4-1 victory in the 2021 DFB-Pokal Final in Berlin's Olympiastadion. Guardiola's prediction proved to be right in the first leg in the sold-out Red Bull Arena, reduced to a 42,600 capacity for European games, despite a first half dominated by City which only brought a solitary goal for Riyad Mahrez in the 27th minute.

The Algerian made the most of Grealish's pass and İlkay Gündoğan's flick to bury an assured left-footed finish the day after celebrating his 32nd birthday.

City had 72 per cent possession in the first half, but that would drop to 49 per cent after the break when Leipzig coach Marco Rose sent on attacking wing-back Benjamin Henrichs and ordered his team to press their opponents higher up the pitch. Haaland struggled to shake off the attentions of highly rated Croatian centre-back Joško Gvardiol all evening. He managed just 22 touches of the ball on a night when every other outfield player had at least 60. His one attempt at goal was a weak right-footed shot dragged wide of the far post in the 68th minute after Grealish's pass gave him the chance to test his marker's pace. It was Gvardiol who headed home a deserved equaliser two minutes later, although he appeared to be climbing on the shoulders of Aymeric Laporte when Marcel Halstenberg worked a short corner to whip over a left-footed cross. Gvardiol's performance impressed Guardiola so much that after the game he urged director of football Txiki Begiristain to investigate the possibility of taking him to Manchester ahead of the following season. The move was completed in August 2023 with Gvardiol stating on his arrival at the Etihad that he was pleased he was no longer playing against Haaland.

* * *

'We need to look for Erling a little more'

Guardiola appeared to be berating his players on the pitch when he called them into a huddle after the final whistle. He insisted later, 'I said to them, "Why do you have your heads down? Heads up, it was good."' He also shouldered the blame for the drop in Haaland's output. 'It's my fault,' he said. 'Erling has been so good all season and I am not talking about his metrics. When we finish the game, one second later I know if he was involved or not and whether he should be involved more. I don't need to see numbers to know that. I know exactly. We need to look for Erling a little more. Striker is the most difficult position, with one man against two defenders – and with Erling sometimes there are even more defenders. It's fine for him to be frustrated – I'm frustrated too. But I also say that happiness is overrated!'

And to prove his point, Guardiola – ever the ultimate perfectionist – even managed to find himself unhappy in the subsequent demolition of Bournemouth on the south coast.

After the frustrations of consecutive draws, Bournemouth were to prove to be the perfect opponents for a City side looking to maintain the pressure on Arsenal at the top of the Premier League and for Haaland to end a relatively barren spell of just one goal in six matches. When he did force home City's second from close in it took him on to 27 league goals, one more than Sergio Agüero's highest total in 2014/15.

City had won the previous 11 matches between the sides and the result was therefore no surprise. Indeed, when they had met earlier in the season, City had scored four without reply in a relatively straightforward victory that did not bode well for the defeated Cherries under Scott Parker who was sacked soon after when Liverpool chalked up a record-equaling 9-0 victory against them at Anfield. Gary O'Neil was appointed and won his first away game, 3-2 at Nottingham Forest.

Bournemouth had recorded their second away victory, 1-0 at Wolves, in the weekend prior to City making the trip south. Any hopes of an upset however were blown away in a commanding first-half performance by Guardiola's men who scored three times without being troubled by the hosts. First, on 15 minutes Julián Álvarez snapped home a rebounded Haaland shot that was the result of a probing

Erling Haaland scoring the second Manchester City goal in the 6-3 hammering of Manchester United at the Etihad Stadium on 2 October 2022. Haaland and Phil Foden each scored three for City.

Haaland scores Manchester City's third goal in a 3-0 defeat of Bayern Munich at home in the first leg of the Champions League quarter-final on 11 April 2023.

Rodri celebrates scoring Manchester City's winning goal in the Champions League Final in Istanbul against Inter Milan with Jack Grealish and Erling Haaland ecstatically joining him.

On his Premier League debut Haaland celebrates his second goal in front of the travelling City fans that included his father Alfie in a 2-0 victory at West Ham United.

In the second game of the Champions League group stages Erling Haaland shows what his former side Borussia Dortmund are missing by scoring a spectacular winner on 14 September 2022. His manager later compared it to a goal that Johan Cruyff had scored in 1973 against Atletico Madrid and which is rated the best goal the Dutch genius ever scored for Barcelona.

Accompanied by his manager Ole Gunnar Solskjaer an 18-year-old Salzburg-bound Erling Haaland bids farewell to fans of second-place Molde FC following a 1-0 home victory against the champions Rosenberg in the final game of the Norwegian Championship on 30 September 2018.

On 3 October 2019 Erling Haaland sparked wild celebrations amongst Salzburg fans when he tapped home an equaliser with his left foot – his 18th goal of the season – to draw his side level at 3-3 in a Champions League group-stage thriller at Anfield that ended in a 4-3 defeat.

In the 2017 Under-17 Championship in Croatia Phil Foden was pitched against Erling Haaland in a match that England won 3-1.

Norway beat neighbours Sweden 2-1 on 5 June 2022 in a 2022/23 UEFA Nations League match in which Haaland converted an 18th minute penalty with a left-footed shot to the bottom left corner. He later scored Norway's second on 69 minutes.

In a bid to keep Erling Haaland quiet at the Champions League Final in Istanbul the Inter coach Simone Inzaghi's game-plan involved surrounding the City striker with central defensive trio Matteo Darmian, Francesco Acerbi and Alessandro Bastoni, seen here battling in the air with the City number 9.

In the 2020/21 Champions League competition Erling Haaland scored ten goals in eight games for Borussia Dortmund and is shown here celebrating one of his two on 9 March 2021 in a 2-2 draw at home to Sevilla in the last 16 of the competition that put the German side through 5-4 on aggregate.

With his side 2-0 down at half time Erling Haaland scored three times as Manchester City beat Crystal Palace 4-2 on 27 August 2022. Haaland is seen here celebrating his first goal with Kevin De Bruyne in a season in which at times their understanding was almost telepathic.

On his first appearance at Wembley, Erling Haaland was part of the Manchester City side that thanks to three goals from Riyad Mahrez swept Sheffield United aside 3-0 in the Emirates FA Cup semi-final and during which Haaland was greeted with a hug from his manager Pep Guardiola when he was substituted late on.

The faces of two confident players. Kyle Walker and Erling Haaland prior to kick-off before the first leg of the Champions League semi-final 1-1 draw at the Bernabeu Stadium that set up Manchester City to sweep away holders Real Madrid 4-0 in the second leg.

Erling Haaland was at the forefront of City's trophy parade in Manchester on 12 June 2023. By winning the Premier League, FA Cup and Champions League Pep Guardiola's squad had equalled the feat of Manchester United in 1999.

move by Gündoğan and Foden that began with a fine tackle and pass by Rico Lewis.

Fifteen minutes later Haaland finished off a Foden shot that had cannoned to him from Jordan Zemura. It was one of seven chances created by Foden on the day, the most by any City player in two seasons. Any remote possibility Bournemouth might have entertained of getting back into the game were destroyed just before the break when the ever-alert Foden, returning to the side after missing the Leipzig game, slotted home a square pass across his own box by Philip Billing.

On the return, City were then presented with a further helping hand when Chris Mepham, later guilty of a poor challenge on his tormentor-in-chief Jack Grealish, put the ball into his own net from an Álvarez shot.

A late Jefferson Lerma goal that angered Guardiola was deserved reward for a spirited performance by O'Neil's side. Yet the gulf in class was obvious on an afternoon when City did what they needed to do to stay two points behind Arsenal who had 21-year-old Gabriel Martinelli to thank for the Gunners edging beyond Leicester City with a 46th-minute goal from Leandro Trossard's neat pass. The margin of the victory did though strengthen City's goal difference to ten superior than Arsenal's, who in midweek used their game in hand advantage by beating Everton 3-0 at home with Saka opening the scoring.

Guardiola had calmed down by the time he met the press afterwards and had been impressed by how his side had, despite playing so many games and travelled so far in recent weeks, 'played incredibly aggressive. Our attack was more dynamic and we got a good result.' He also praised teenager Rico Lewis, saying he 'had quality and intelligence … he moves in small spaces, to play in pockets that we need he is unique. He is really good at that.'

According to Guardiola, Haaland's impact had 'been incredible. We love him and he is helping us, today we found him more and he is an incredible threat.' The winning manager was also delighted with Foden's return, saying 'We need Phil – his work ethic, his goals, his assists. Step by step he will be back [to his best form.]'

* * *

As in 1936/37, could City overtake Arsenal in the title run-in?

City thus remained in a perfect place to do what their first team to win the top flight had done in 1936/37 and overtake leaders Arsenal in a season when one of the key fixtures was a late match between the pair that City won to go to the top of the table for the first time. Could history repeat itself?

With potentially tougher fixtures to come, Haaland was rested for the FA Cup fifth round tie at Bristol City where the City starting line-up included only two players in De Bruyne and Silva who had played the last time Guardiola's side had travelled to Ashton Gate five years earlier to clinch a place in the EFL Cup Final with a 3-0 victory in the second leg of the semi-final following a 3-2 success in the first leg. Leroy Sané, Sergio Agüero and De Bruyne had scored the goals that night.

Nigel Pearson's team had been in good form in the Championship and were unbeaten in 12 games. A capacity West Country crowd gave their players magnificent backing but with Foden scoring twice and De Bruyne once it was City who made it through to the quarter-finals.

The game was covered by ITV Sport, who Guardiola was speaking to after the game when discussing Foden, 'Dynamic, rhythm, work rate, he's quality. His career was always up, up, up. This season he struggled a bit and was a bit down. But now he's back for the best bit of the season.

His impact has been amazing. Football pays off when you work like he does.'

Guardiola also praised his opponents, who in 1909 reached their only FA Cup Final where they were beaten by Manchester United 1-0 thanks to a goal by former City man Sandy Turnbull, and their supporters, 'It was really tough. Bristol showed us how good they can be. I was impressed by some players; I didn't know them. The second half was much better.

'Incredible fans at Bristol. We came here five years ago in the Carabao [EFL] Cup and it was amazing. I remember it perfectly.'

Haaland was back at number nine for the home match with Newcastle and in what was a quiet game for him he showed he could see the funny side of football, create goals and defend his colleagues.

Newcastle travelled to the Etihad having never won there but having become another oil-rich state-owned club they had cut the gap on City and arrived in a good place to make it into the Champions League for 2023/24. They had also provided tough opposition earlier in the season at St James' Park.

Yet, despite creating two great first-half opportunities which were spurned by Sean Longstaff and Callum Wilson, the Magpies, recently defeated by Manchester United at Wembley in the EFL Cup Final, rightly left the field at half-time losing to a Foden goal. This came on 15 minutes following a marvellous run and although the wide man's shot did take a nick off Sven Botman to send Nick Pope the wrong way it was no more than the England international deserved. If Foden's hero Paul Gascoigne was watching then he would have been impressed. Foden went on to have a great match.

On 65 minutes the result was tied up when Grealish found Haaland whose instant ball was controlled by substitute Bernardo Silva whose subsequent forensic shot flashed into the bottom right.

Silva had only two minutes earlier been introduced to the play as Guardiola sought to respond to Eddie Howe's three changes in an attempt to grab an equaliser.

At 2-0 up City were set for a precious three points. Playing as a lone striker in a 4-2-3-1 formation Haaland had earlier headed and then shot well wide as he struggled to escape the attentions of Botman and Jamaal Lascelles.

* * *

Booked for defending his team-mates

With City needing as many players as possible to be fit for the run-in, on 73 minutes when Dan Burn took Grealish's ankle before glaring over the injured City winger it was Haaland who came to his colleague's rescue when he squared up to the big Newcastle defender. Fortunately, just as the incident looked like it might turn nasty, referee Simon Hooper stepped in and booked both men who even enjoyed a laugh together once they had calmed down.

There was then an attempt to rile the big Norwegian striker even more when he was wrestled to the floor by Lascelles. Having initially glared menacingly at the centre-back Haaland showed his professionalism by calming down and then bursting out in laughter. It was the perfect response to a crude attempt to get him sent off.

With Newcastle thereafter rarely looking like scoring, the game petered out for a result that meant having conceded several goals in recent games Ederson recorded his 100th clean sheet in the Premier League. Pressure was thus maintained on Arsenal who the following day played poorly and were only rescued by a last-minute Reiss Nelson effort to defeat Bournemouth 3-2.

Before the game Guardiola recognised that Newcastle's newfound wealth meant they were certain to become a 'future title threat' to his side. He repeated this afterwards and said it had been a 'tough game' in which 'the solidarity between the players was amazing' and 'big actions for both goals had made the difference'. He praised his goalkeeper who, like the rest of the players, was, with no game in the next seven days, given time off before the tricky Saturday evening encounter at Crystal Palace on 11 March. Guardiola has always believed in giving his players successive days off when the fixture schedule allows so that they can travel back to their home countries to visit family and friends when practical. Guardiola used the break to visit his wife and youngest daughter in Barcelona. Unfortunately, not all of his players used their rest and relaxation in the same way and England defender Kyle Walker was questioned by police after an incident in a Manchester bar went viral after being captured on a security camera. Walker was not charged over the alleged offence – and when Guardiola faced the media 24 hours before the trip to Selhurst Park, he found himself facing questions about the behaviour of his players rather than the form of his top goalscorer.

When Guardiola was asked whether Haaland was struggling to adapt himself to City's philosophy, he replied, 'In our process, I would like to see him more involved, but that's up to him. It's not good or bad. It is what it is. I love him and we love to have him. That is the reality but Erling has some moments – like in the past when we had Gabriel [Jesus] and Sergio [Agüero] when we didn't look for them a lot. Now we must try to do it. We must see that he is there and a good target for us – and so the first vision has to be to look for him.

'But sometimes when you look forward too quickly, you are less precise and you lose the ball and allow transitions for the opposition. This balance is what we have to find in the right way because when he runs, with his power, the tendency is to give him the ball because we think he will score a goal.'

But if he doesn't get it – like happened against Newcastle – it becomes a transition for the other team. It's the question of time but he gives us a lot. I would say in Germany, in Spain, in Italy, in Norway or in the Congo that these types of players can adapt everywhere. Africa, South America? No problem.'

This was an evening when City's players really did have to trust the process – and they were rewarded when Haaland won the game from the penalty spot 13 minutes from time after İlkay Gündoğan had been caught late by Palace winger Michael Olise. He had missed a golden chance in the first half when he lifted Nathan Aké's low cross over the crossbar from ten yards. 'I don't like to miss chances,' said Haaland after the match. 'I should have scored, but there was a small thing in the grass that made the ball bounce higher!' Haaland didn't speculate on what the unidentified object could have been. But when TV cameras showed him looking to the sky after referee Rob Jones spotted Olise's foul on Gündoğan, there were suggestions that he was asking for some divine intervention. 'I was not looking to the heavens,' insisted Haaland after he had sent Palace keeper Vicente Guaita the wrong way from 12 yards. 'I looked at the big screen, honestly. I don't know, where else should I look? I don't have to look at the keeper. I just breathe at that moment.'

* * *

Loving the title race

Haaland's knee-slide celebration in front of City's travelling fans spoke volumes. At the final whistle, after hugging team-mates Gündoğan, Grealish and Álvarez, he gave Palace defender Joel Ward a squeeze, presumably mistaking him for another City player. But while Haaland made it clear how important it was for him to be back in the goals, he also made a point of telling anyone questioning his desire to mix it in the Premier League that he was loving the challenge.

Haaland said, 'Nothing is decided yet, but I am loving this title race. This is England. This is what I've been watching my entire life. I enjoy every single second of it. It's good to be in the middle of it. Every game is a fight. Today we fought, so I am happy. Everyone knows how important this win is for us, but we have to keep going. Other teams know how City play, of course, because in the last five years we have won four Premier Leagues. I just do what I can do.'

16

High-Energy Performances in Europe and FA Cup as it's Unlucky 13 for Leipzig and Burnley

PEP GUARDIOLA insisted that Haaland had not been signed just to make City European champions. He correctly pointed out that his team had been knocked out of the Champions League on away goals despite scoring six times over two legs against Monaco in 2017, then the following year they lost 5-1 on aggregate to Liverpool before another away goals loss to Tottenham after winning a thrilling second leg at the Etihad 4-3. The near-misses continued; a 3-1 quarter-final defeat to Lyon in the 2020 mini-tournament played in Lisbon because of the Covid-19 pandemic was a loss that shook Guardiola after he had tinkered with his team. Then City's first appearance in the final ended in another pitiful performance and a 1-0 defeat to Chelsea in Porto after the Catalan had experimented with a team that had playmaker İlkay Gündoğan as a defensive midfielder with Rodri and Fernandinho on the bench. Guardiola had never played that XI before – and didn't do so again after being outwitted by Thomas Tuchel. In 2022, old flaws resurfaced when City found themselves 5-3 up on aggregate going into the last minute of the second leg of the semi-final at a stunned Bernabéu. Then Rodrygo scored twice inside two minutes to take the game to extra time where Karim Benzema's penalty sent Real Madrid through to a Paris match against Liverpool and a 14th European crown.

Guardiola had started employing a back four comprising entirely of centre-backs to bring his team more defensive solidity, although John Stones would often be asked to move forward into midfield and Kyle Walker would also be deployed in his favoured right-back role if the boss decided his blistering pace was required. It was a ploy that often went unnoticed because most eyes were focused on the struggle to introduce Haaland into a system that relied heavily on using a deep-lying striker to ensure City could overload the midfield.

After the 1-1 first-leg draw in Leipzig, the Blues were big favourites to reach a sixth successive Champions League quarter-final. The German club's only visit to the Etihad had seen them despatched 6-3 in the group stage in September 2021 – although they restored some pride with a 2-1 home win with City's passage already assured. Even with the away goals rule now a thing of the past, Guardiola was taking no chances. Stones, Rúben Dias, Manuel Akanji and Nathan Aké would give his team a defensive platform which enabled his attacking players to run riot. Haaland was Leipzig's worst nightmare – although the rejuvenated Kevin De Bruyne also piled on the misery.

* * *

Five goals

Haaland became only the third player to score five times in a Champions League tie, emulating the nap hands of Lionel Messi for Barcelona against Bayer Leverkusen in 2012 and Luiz Adriano for Shakhtar Donetsk against BATE Borisov two years later. Haaland's goals came in a 35-minute blitz either side of half-time, before Guardiola decided to replace him with Julián Álvarez in the 63rd minute with history beckoning. 'I told Pep when he took me off that I would have loved to score a double hat-trick,' said Haaland. 'But what can you do?' Guardiola said, 'I didn't know he could equal Messi until after the game. But if Erling sets a milestone like that at his age, the rest of his life will be boring. Now he has the target of doing it again in the future.' It was tough to tell whether the City manager was joking.

But even Haaland couldn't suppress a laugh when former City defender Joleon Lescott asked him in his role as a BT pundit what his super-strength was. He replied, 'My super-strength? I think that after scoring five goals, I have to say scoring goals! A lot of the goals today, I didn't even think about. I was just doing it. A lot of what I do is about being quick in the mind and doing the right thing by putting the ball where the keeper isn't.'

During the build-up, Guardiola had repeated his mantra that Haaland needed to involve himself more in aspects of the game other than scoring goals. 'I don't like a player just being in the box scoring goals,' he said in the official UEFA press conference. 'Of course, it is important and the main thing we need from Erling, but part of his game when we are not near our opponents' box and he cannot score a goal is to be active and become involved in everything we are doing. Erling has improved that – but he can improve some more and be even better.'

Haaland followed Guardiola's demands to the letter – and this time his pace, power and movement were just too much for Joško Gvardiol to handle. He had already forced Leipzig keeper Janis Blaswich into a fine save by the time he put City ahead in the 22nd minute from the penalty spot after Slovakian referee Slavko Vinčić had been advised by VAR official Alejandro Hernández to look at the pitchside monitor after Akanji's header had brushed Benjamin Henrichs's hand. The German defender had been fortunate to escape having a penalty being given against him in injury time in the first leg – this time his luck ran out.

Haaland scored again just 78 seconds later when he forced Blaswich into a hurried clearance and then laid the ball back into De Bruyne's path to strike a 20-yard shot against the underside of the crossbar. The Norwegian was already on the move as De Bruyne took aim and was then to head the loose ball into the unguarded goal. His fifth Etihad hat-trick came in the second minute of first-half injury time when Rúben Dias sent a header against the inside of the post and Haaland was able to force the ball over the line as Amadou Haidara desperately tried to clear. He was also involved in the move which saw İlkay Gündoğan score City's fourth goal four minutes into the second half before shooting home from close range again in the 53rd minute after Blaswich had saved Akanji's effort and Haaland's initial follow-up.

Then, in the 57th minute, came another piece of history. Akanji forced Blaswich into a smart save when he flicked on Riyad Mahrez's cross, but there was Haaland to bury the rebound with a fierce, instinctive finish with his right foot. It was his 39th goal of the season – and it broke the club record set 94 years earlier by Tommy Johnson. Guardiola said, 'The problem for Erling is that every time he doesn't score three goals he will be criticised for the rest of his career. This is the reality. It is a lot of pressure to have but he has made an incredible season so far. But what I really like about him is the way he celebrates all of his goals and how he celebrates the same way when his mates score. That shows how happy he is here.'

After Haaland was removed from the action City eased off before De Bruyne made it 7-0 late on as Leipzig were condemned to their heaviest European defeat.

Haaland marched on to the pitch at the final whistle to retrieve the match ball from referee Vinčić. The following day he posted a photograph of himself taking a nap on a couch with his arm resting on the ball.

Jeering the Champions League anthem has become a pre-match tradition for those City fans who still feel their club was unfairly treated by UEFA over alleged FFP irregularities, but their favourite number nine changed the ringtone on his mobile phone to the distinctive tune written by English composer Tony Britten in 1992 and based on Handel's 'Zadok the Priest'.

'I love this competition,' said Haaland just minutes after delivering the statement performance that shook the rest of Europe. 'It is always such a big night when you play in the Champions League. To score five goals and win 7-0 makes me so happy.' Team-mate John Stones admitted, 'I knew Erling was good – but I didn't know he was this good. I'm running out of messages to write on the match balls he keeps winning. He's a great player but an even better person – and that's why everyone at the club is so happy for him.'

You had to fear for City's next opponents, Burnley, the runaway Championship leaders who arrived at the Etihad for an FA Cup quarter-final; the Clarets had won the competition back in 1914.

The pre-match build-up was to be centred around the return of City legend Vincent Kompany as the Burnley manager but long before the final whistle the headlines were again about Haaland as he made it eight goals in two matches.

He had now scored a remarkable 42 goals in 37 appearances in all competitions, thus sparking speculation that while he could not hope to overtake Dixie Dean's 60 goals in a single top-flight league campaign, he might just overtake the all-competitions record of 63 goals recorded by the Everton centre-forward in 1927/28.

His hat-trick against Burnley was also his sixth already, having reached that mark in his 37th game. City's all-time record goalscorer Sergio Agüero had needed 175 games to score the first half a dozen of his club-record 16 career trebles.

Haaland had already set a new City record for most goals scored in a single season, easily eclipsing the 38 Tommy Johnson scored in 1928/29.

With Haaland being so prolific in the cup competitions, he was also moving in on the record for most goals in all competitions scored in a single season since the Premier League kicked off in 1992/93. That total, 44, was jointly held by Manchester United's Ruud van Nistelrooy in 2002/03, and Mohamed Salah in 2017/18.

The outcome of the tie was that City thrashed the visitors to move into the FA Cup semi-finals.

Burnley started the match well and in a reshuffled back line Stefan Ortega was almost caught out as he was rushed into a pass and gifted the ball to Ian Maatsen. Fortunately for the goalkeeper Rico Lewis raced back to avert the danger and Ortega soon after made amends when he pushed away a long-range effort from Nathan Tella.

Indecisive at the back, City were devastating up front. Haaland misdirected a header from a Phil Foden cross and only a good tackle from Jordan Beyer prevented Álvarez from shooting.

Burnley might have considered they were doing well when they reached the half-hour mark without conceding but then in a flash, they were two down. First, Haaland was fed on the edge of the area by Álvarez and, although Bailey Peacock-Farrell rushed out, the number nine instinctively poked the ball beyond the keeper.

Then Foden was the provider; charging down the left, his low ball into the area was perfect for Haaland who lifted it neatly over Peacock-Farrell. The Burnley stopper blocked a Riyad Mahrez volley before beating away a strike from

Haaland who could though not be denied and completed his treble just before the hour when he was in the right place to pounce on a rebound after Foden hit the post.

It was swiftly 4-0 as De Bruyne burst into the area and squared for Álvarez to tap home.

Haaland, like against RB Leipzig, was taken off in the 63rd minute. In just 126 minutes of football over two matches he had scored eight times.

There was still no respite for Burnley as Foden's cross was pushed into the path of substitute Cole Palmer who turned it home before Álvarez raced on to a De Bruyne through ball and turned inside Ameen Al-Dakhil to thump home the sixth goal.

Haaland's continuing ability to find the net had the Premier League record goalscorer Alan Shearer purring on *Match of the Day*, 'Haaland is a beast, he is a goalscoring machine. He lives and breathes goals. If he doesn't score, he doesn't sleep at night. He wants another one, then another one, then another one.

'He's fantastic, and this team must be a dream with the chances they create. He might get 50 goals, maybe even 60. It's bonkers.'

17

Make-or-Break in April 2023

CITY FACED a make-or-break 29 days in April in which they would play eight games that would define their season. It started with a home match against a Liverpool team that had become their major rivals for trophies under Jürgen Klopp. There were other tricky Premier League fixtures against Southampton, Leicester and Fulham as well as a mouthwatering title-deciding return with Arsenal at the Etihad. Two quarter-final legs with Pep Guardiola's former club Bayern Munich would decide their Champions League fate and Championship promotion chasers Sheffield United awaited them in the FA Cup semi-final.

Erling Haaland's groin injury against Burnley gave City so much cause for concern that the Norwegian FA were immediately informed that the striker would not be available for his nation's two opening Euro 2024 qualifiers against Spain and Georgia, and he was flown out to Barcelona to be assessed by Guardiola's trusted aide Dr Ramon Cugat. Haaland was advised to rest before undergoing any treatment and so immediately flew to Majorca to enjoy some recuperation in the Balearic sunshine. City insisted that he could still be fit for the visit of Liverpool on 1 April – but no one was fooled when Alfie revealed his son was unlikely to face the Merseysiders. He said, 'I'm not a doctor, but you can't just go two weeks without training and then jump straight into a fight. They can gamble on it, but if Erling doesn't get the proper training with the team then he won't play.'

Guardiola wasn't ready to take any chances with the business end of the season approaching. Haaland insisted he was feeling fit 24 hours before Liverpool arrived at the Etihad – but his manager decided that his team could handle the Merseysiders without the star striker, who was later captured on camera celebrating wildly and joining in the Poznań at full time as City, exploiting Trent Alexander-Arnold's defensive weaknesses at full-back, ran riot against a side now well past its best.

Yet the game started well for Liverpool, England's most successful club with a bagful of trophies, when Diogo Jota beat the offside trap to set up Mohamed Salah, who a few weeks earlier had become the Reds' all-time top scorer in the Premier League after scoring twice in a 7-0 thrashing of Manchester United, after a perfectly timed run. Liverpool had not lost in the Premier League when taking the lead since February 2021 so the goal was a blow to City.

It looked like things might even get worse when the Egyptian genius again found space only to be denied by a crucial intervention by Jack Grealish. Moments later Grealish was down the other end to provide the final assist in a lightning-fast City move that concluded with Julián Álvarez equalising on 27 minutes.

With Guardiola 'adjusting our process a little bit at half-time', City benefited immediately when with just 57 seconds gone an impressive Álvarez provided Riyad Mahrez with a measured pass out wide and from the resulting cross Kevin De Bruyne put his side ahead.

The Argentinian was involved in the third too but when his left-footed shot was blocked close in by Alexander-Arnold, İlkay Gündoğan had time to compose himself to double City's lead and ease the tension around the Etihad

Stadium. Back in February 2021 the skipper had scored twice in a historic 4-1 win at Anfield that established a decisive hold on the title race and now on April Fool's Day 2023 no one in the red of Liverpool or Arsenal was laughing as City showed that with or without Haaland they had the momentum to steamroll their opponents and take a third title in three years.

As the game moved on, Alexander-Arnold must have been sick of the sight of Grealish, who had been unwell on the morning of the game. It was fitting that the former Aston Villa man, whose great-great grandad Billy Garraty had won the First Division title and FA Cup at the start of the 20th century with the Birmingham side, grabbed the goal his performance deserved from a perfectly timed run that left him on the end of De Bruyne's cross to send Liverpool back along the M62 well beaten.

A downcast Klopp had to admit that his side were well beaten stating, 'Four performances were OK, the two midfielders, Hendo [Jordan Henderson] and Fab [Fabinho], worked a lot, Cody [Gakpo] and Ali [goalkeeper Alisson], and that is very difficult. If you want to get something here, 14 or 15 players have to be on top of their game and that was not the case.'

* * *

'One of our best performances'

In comparison Guardiola was in a very good mood, stating, 'When we conceded the goal, we were playing really well. Of course, they are always a threat in the transitions, but we played really well in all departments. It was one of our best performances in these seven years [since he had taken over].'

With his form now fully showing why City had spent big to bring him north, man of the match Grealish indicated how important the occasion had been for the remainder of the season, 'We knew it was going to be a tough game. We wanted to start this last period of the season right. We responded brilliantly to going behind and we were excellent in the second half.'

The win narrowed the gap on Arsenal to five points – this was to rise when the Gunners cruised past a sorry Leeds United later that day – and offered a timely reminder that Guardiola's team remained a potent force even without the watching Erling Haaland.

Guardiola had already decided that City's players and staff would need to recharge their batteries before the long sprint to the finish line and with a week before the trip to face Southampton he informed them in the dressing room that the reward for overwhelming Klopp's side was a three-day furlough that would allow them to spend valuable time with family and friends.

Haaland stayed behind to continue having treatment and also had a date in his diary to launch the new boot deal with sportswear giants Nike that would net him a cool £20m over the next ten years. He travelled to NikeTown, the company's flagship store on London's Oxford Street, with his girlfriend Isabel Haugseng Johansen to collect his Luminous Pack Phantom GX boots at an invite-only event that saw him arrive on an escalator to much fanfare as the song 'Sky's the Limit' by murdered American rapper Biggie Smalls boomed out of the sound system. 'I think the song fits me really well,' Haaland told Alex Scott, the former England women's international who is now an assured and expert broadcaster. During a Q&A session with Scott, the striker revealed his own icons and his hopes of the future. 'My heroes were the players who scored goals,' said Haaland. '[Zlatan] Ibrahimović was a big one. Cristiano Ronaldo and [Sergio] Agüero as well.' Haaland later admitted, 'I know Arsenal are so many points in front of us, but I don't think too much about it. In the end, it's about ourselves. In the end, we will see if I can catch [Norway international team-mate Martin] Ødegaard or not.'

There was also a shot across Alan Shearer's bows with Haaland about to embark on another scoring spree that would take him past the record held jointly by the England striker and former international team-mate Andy Cole of 34 Premier League goals in a single season. 'Shearer has talked to me in a few interviews about the record,' said Haaland. 'I just try to do my best in every single game.' Haaland's next outing, against relegation-threatened Southampton at St Mary's on 8 April, would see him score twice – including the goal he later rated as his best of the season. His performance would also prompt Guardiola to compare Haaland to Cristiano Ronaldo and Lionel Messi, the Argentine superstar who was the jewel in his crown at Barcelona.

* * *

Best goal of the season

Haaland calmed City's nerves at the end of the first half by ghosting off the shoulder of Saints defender Armel Bella-Kotchap to steer home Kevin De Bruyne's cross from inside the six-yard box. It meant De Bruyne had become the fastest player to provide 100 Premier League assists, his century coming up in 237 appearances – taking 56 games fewer than Cesc Fàbregas.

But it was Haaland's second goal, to put City 3-0 ahead in the 66th minute, that really took the eye. He could have taken a controlling touch when Grealish picked him out at the far post, but the cross was too tantalising for the Norwegian to resist launching himself into a spectacular scissored volley that flew past home keeper Gavin Bazunu.

Haaland, asked about his 'goal of the season' when he was receiving the FWA Footballer of the Year award, confessed,

'I scored a lot of nice goals and I really liked the goal at home against Manchester United, with the pass from Kevin [De Bruyne] when I was sliding in and the ball bounced perfectly. But the bicycle kick against Southampton was truly something special. It's difficult to choose one but I'll take the bicycle kick. To have this big body up in the air for this long is not easy!'

Haaland was also involved in the move that allowed Grealish to get on the scoresheet and would have had a chance of another hat-trick had Guardiola not decided to substitute him for Julián Álvarez in the 69th minute – leaving the Argentine to complete the scoring in a 4-1 victory from the penalty spot just six minutes later. Guardiola is not a manager who lavishes praise on individual players, but he was gushing about Haaland after he had taken his Premier League goal tally to 30. 'We have lived with Messi and Cristiano for two incredible decades – and now Haaland is on that level,' cooed Guardiola. 'You see how many games Erling has played during his professional career and you compare the goals he has scored in that time to Messi and Cristiano, it's quite similar. I think Messi is a more complete player. The other two, Cristiano and Haaland, are like machines. But Erling knows the other two guys have dominated for two decades, not just one year. They have scored goals, won titles and done absolutely everything. Erling is just 22 years old and he is doing it in the toughest league in the world. I can talk because I've been in other leagues. Doing what he is doing is remarkable. To reach the level of Cristiano and Messi takes a lot of work. But Erling puts pressure on himself like Messi and Ronaldo. The numbers he has at his age are unbelievable.'

Haaland's double on the south coast was the start of a sequence which saw him score ten times in ten games. But there were also compelling signs that he had adapted himself to Guardiola's very specific passing philosophy, with the Norwegian starting to provide assists for his team-mates. Questions were asked how Guardiola would be able to exploit the pace and power of Haaland from the moment it was announced he was heading to the Etihad. RB Salzburg and Borussia Dortmund both played a counterattacking style that suited Haaland's natural instinct to get himself in behind defenders, while City's possession-obsessed gameplay prompted opposition teams to sit deep and limit space.

* * *

False nine

To combat this, Guardiola had taken to playing without a recognised central striker, often using an extra midfielder in a false nine role first perfected by Hungary in the 1950s to draw defenders out of their natural habitat. From the moment Guardiola arrived in Manchester in 2016 there were suggestions that Sergio Agüero would struggle to adapt to the demands of the Catalan. Despite an uneasy relationship between the pair, the Argentine proved the doubters wrong by bending himself to the manager's will while still providing a lethal goal threat. In five seasons playing under Guardiola his goals-per-season output in all competitions was 33, 30, 32, 23, six. Agüero's tenth and final campaign at the Etihad was decimated by injuries that limited him to just 20 appearances. But when he came off the bench as a second-half substitute against Everton in his final appearance at the Etihad, he scored twice in four minutes to take his goal tally to 260 goals. Agüero became City's record goalscorer in November 2017 when he struck in a Champions League tie against Napoli in the Stadio San Paolo to break the 177-goal standard set by Eric Brook 78 years earlier.

Agüero scored the most iconic goal in Premier League history in May 2012 when his injury-time strike against

Queens Park Rangers at the Etihad sealed the dramatic victory that made City champions for the first time in 44 years, on goal difference at the expense of rivals Manchester United. It was the 30th goal of his debut season with the club following his £35m arrival from Atlético Madrid the previous summer and a statue of him celebrating the goal was unveiled outside City's stadium to mark the ten-year anniversary of the event. A lounge inside the ground is named 93:20 to mark the time of his strike. Yet despite his incredible consistency, Agüero only won the Premier League's Golden Boot award once, in 2014/15 when he scored 26 times.

The last of his 390 games for the club was as a late substitute as City were beaten 1-0 by Chelsea in the 2021 Champions League Final in Porto, and later that summer he joined Barcelona when his contract expired. But by then, Agüero's injuries had prompted Guardiola to play without a recognised central striker so that he could consistently establish overloads in midfield areas. In the 2020/21 season, played in empty stadia due to the ongoing Covid-19 pandemic, City reclaimed the Premier League title from Liverpool by finishing 12 points ahead of second-placed Manchester United and also lifted the EFL Cup by beating Tottenham at Wembley. Their first European final since winning the Cup Winners' Cup in 1970 ended in disappointment and they reached the semi-finals of the FA Cup before a weakened team succumbed 1-0 to a Chelsea team that beat them three times in the final weeks of the campaign.

City scored 131 goals that season – but it illustrated how Guardiola was winning games by the fact that midfielder İlkay Gündoğan finished as top scorer with 17, the German also finishing as the club's most prolific scorer in the Premier League with just 13. Phil Foden (16), Gabriel Jesus (14), Riyad Mahrez (14), Raheem Sterling (14), Ferran Torres (13) and Kevin De Bruyne (ten) confirmed how the responsibility for scoring goals was now being shared.

Guardiola recognised, however, that his policy of playing without a more prolific goalscorer could only be a temporary solution. Opposition teams were organising themselves better to cope with City's slick-passing style and their tactic of flooding the box with attacking midfielders when the time arose – but he needed a forward capable of scoring the 'heavy' goals in the biggest games. City wanted to buy Tottenham's England captain Harry Kane in the summer of 2021, and were willing to break the British transfer record to get their man despite already triggering the £100m clause in Jack Grealish's contract at Aston Villa to make the midfielder the most expensive player in the country. Spurs chairman Daniel Levy insisted Kane was not for sale – and was so entrenched in his position that at one point he refused to answer his phone unless he was sure it wasn't City's director of football Txiki Begiristain making the call. Even when Kane failed to report for pre-season training in a bid to force through the departure from the London club, Levy would not budge on his position.

If Kane had become a City player that summer, then Erling Haaland's career path would have taken a different route. Guardiola made it clear after missing out on the man who would later become England's record goalscorer that the only alternative was to enquire whether Dortmund would cash in on their Norwegian number nine a year before the £51m get-out clause in his contract could be triggered. Officially, Dortmund confirmed that Haaland was not for sale – but City were made aware then an offer of £150m would persuade the German club to sell. City felt they could not justify paying such an extortionate premium and so launched a charm offensive with the player and his entourage while Guardiola set about perfecting his striker-light formation.

Liverpool, as in 2019 when City had to come from behind to beat Brighton & Hove Albion at the Amex Stadium on the final day to post a 98-point total that saw them prevail over the Merseysiders by a single point in the title race, would once again emerge as the biggest threat to Guardiola's dominance of the Premier League. Indeed, Jürgen Klopp's men went into the final six days of the campaign dreaming of an unprecedented Quadruple after beating Chelsea on penalties in both the final of the FA Cup and EFL Cup and reaching the Champions League Final to face Real Madrid. When City fell two goals behind to Aston Villa in their final game, it needed an Etihad miracle to rival the Agüero moment a decade earlier for them to retain the championship. Gündoğan scored either side of a Rodri equaliser in the space of five tumultuous minutes as a Villa side managed by Kop legend Steven Gerrard folded under the onslaught. Liverpool, who also came from behind to beat Wolves, won 92 points but still finished a point behind City. Their agony was then compounded when they lost 1-0 to Madrid in Paris.

By then Haaland was Manchester-bound. City scored 150 goals that season; Mahrez finished top of the club's goal charts with 24 and De Bruyne managed 19, his 15 in the Premier League being more than anyone else in the squad. But Guardiola picked a weakened team when faced by Liverpool in the FA Cup semi-final just three days after refusing to bow to Atlético Madrid's dirty tricks in a bruising goalless draw at the Wanda Metropolitano Stadium that secured a 1-0 aggregate victory and took them through to a Champions League semi-final showdown with Real Madrid. City were blown away by Liverpool, who scored three times in the first half, but hit back with goals by Jack Grealish and Bernardo Silva only for Fernandinho to miss the chance to take the game into extra time.

City's need for a more regular goalscorer was even more profound against Madrid. They won a thrilling first leg in Manchester 4-3 but wasted a catalogue of chances that would have put the tie beyond the Spaniards. When Mahrez crowned a dominant performance in the Bernabéu in the return by putting City ahead with just 17 minutes to go, an all-Premier League Champions League Final appeared to be a formality. But Grealish failed to take two glorious chances – and when Madrid substitute Rodrygo scored twice in the final minute to send the game into extra time, it allowed Karim Benzema to score his third goal of the tie from the penalty spot to send Carlo Ancelotti's men to Paris and their destiny of a 14th European crown. The fates had again conspired against the Blues and Joe Mercer's Lions of Vienna still stood alone as the only City team to lift a European trophy.

By February 2023 it was clear that only injury would prevent Haaland smashing a fistful of goalscoring records – but when former Liverpool defender Jamie Carragher asked if the striker had signed for the wrong club, he was only expressing the reservation held by several observers. After 21 games, Haaland had scored 25 of City's 53 goals, which was exactly the same number they had scored as a team at the same stage of the previous season. Carragher, in his role as a Sky Sports pundit, reasoned, 'Haaland has come from a counterattacking league where it's end-to-end. You saw his blistering pace there – we don't see it here. He might have picked the wrong club to actually get the best out of him. We're not seeing everything of Haaland. City have scored exactly the same number of goals as last season. He's got 25 of them, but overall City have scored the same number. They have also conceded more and are easy to counterattack against. They are a different – and a lesser – team with Haaland in the team. That's not his fault. City won't play end-to-end football. That's not Pep Guardiola's way. His players don't have the energy to play that way. They build up slowly and push opponents back to their box and play from there.'

But Haaland knew it would be a challenge playing under Guardiola – and was happy to accept it because he understood the Catalan would make him a better player. He told the Football Writers' Association, 'Winning the Premier League for the third time in a row was a relief for me. I joined a club that had already won it two years in a row and if we didn't win it after I signed, it would not be so good for me. It was a big relief. In my first season to play the way I have and to play beautiful football with my team-mates means a lot. I think I'm developing really well under Pep and his team. I must thank my team-mates. Without the passes of Kevin [De Bruyne] and all the beautiful passes I've been getting it would not be possible. I didn't expect to score as many goals, but the most important thing is that Manchester City plays well. If the team plays well then, the striker will score goals. They scored over 100 goals last season, so they have always scored a lot.'

But Haaland was also aware that pressure was building on City to become champions of Europe for the first time after a catalogue of heartbreaking near-misses. The draw for the last eight and semi-finals meant they would have to do it the hard way, facing Bayern Munich in the quarter-finals for the right to meet Real Madrid or Chelsea for a ticket to the Atatürk Stadium in Istanbul where Liverpool had so memorably beaten AC Milan in the 2005 final. 'I will handle the pressure like I have been doing my whole career,' Haaland had told a packed press room at City's academy when he was unveiled in July 2022. 'The way I do that is to enjoy every single minute and try not to overthink things. What I will say is that the Champions League is my favourite competition – so I think you have the answer right there.' Haaland was still to taste victory in a competitive game against Bayern, despite scoring the winning goal on his debut against them for City in a pre-season game in the USA. Bayern forward Thomas Müller came to regret bringing the subject up in an ESPN interview before the first leg, 'He [Haaland] is an unbelievable striker, but in a team like Dortmund he had no chance against us.'

City faced a Bayern team managed by Thomas Tuchel, the man who had masterminded three successive Chelsea victories over City in the final weeks of the 2020/21 season, outwitting Guardiola in the semi-final of the FA Cup, a Premier League fixture at the Etihad when a win would have confirmed the home team as champions, and in the Champions League Final. The German had been sacked by the London club after winning just three of their first seven games of the season, but was appointed by Bayern six months later following the controversial decision to relieve Julian Nagelsmann of his duties when his team were top of the Bundesliga. Guardiola had won all seven of his other head-to-head meetings with Tuchel. Twenty-four hours before the first leg in Manchester, the Bayern boss admitted, 'I will try to go to bed early and hope I will be able to sleep. This morning I woke up really early and decided to go into the training ground because I was thinking of the game too much. The style of Erling Haaland is very unique and City have adapted to fit him in. He offers them something they haven't had in recent years.'

Tuchel may have talked up the opposition – but even he was shocked by the tempo and ruthlessness that led to his team's destruction. City got the breakthrough their fast start had threatened in the 27th minute when Rodri collected Bernardo Silva's pass 25 yards out and found the top corner of Yann Sommer's goal with a curling left-footed finish. Bayern threatened parity, with former City winger Leroy Sané twice forcing Ederson into saves before Haaland broke his shackles and the home team scored twice in the space of six minutes to leave the Germans stunned. Haaland was the provider in the 70th minute, collecting Jack Grealish's back-heel after the midfielder had dispossessed Dayot Upamecano.

Haaland appeared to be setting himself to shoot as Upamecano and team-mates Leon Goretzka and Matthijs de Ligt tried to retrieve the situation. But with Joshua Kimmich also concentrating on the imminent danger to Bayern's goal, Haaland clipped a glorious cross to the far post which invited the 5ft 8in Bernardo Silva to head powerfully into the top corner without breaking stride. Haaland celebrated like he had scored himself – which he duly did when Julián Álvarez's cross from the right was headed back across goal by the leaping John Stones and there was the prolific ponytail to use his instep to volley home as he slid in. It was Haaland's 45th goal of the season in all competitions – a tally no other Premier League player had managed. There was uproar in Bayern's dressing room after the game, with former Liverpool forward Sadio Mané punching Sané. The Senegal international avoided having his contract terminated after issuing an apology, but was put up for sale at the end of the season.

Guardiola said, 'The thing I like most about Erling is the joy he gets from the goals we score. I am not just talking about the goals he scores. Watch his celebration when one of his mates scores. It means just as much to him. That's why he is loved by everyone in the dressing room. A lot of strikers are not happy if the team wins but they don't score. Of course, Haaland wants to score goals. It's what he lives for. But the most important thing for him is that he goes home with the game won.'

* * *

Cracks appear in Arsenal's belief

The following day, cracks started to appear in Arsenal's belief that they could hold off the champions when they surrendered a two-goal lead to draw 2-2 at Liverpool. The Gunners appeared on course to deliver a statement of intent by claiming their first Premier League win at Anfield in almost 11 years when Gabriel Martinelli and Gabriel Jesus both scored in front of the Kop inside the first half an hour, only to fold under an onslaught which saw Jürgen Klopp's side hit back through Mohamed Salah and Roberto Firmino, the equaliser arriving three minutes from the end after Salah had missed a second-half penalty. Once again, the destiny of the title was in both City's and Arsenal's hands just 17 days ahead of their Etihad showdown – but City had been here before.

Guardiola warned his players what was at stake when struggling Leicester arrived in Manchester the following Saturday. 'If we lose this game then we cannot be champions,' he said. 'We are six points behind Arsenal – a team that has dropped only a few points all season and only plays one game every week. If we lose, it's over – but I have always believed that is the best way to compete.' Haaland had missed just four games all season, compared to the 16 he had been sidelined for during his last year in the Bundesliga. But Guardiola revealed that City's medical staff were taking optimum care of the striker. He said, 'I don't know what Erling did at Dortmund, but we take care of him for 24 hours a day. He has incredible physios and doctors looking after every single detail. With this demanding schedule, playing every three days, he has an incredible entourage to take care of him. It is so demanding today that you need nutrition, rest, sleep, the right food and training. There are days when he only trains for ten or 15 minutes, otherwise it would be a risk. People ask why I substituted him against Leipzig when he had scored so many goals. But he stayed on against Burnley and was out for ten or 15 days. Erling is so big. To play he has to have massages on his back, his shoulders and his tendons.'

It was an early warning of what was to come against a Leicester side being managed for the first time by Dean Smith following Brendan Rodgers' sacking. Smith was ultimately unable to save the 2016 Premier League champions from the ignominy of relegation, but was encouraged by the spirit his team showed in the second half at the Etihad. Unfortunately, by then City were about to close the gap on Arsenal to three points.

The Gunners once again had to endure watching their rivals in action before they travelled east for a London derby with West Ham – and they would have been forgiven for turning the TV off after just 25 minutes. By then Haaland had struck twice after John Stones's volleyed opener in the fifth minute, the Norwegian steering home a penalty after Wilfried Ndidi had handled Jack Grealish's cross and then clipping a masterful finish over Foxes keeper Daniel Iversen after De Bruyne's pass had invited him to race through on goal. It meant Haaland had equalled Salah's record of scoring 32 goals in a 38-game season – and it was the tenth time that De Bruyne had assisted him. Haaland had scored from 16 of his last 21 shots on target, but he was denied the chance of another match ball when Guardiola substituted him at half-time – one of five changes made that led to Leicester responding with a late riposte that could have brought more than a consolation tap-in by former City striker Kelechi Iheanacho 15 minutes from time.

Guardiola said, 'I desire that Erling breaks all records possible because that means he has scored goals to help us. But I think that what he wants the most is to win titles – and he still has eight or nine games to break a lot of records. His reaction [to being substituted] was excellent, as always. Look at his body language and face when he's been substituted.

He has just recovered from an injury to play 90 minutes against Bayern, so that's why after 45 minutes it was good to rest him.'

All eyes were now on Arsenal – and once again Mikel Arteta's men buckled after taking an early two-goal lead through Gabriel Jesus and Martin Ødegaard inside ten minutes. The Gunners could not keep possession as West Ham pressed and Saïd Benrahma converted a penalty before Jarrod Bowen grabbed an equaliser nine minutes into the second half. It was now advantage Manchester City – and five days later their London rivals surrendered two more precious points when they were held to a 3-3 draw by Southampton, with City also in the capital to prepare for their FA Cup semi-final with Sheffield United at Wembley the following day. It could have been worse for the Gunners, who trailed 2-0 and then 3-1 with just two minutes of the 90 to play against a Saints team destined for relegation before Ødegaard and Bukayo Saka struck to salvage a point. Arsenal were now five points clear at the top but had played two more games than City and now appeared riddled with self-doubt with their trip to Manchester looming next.

It was the perfect week for the reigning champions. Guardiola's men had shown their mettle by reaching the Champions League semi-finals after withstanding a furious Bayern Munich barrage as the German giants reacted to their humbling at the Etihad in a way their fans demanded. They also reached the FA Cup Final by beating Championship promotion chasers Sheffield United 3-0. The quest for the Treble was still on.

Guardiola called on his team to embrace the chance to make history rather than be paralysed by what had happened before. Before the return against Bayern, he admitted that he was braced for a backlash from the German champions following the 3-0 win in Manchester – but his warning came with a caveat. Guardiola said, 'We had to defend at home and we will have to defend again – but if we were playing history we could not win because Bayern have more history in Europe than we have. I was the manager at Bayern. I know how they think at this club because they have done it so many times before. They will believe it can happen again. But when I talk about the game to my players, I will talk about what's in front of us. Not last week and not history.' Guardiola also revealed the influence Haaland was exerting in the dressing room, 'I think Erling has adapted so quickly from day one, first of all in the locker room with his mates. We felt it in the way he introduced himself, not just to the players but to the backroom staff and other staff at the club. It has been so natural, nothing forced or complicated.'

Haaland's return to Germany was a rollercoaster of emotions. He missed a penalty in the 34th minute, blazing his shot over from 12 yards after French referee Clément Turpin adjudged that Dayot Upamecano had handled İlkay Gündoğan's shot. It was a harsh decision – but not the worst of the evening – and after Haaland had placed the ball on the spot his concentration was broken when Bayern midfielder Leon Goretzka interrupted his preparations by walking back into the area to remove a piece of debris he had spotted. Guardiola said, 'Erling will learn from this situation. He should have disappeared and taken himself out of his process before putting the ball down again. He is 22 and an incredible machine, but I am pretty sure he will learn from it in the future and be more secure and confident to take the penalty.' The injustice of it – and Haaland's subsequent miss – reignited the atmosphere in the Allianz Arena after City had soothed a febrile crowd by controlling the early exchanges. When opportunity knocked again, in the 57th minute, this time he kicked the door down and grasped it. The visitors went ahead just seconds after Ederson had only half-blocked Kingsley Coman's angled shot and seen the ball roll agonisingly across the face of his goal before Stones hacked it clear in the general direction of Haaland.

The Norwegian lost his aerial challenge with Matthijs de Ligt, but the Dutchman's header fell to De Bruyne – and his pass gave Haaland the chance to test the nerves of the back-pedalling Upamecano. The Frenchman wasn't up to the task and lost his footing, allowing Haaland to burst past him and lift a composed finish into the roof of the net. Haaland had scored for the seventh successive game and he celebrated by lifting his finger to his lips to challenge the stunned Bayern fans to jeer him some more. Bayern equalised seven minutes from time after Turpin ruled following a VAR check that Manuel Akanji had handled when Leroy Sané's cross bounced up off his boot and struck his arm. This time justice wasn't done and Joshua Kimmich scored from the spot. But City were through – and in the last four they would meet Real Madrid again after the reigning champions beat Chelsea 4-0 on aggregate. De Bruyne said, 'We've done what we needed to do. We dealt with all the pressure by defending during the tough moments and then the goal from Erling virtually sealed it. Knowing Erling, he won't be happy about missing a penalty, but you have to go again – and when he got another opportunity, he came up with a class finish to help us win the game.'

City had been scheduled to be playing Brighton at the Amex Stadium on 22 April, but the game was postponed when they reached the FA Cup semi-final. Phil Foden was on the bench in Munich after missing four games following an operation to have his appendix removed after being taken ill while on international duty with England.

To reach the FA Cup Final again meant beating Sheffield United at Wembley. It was to be a routine win as after Cup semi-final defeats Guardiola's side were to be carried to a victory thanks to a marvellous Mahrez performance in which he became the first player to score a hat-trick in the last four of the competition since Alex Dawson achieved the feat for Manchester United in 1958. City thus remained on course to win the Premier League, FA Cup and Champions League.

With Guardiola having professed that his players were 'exhausted' following the midweek success against Bayern Munich and with the Premier League clash with leaders Arsenal four days away, many had felt that Haaland would be either benched or left out of the squad altogether for the semi-final.

Instead the sight of the number nine running out at Wembley was a clear intent that Guardiola was not, even in a game that failed to anywhere near fill the national stadium, risking a fourth consecutive defeat in the last four after losses to Liverpool, Chelsea and Arsenal.

With 80 per cent of the ball, it was a surprise that half-time was almost reached before the Blades were finally breached when Mahrez scored from the spot following an unnecessary foul in the box by striker Daniel Jebbison on Bernardo Silva.

On the return, Haaland was unable to turn in a deflected Sergio Gómez shot before Mahrez converted his second after United, winners of the FA Cup at Wembley in 1925, backed off.

Mahrez then met Grealish's centre sweetly on 63 minutes for his 12th goal, plus seven assists, in 23 appearances since returning from the World Cup. Five minutes later Haaland was replaced by Foden.

Mahrez drew praise afterwards from Guardiola, 'He is always grumpy with me when he doesn't play all the time, he makes me notice how grumpy he feels. Today no. He is an exceptional player, a big stage player and has the mentality to score the goal. The composure for the penalty was important to go in after the first half at 1-0 and the second and third goal was brilliant.'

* * *

Neighbours are always nice to each other

Guardiola was also in a playful mood when asked if Manchester United had anything to fear about City equalling their 1999 Treble.

'They don't have to be scared, we are neighbours, the neighbours are always nice to each other,' he said. 'We are far away; people cannot believe that we are far away with this kind of situation. It is OK for people to discuss it for a funny moment, but the reality is different. The reality is to come here and perform.'

With United somewhat fortunately beating Brighton in the following day's semi-final, Erik ten Hag's side would have a chance to protect his club's unique record.

Before the return to Wembley in the FA Cup, City next faced Arsenal and it was to be fitting that they should produce their best Premier League performance of the season against their closest title rivals. The atmosphere at the floodlit Etihad was febrile, with the fans unveiling a huge surfer flag before kick-off that read 'We'll Follow You Everywhere', a reference to a new terrace chant based on Fleetwood Mac's 1980s hit 'Everywhere'. Guardiola's team then plugged themselves into the frenzy to blow Arsenal away with a barrage of brilliant goals. It was also Haaland's best all-round performance in a sky blue shirt, the Norwegian repaying De Bruyne for his service by setting up the Belgian for a goal in each half and then getting on the scoresheet himself to break Salah's record for a 38-game Premier League season. As well as scoring his 33rd league goal of the season, the striker had also made seven assists – only five players in the division had made more at that stage of the season. Haaland had either scored or created a goal at an average of every 58 minutes.

Guardiola was asked before the game about how Mikel Arteta could deploy his forces to stop Haaland, and replied, 'It is so difficult to stop Erling but what we did when we played Dortmund was to try to make sure he was involved as little as possible by having 70 or 80 per cent of ball possession. If we have the ball, he has less chances.' Even more worrying than the fact that the boss was confident enough to give advice on how to combat his biggest goal threat was that he also appeared to sense what Arteta's gameplay would be and had drawn up a tactical plan that would make the man who had previously been his assistant at the Etihad for three years look like a virtual novice. Guardiola knew that Arsenal would play a high defensive line and look to press City into mistakes. Arteta's theory had worked in the first 45 minutes in the game at the Emirates because the visitors tried to free Haaland in behind too early. This time, it was clear from the opening exchanges that the Londoners were in for a whole lot of pain. The ease with which City switched from 4-2-4 to 4-2-3-1 to 3-2-1-4 in a blur of movement was just too much for Arsenal to cope with. City only had slightly more of the ball – 52 per cent to 48 per cent – but this was such a chastening evening for Arteta and his players that Opta's estimation after the game that the champions now had a 78 per cent chance of retaining the title proved generous. To the Gunners.

City felt they should have had a penalty when Thomas Partey barged over De Bruyne, although referee Michael Oliver was unmoved. But when they did go ahead in the seventh minute, it was an illustration that the link-up between De Bruyne and Haaland now went both ways. Arsenal thought they had penned the home team in close to their corner flag when Ederson played a square pass to John

Stones on his right. But as four Gunners players went hunting in a pack, Stones sent a long ball up towards Haaland on the halfway line and his strength and first touch were, like in the FA Cup at the Etihad, too much for Rob Holding to cope with. De Bruyne could smell the possibilities and escaped Partey with a change of pace that enabled him to collect Haaland's pass before powering forward to work a yard of space to the right of Gabriel Magalhães and then using the Brazilian as a shield to work a wonderful shot past Aaron Ramsdale's left hand from 20 yards.

The next time Arsenal pressed, Stones, Bernardo Silva and Kyle Walker kept the ball with the kind of patience that their manager had demanded and when Haaland once again sent De Bruyne storming through the middle, only a desperate block by Ben White prevented another goal. Haaland was then denied by two Ramsdale saves before another combination with De Bruyne ended with the Norwegian placing his shot wide when he appeared certain to score. His cry of anguish spoke volumes. Haaland then earned the free kick in first-half injury time from which Stones despatched De Bruyne's delivery past Ramsdale – the goal standing after a VAR check showed Holding playing the City defender onside by the width of his boot. It was a defining moment in the title race and as City fans belted out a chant in honour of the scorer a pitchside camera picked out Haaland joyously joining in.

Earlier in the month the big Norwegian had had fans laughing when he perfectly mimicked the English international's Yorkshire accent on a viral clip in which the pair and Gündoğan discussed some of their favourite travel destinations in the world.

The Louvre Abu Dhabi, run under an agreement between the UAE and France, is the most visited museum in the Arab world.

When Stones, much to the joy of his team-mates, butchers the pronunciation of the building, Gündoğan looks to provide the stylish South Yorkshire-born defender with a more fluent pronunciation.

West Yorkshire-born Haaland then joins in to mimic his team-mate in quite hilarious fashion with a perfectly executed impression of Stones that sounds more like Stones than Stones himself.

This was not the first time that Haaland had mocked Stones's accent having earlier been filmed doing so as he entered training with Grealish.

No one in Arsenal colours was laughing at half-time at the Etihad in a game they could not afford to lose, and things though were set to get worse. Haaland opened the second half by shaking off Gabriel on the halfway line only to shoot against Ramsdale, but moments later he put the game beyond doubt after his exchange of passes with De Bruyne enabled the Belgian to expertly find the bottom corner by shooting through Holding's legs. It was game over – and after Holding had given Arsenal a crumb of comfort with a smart finish, it was left for Haaland to quite literally let his hair down to make history in the dying seconds. Perhaps the Norwegian was expecting the final whistle when he took out the band that was holding his ponytail in place – but when Phil Foden poked the ball forward, he hooked home his 34th Premier League goal to take the record for a 38-game season.

City were still two points behind the Gunners in the table, but now had two games in hand. 'After what happened at the Emirates, we had to adjust something,' said Guardiola. 'Erling is a master of winning the long ball and then he can involve Kevin [De Bruyne]. When that happens, they are unstoppable. It isn't something I have taught them in training. The game belongs to them because football is a natural thing. Kevin the master of the assist, even without

Erling. And Erling will always score goals, with or without Kevin. Tonight, when Arsenal pressed high and there is space in behind, Haaland and De Bruyne can be so, so dangerous. Erling's goals are fantastic, but he also has to be involved in the game. We asked him to come and play. We didn't want him to lose his identity for scoring goals but I don't like a player who just stands there and lets his ten team-mates control the process so that he can score all the goals. Erling is doing really, really, really well.'

18

Nine Points From Nine as Haaland Breaks Shearer and Cole Record

UNTIL ERLING Haaland's sensational debut season at Manchester City, the last top-flight player to score 50 goals in English football was Aston Villa striker Tom Waring – 92 years earlier. Waring, who was nicknamed 'Pongo' after a cartoon dog that was popular at the time, scored 49 goals in the First Division and another in the FA Cup as Villa finished runners-up in the title race, seven points behind champions Arsenal. Ironically, Waring scored his 50th goal to great fanfare in a 4-2 victory over Manchester City at Villa Park in April 1931. When the England striker died at the age of 74 in December 1980, his ashes were spread in front of the Holte End stand. Six months later Villa became champions for the first time in 70 years and they would go on to win the 1982 European Cup. At the height of his fame, Waring was earning 30 shillings a week and when he went into training on a Monday morning he would search the terraces and drink any beer slops that had been left behind by fans at the weekend.

Arsenal's title win of 1931 was the first of four championships in five years. They would later finish top in three successive seasons between 1933 and 1935, emulating the achievement first completed by Huddersfield Town between 1924 and 1926. Huddersfield manager Herbert

Chapman had quit the Yorkshire club to take charge at Highbury in the summer of 1925, just as Town were about to embark on their history-making season. When he died suddenly of pneumonia at the age of 55 in January 1934, his defending champions went on to win the next two First Division titles under the stewardship of Joe Shaw and George Allison. It was 49 years before three in a row was achieved again, Liverpool lifting the title under Bob Paisley in 1982 and 1983 and with successor Joe Fagan in 1984. Sir Alex Ferguson, the game's most successful manager, then did it twice with Manchester United. United became the first club to win the Treble of Premier League, Champions League and FA Cup in 1999 and then successfully defended the title in 2000 and 2001. Their three title wins between 2007 and 2009 included another Champions League triumph in 2008, when a shock home defeat to Portsmouth in the quarter-final of the FA Cup ended their Treble hopes.

Waring was born in October 1906 in Birkenhead, the town on the Wirral peninsula by the banks of the River Mersey that also produced Ralph Dean. Dean, nicknamed 'Dixie', was three months younger than Waring, but even more of a goalscoring phenomenon. When he was staking his claim for greatness with local club Tranmere Rovers, Waring was standing on the Prenton Park terraces watching his hero in action, dreaming that one day he could follow in his footsteps. By the time Waring signed for Rovers in 1926, Dean had moved across the Mersey to sign for Everton in a deal worth £3,000 – a record at the time for a Third Division player. He scored 21 goals in his debut season at Goodison Park as the Toffees narrowly avoided relegation. The following year, Dean became the greatest goalscorer in the history of English football, finding the back of the net 60 times in 39 First Division games as Everton were crowned champions. He also added another three in the FA Cup.

There were times during the 2022/23 season that Dean's record appeared to be under threat. Haaland may have had fewer league games at his disposal, but the Champions League and EFL Cup gave him more scope to score goals than the striker who is commemorated in bronze outside Goodison. It was at Everton that Haaland would score his 52nd and final goal of the season; his 50th had come at another famous old ground designed by Archibald Leitch, the Scottish architect who also drew up plans for some of the most iconic stadia in football, including Old Trafford, Anfield, Highbury and Hampden Park. Haaland's seventh penalty of the season, scored in the third minute after strike partner Julián Álvarez had been upended by Fulham skipper Tim Ream, sent City on their way to a 2-1 victory at Craven Cottage. He was clearly emotional after the landmark strike, looking to the heavens after making history on a day that also marked the first anniversary of the death of his agent Mino Raiola.

Haaland had scored a penalty in the last minute to give City a 2-1 win at the Etihad in November after Álvarez had equalised for the ten-men Blues against the Cottagers. This time it was Álvarez who hit the decisive strike, working space with a drag-back when he was surrounded by six home defenders before curling a glorious shot over keeper Bernd Leno from 25 yards in the 36th minute. Fulham had equalised with their only shot on target 12 minutes after Haaland's opener through Carlos Vinícius' fierce volley, but Álvarez had the last word.

The young Argentinian was in his first season with City having signed from River Plate on his 22nd birthday in January 2022 before being loaned back to the Buenos Aires club until the summer. He scored 23 goals during the Treble campaign – despite playing second fiddle to Haaland – and had arguably the most successful season of any player in world football. Álvarez was a key figure as Argentina won the World Cup in Qatar in December 2022, scoring four goals during the tournament and becoming the youngest player since Pelé to score twice in a World Cup semi-final as the South Americans defeated Croatia 3-0. Álvarez started the final against France in the Lusail Iconic Stadium and provided the assist from which Ángel Di María put the South Americans 2-0 ahead following Lionel Messi's opener from the penalty spot. Kylian Mbappé revived the French by scoring twice in two late second-half minutes to send the game into extra time, where Álvarez was substituted after 103 minutes and watched from the sidelines as Messi struck again only for Mbappé to become the first player since England's Sir Geoff Hurst to score a World Cup Final hat-trick with his second penalty. Mbappé struck again in the shoot-out, but Messi lifted the trophy after Argentina prevailed 4-2. Álvarez offered Guardiola something different to Haaland with his low centre of gravity and ability to adapt himself to operate in a deeper role or out wide. He often proved an effective foil for the Norwegian – but both shared an ability to finish with deadly effect.

City's win in west London hoisted them back to the top of the table, although Arsenal responded two days later by winning for the first time in five games with an impressive performance in a 3-1 victory over Chelsea that saw the struggling Blues dismantled at the Emirates Stadium. But all the talk now was about the goalscoring Norwegian phenomenon in sky blue. Guardiola had clearly studied the history books. 'I know that Winston Churchill was not even the prime minister the last time the record was set that Erling has broke,' he said. 'This group of players don't need a leader like Churchill – they know what they have to do. Erling missed his last penalty against Bayern [Munich] so he had to show his mentality. It is amazing the amount of goals he scores, but that's why we are still fighting for three competitions. He has a love for the game, he enjoys being here – and he has the capability to score goals for us in good moments and bad moments.'

When Haaland collected the Football Writers' Association Footballer of the Year award at a gala dinner at London's Landmark Hotel at the end of May, he told FWA chairman John Cross that he did not expect to be so efficient in front of goal, despite his belief that playing as the number nine in Manchester City's formation is a striker's dream job, 'Of course I wanted to score as many goals as possible, but the first thing I want is for the team to play good. If Manchester City plays good then the strikers will score goals. So I knew I would score goals, but I didn't expect so many. It is my team-mates who make it possible.'

Haaland made more history three days later when he scored his 35th Premier League goal of the season to break the record held jointly by Alan Shearer and Andy Cole, both having reached the figure in the first half of the 1990s when a top-flight campaign consisted of 42 games. It was fitting that the landmark strike should come in a 3-0 victory over West Ham, the team he had opened his account against with two goals at the London Stadium 270 days earlier.

Cole was first to set the standard when he made 40 appearances for newly promoted Newcastle in the 1993/94 season. Not one of his goals came from the penalty spot. Twelve months later, Shearer equalled the record from 42 outings as Blackburn won the Premier League title. His tally included ten penalties. Haaland scored all seven of the spot-kicks he took in the Premier League.

It's fair to say that Shearer greeted Haaland's heroics with more magnanimity than the man he replaced as Newcastle's number nine when Cole joined Manchester United in 1995. *Match of the Day* host Gary Lineker delivered a gentle reminder by tweeting, 'A Premier League record for Erling Haaland. 35 goals. That's nuts. Thoughts are with Alan Shearer at this difficult time.' Shearer's classy response was, 'Couldn't have wanted it to go to a nicer guy. It's only taken 28 years. He's the best!!!' Haaland then joined the exchange by tweeting, 'Thank you legend.' Shearer had interviewed Haaland during the season in his role as a pundit with the BBC and Amazon and had been rich in his praise.

Cole's take on Haaland's achievement was less ebullient. 'If I answer how many goals I'd get in this Manchester City side, I'll get made out to be arrogant,' said Cole. 'No one's actually mentioned I did it in a newly promoted side, it would be interesting to see how Erling Haaland would do in a newly promoted team. My record is seen as nothing because someone has broken it. But Haaland can't be greater than the first person who set the record. It's like Neil Armstrong, who was the first man who landed on the moon. He was the greatest because he was the first man to do it. You can't be greater than the first individual who set those standards. But it is what it is. The way my record has been perceived is as if it wasn't worth two bob, but now Haaland broke the record, he's now a "phenomenon". 'I couldn't give a fuck if I'm being honest. I am not anal in any way, shape or form about someone breaking goalscoring records, because records are set to be broken. But people say I must be disappointed. Why? Because someone has scored more goals than me? It's taken 20 years for someone to get that close. Am I going to rock myself to sleep and think, "Oh God, someone has broken my record?" No, I'll take my hat off to him. I'll salute him. He's done it in a team that creates chance after chance. At some stage, your record's going to be broken.'

* * *

Special moment

Haaland's special moment came in the 70th minute, with City leading 1-0 after Nathan Aké had broken West Ham's resistance with a far-post header five minutes after half-time. There was a huge roar of anticipation when Jack Grealish collected Bernardo Silva's pass and broke into space just inside the Hammers' half. City's fans recognised that Haaland was making his trademark burst in between centre-back pair Angelo Ogbonna and Thilo Kehrer and when Grealish delivered a ball that meant the striker didn't have to break stride, he beat oncoming keeper Łukasz Fabiański with a deftly lifted finish. The celebratory roars of 'Haaland, Haaland' shook the stadium, while dad Alfie joined in the celebrations with family and friends from the family's executive box in the Colin Bell Stand.

When Phil Foden completed a 3-0 victory with a 20-yard volley that was deflected past Fabiański by Emerson Palmieri, it was the 1,000th goal that City had scored during Guardiola's reign. But the manager recognised this was Haaland's evening and he joined his players and the rest of his staff in forming a guard of honour for the record-breaking striker at the final whistle.

Haaland repaid the gesture by calling his team-mates and Guardiola's backroom staff together in the dressing room. 'I don't know what else to say, but thank you guys so much,' he said before being swamped by hugs and high-fives. 'It's a special night and a special moment,' Haaland told Sky Sports. 'I am really happy and proud. I don't know what else to say. I knew about the record, of course, but we tried to create chances to score and it wasn't easy because they wanted to defend. We struggled in the first half but they eventually came. I spoke with Jack [Grealish] before the game and he said he wanted to do the assist for the record-breaking goal. It was a perfect bounce, I didn't think to chip but the opportunity was there so I did it.' Haaland didn't celebrate with a flute of champagne, a glass of milk or a slice of his dad's lasagne. Instead, he drove the 200 yards back to the City Football Academy with team-mate Rúben Dias for some treatment on a minor knock, a massage and an ice bath.

At the same time, Guardiola was falling into his habit of paying another glowing tribute to his star scorer. 'Erling deserved the guard of honour,' he said. 'But all the team deserved it, because without the team he couldn't do it. But he's a special striker. We are very pleased for him, because he's a joy, not just to work with him as his manager, but I think everyone is happy to have him with us. I think in football when there is a special occasion, we have to show how special it is. To overcome Andy Cole and Alan Shearer, two incredible top, top strikers, it is very special.'

Nike marked the occasion by giving the Aurora Borealis, commonly known as the Northern Lights, to Manchester – although it has to be said the publicity stunt came with something of a twist. Using hologram technology, the sportswear company's ad agency Wieden + Kennedy Amsterdam used a mixture of smoke, lasers and 'Hologauze' technology to beam images of Haaland from the roof of the National Football Museum. He was wearing his Nike-manufactured Norway kit rather than the Puma-made City strip.

When City faced Leeds on 6 May, Guardiola felt some of his players were looking fatigued and with the first leg of the Champions League semi-final against Real Madrid in the Bernabéu just three days away he opted to make seven changes to his team. Haaland would play for the full 90 minutes for the fourth successive game. Once again, the opposition had a new manager in charge, with the Yorkshire club bringing in escape artist Sam Allardyce to replace Javi Gracia after the Spaniard had won just three of his 11 games at the helm. It was a desperate throw of the dice by Leeds, who agreed to pay the former England manager £500,000 to end his two-year absence from the game and also offered him a £2.5m bonus if he could beat the threat of relegation. Allardyce had lost none of his old confidence and on the eve of the game he proclaimed himself the equal of Guardiola, Jürgen Klopp and Mikel Arteta. 'There's no one ahead of me in football terms – not Pep, Klopp or Arteta,' said the 68-year-old. Guardiola insisted that Allardyce was right – but the Spaniard was also careful to point out that he himself had never faced a relegation battle.

City's 2-1 victory was more comfortable than the scoreline suggests – and it brought Haaland's first public rebuke from his manager. There was nothing revolutionary about Allardyce's tactic of sitting players behind the ball in an attempt to frustrate the home side. The visitors had ten players camped inside their own penalty area on both occasions when İlkay Gündoğan scored twice inside the opening 27 minutes to put City in control as they dominated with 81 per cent possession. But Guardiola was furious when his team were awarded a penalty with six minutes remaining after Phil Foden was barged over by Leeds defender Pascal Struijk and both Haaland and Riyad Mahrez stepped aside to allow Gündoğan the chance to score the first hat-trick of his career. When the German struck the post with his effort from the spot, Guardiola was picked up by the TV cameras pointing furiously in the direction of Haaland while shouting, 'You have to take it, you have to take it.' Guardiola's mood darkened further when just 54 seconds later, Leeds grabbed another lifeline when Spanish striker Rodrigo scored with his team's second effort on target. City closed out the final minutes with an assuredness that wasn't felt by the Etihad fans. Leeds remained outside the drop zone on goal difference, but took just a point from their final three games and were relegated while Allardyce went back to his holiday home in Spain. 'I didn't mean what I said about being Pep's equal,' he later confessed. 'I was just trying to take the pressure off my players.'

When Guardiola was questioned by BBC Sport just a few minutes after the final whistle, his annoyance was clear. 'At 2-0, you have to close the game,' he said. 'I admire that Gündoğan wanted to score, but the taker is the taker – so Erling has to take it because he is our specialist. The game was not over. It shows how nice and generous Erling is. If it is 4-0 with ten minutes left then OK. But at 2-0? At 2-0, especially in England, it is never over. Business is business.' Guardiola's temper had cooled by the time he faced up to national newspaper journalists in the Etihad press room. Or perhaps his omnipresent adviser Manuel Estiarte had offered him counsel about the next day's headlines, which would emphasise a bust-up between the manager and his most high-profile player rather than the fact that City were now four points clear of Arsenal at the top of the Premier League.

Asked about 51-goal Haaland deciding to hand penalty duties to the captain, Guardiola now preferred to concentrate on the generosity of the striker, 'What happens if Erling had taken the penalty and missed it? Or Riyad Mahrez had taken the penalty and missed it? The normal taker is Erling or Riyad so they have to take it. But the point is, what does this say about Erling as a person? All the time he wants to score goals, but his mates are also important. Erling had other chances to score. He didn't convert, but he had an outstanding game. But I want a taker, someone who has a routine and is more of a specialist than other players to take our penalties.' Guardiola then turned his ire on *Guardian* journalist Jamie Jackson when he was asked whether the incident had exposed a flaw in Haaland. 'Do you know, what Erling did after the game against West Ham, when we finished at 10.30 or 11 o'clock? He went directly to the training centre to get treatment. At 11.30 to 12 at night he was getting treatment with [Rúben] Dias. Of course he is professional. He is ruthless. But at the same time, he said, "OK, İlkay has never scored a hat-trick." He is so generous and so nice. Erling could have taken it and missed. Who knows? But my feeling is that he has more confidence now because he has taken ten or 11 penalties and Gündoğan doesn't have that feeling right now. I understand both sides.'

Gündoğan, however, gave the game away. Guardiola had reminded Haaland of his responsibilities – and then turned his sights on his captain. 'At first, Pep showed he was quite mad at Erling,' said the captain. 'And then he had a go at me. It is what it is. The moment Erling grabbed the ball, I was sure he was going to take it but he looked out for me. I checked with him a few times to make sure he was sure. He was certain about handing the ball to me. I was confident to score. I can't even remember if the keeper saved it or it was the post?'

Haaland was now reaping the benefits of the care and attention Guardiola had lavished on his striker by substituting him when more goals and match balls appeared there for the taking. The boss explained, 'Erling feels so strong now. People say he has a magic potion – milk. I also drink this magic potion and I don't score 50 goals, that's for sure. I would recommend little boys who want to emulate Erling should emulate what he drinks.'

19

Fine Performances in Madrid and on Merseyside

REAL MADRID wanted to sign Erling Haaland. They still do. The *Galáctico* dream of club president Florentino Pérez that once took players like Ronaldo, Luís Figo, Zinedine Zidane, Robinho and David Beckham to the Bernabéu at the start of the millennium has never been sated. Pérez would love nothing more than to see Haaland leading Real's attack in tandem with Kylian Mbappé, with Jude Bellingham just behind. Winning always comes first for Real, but flexing their muscles to buy any player they want is part of the grand machismo of the club.

* * *

Release clause

Haaland had been at Manchester City for a matter of months when Pep Guardiola was forced to deny reports emanating from Spain claiming Haaland had a 'Madrid' clause in his contract which would allow the world's most successful football club to buy Haaland for €200m in 2024 or €175m in 2025. 'It's not true,' said Guardiola. 'He has no release clause for Real Madrid – or any other team. It's not true, what can I say? I have the feeling he is incredibly happy here and we will try to make him happy.' But Haaland does have a release clause in his contract at the Etihad which can be triggered after two years and reduces accordingly with every further season he spends with the club. Before he passed away, agent Mino Raiola did business with City the same way he had operated in his dealings with RB Salzburg and Borussia Dortmund – and that was to ensure Haaland remained in control of his future. Alfie Haaland admitted in *The Big Decision* that his son would choose from one of three clubs – Manchester City, Bayern Munich and Real Madrid. What helped City's cause was that Guardiola had been playing for two years without a recognised central striker as injuries and then an end-of-contract move to Barcelona took away record goalscorer Sergio Agüero. And Bayern still had Robert Lewandowski, while Karim Benzema was winning the Ballon d'Or in Madrid. Erling himself was asked how he could reject the chance to join a club that is considered the kings of European royalty. 'That's a good question,' he said. 'It is not really possible.'

City had given as good as they had got in Champions League head-to-heads with the 14-time champions, winning three, losing three and drawing two. But Madrid had prevailed over two legs in two previous semi-final meetings – and the question was whether losing to the Spaniards over two epic encounters 12 months earlier had inflicted any lasting psychological damage on Guardiola and his team. Of course, they didn't have Haaland at that time. He would have surely taken some of the chances that City spurned when winning the first leg 4-3 at an exuberant Etihad. City were 2-0 ahead after 11 minutes thanks to goals by Kevin De Bruyne and Gabriel Jesus, but Real illustrated their stomach for a fight by replying through Karim Benzema. Phil Foden brought a reply from Vinícius Junior, the supercharged Brazilian winger who was being marked by City captain Fernandinho because Kyle Walker was suspended. And when Bernardo Silva made it 4-2 with 16 minutes left that was enough time for Benzema to score from the penalty spot with a 'Panenka' and keep the Spaniards in the tie. City were just as dominant in the second leg but had to wait until the 73rd minute to make it count when Riyad Mahrez scored to put them 5-3 ahead on aggregate. But Carlo Ancelotti's men had demonstrated remarkable powers of recovery when getting past Paris Saint-Germain in the last 16 by scoring three goals in the last 29 minutes. This time, after Jack Grealish had missed two outstanding chances to seal City's passage to a final meeting with Liverpool, Real scored twice in 90 seconds with the game in its 90th minute through Rodrygo before Benzema won it with an extra-time penalty. Real beat Liverpool in Paris, while City were left to contemplate how the loss of Walker just before Mahrez's strike had given Vinícius room to exploit. The Spaniards also rode their luck against Liverpool in Paris – goalkeeper Thibaut Courtois was the man of the match – but lifted the trophy for a 14th time thanks to Vinícius's second-half goal.

City had also fallen victim to the mystical powers of the Bernabéu when they qualified for the Champions League for the second successive season in 2012 after winning the Premier League for the first time under Roberto Mancini. Their opening group game took them to the mighty amphitheatre in the Spanish capital and a contest with José Mourinho, Cristiano Ronaldo and co. City deserved the lead that Edin Džeko gave them in the 68th minute and even though Marcelo equalised eight minutes later, the visitors were ahead again five minutes from time through Džeko. Then madness took hold. Karim Benzema equalised a further two minutes on and Ronaldo's winner in the final minute prompted the kind of celebratory touchline knee-slide from a suited and booted Mourinho that he would save for special occasions. City drew the return game in Manchester 1-1, but collected just three points overall and finished bottom of a group that also included previous winners Borussia Dortmund and Ajax. The previous season, they had also failed to survive the group stage.

In 2016 came the first of the three semi-final clashes. City, under Manuel Pellegrini, appeared happy to secure a goalless draw in the home leg in the hope that an away goal might be decisive in the return. But once again the Blues failed to perform at their best and were criticised for their cautious approach. Even when an own goal by City midfielder Fernando put Madrid ahead after 20 minutes, the visitors refused to change tactics and it took until injury time for them to threaten with a long-range Agüero strike that was inches too high. Real went on to lift the trophy in Milan by beating neighbours Atlético on penalties after a 1-1 draw.

City did draw some Real blood in the last 16 of the pandemic-affected 2019/20 season, recovering from the shock of conceding a goal to Isco to claim their first win in the Bernabéu thanks to two late goals from Jesus and De Bruyne. Six months later, with the fight against Covid-19 starting to take effect, they repeated the scoreline at an empty Etihad, with Raheem Sterling and Jesus on target either side of a Benzema equaliser. That took City into a mini-tournament in Lisbon, where they suffered a shock 3-1 defeat to underdogs Lyon in the quarter-finals.

Guardiola, of course, had previous with Real during his playing career and his success-filled four-year spell with Barcelona as a manager. He led Bayern Munich to three successive Bundesliga titles but had been beaten in three consecutive Champions League semi-finals at the same time – falling at the hands of Spanish opposition on each occasion. Bayern lost 5-0 on aggregate to Madrid in 2014, 5-3 on aggregate to Barça the following season and lost on away goals to Atlético Madrid in his final year. With his misery compounded by his European record with City, there was a widely held belief that the Catalan's reputation had been burnished by the genius of Lionel Messi. Now, though, he had the most prolific striker in football. Guardiola said, 'I know that it doesn't matter what we do this season, if we don't win the Champions League then I will be called a failure. But I would not like to have a team that won the Champions League one day and then goes down and down and down. Being stable is the most important thing for a club. Last year was tough, but we are not here for revenge, we are here for an opportunity. We were exceptional in the first game against Madrid last season and very good in the second – but sometimes that is not enough. That's football. I think this tie will be decided in Manchester.'

The game was billed as the history makers v the history chasers. Haaland had never faced Madrid before and Real boss Ancelotti tried not to be drawn on how his team would stop him. 'Obviously Haaland is a dangerous player who has shown amazing quality,' he said. 'But to only talk about Haaland means you don't think about the other great players City possess. It's not about stopping Haaland, it's about stopping a team that appears to be unstoppable. But with Haaland, City are a more complete team. They had a forward in Gabriel Jesus, who can be difficult but has different features than Haaland. They have not changed their style, apart from maybe being more direct. They can now use the long ball more, but they remain just as organised in defence and midfield.' Madrid were third in La Liga, 14 points behind leaders Barcelona. But they had demonstrated their readiness for the big occasion in the last 16 by dismantling Liverpool 5-2 at Anfield after conceding two early goals. They had also won 4-0 in the Camp Nou to reach the final of the Copa del Rey, lifting the trophy three days before facing City with a 2-1 victory over Osasuna.

The loss of Brazilian defender Éder Militão through suspension meant Ancelotti had to ask Antonio Rüdiger to tangle with Haaland – something the German would relish. The former Chelsea centre-back showed how ruthless he can be when he broke De Bruyne's eye socket with a cynical bodycheck in the 2021 final and then avoided a red card by faking injury. Rüdiger decided that the best way to stop Haaland was to be constantly in the Norwegian's face – and it worked. Film footage shows Rüdiger dipping his forehead into Haaland's armpits and lower back, constantly tugging at his shirt and trying to disrupt his concentration. This was European football at its most cynical and when Rüdiger recklessly smashed his forearm into the face of İlkay Gündoğan, he was lucky to escape a card and his German international team-mate fortunate not to suffer a serious injury. City's dominance in the opening half-hour failed to produce any clear chances, although Real keeper Courtois thwarted De Bruyne and Rodri from distance. Then, after 36 minutes, Vinícius finally escaped the shackles of Walker to drift inside when the City full-back went to engage Eduardo Camavinga. And when the Frenchman played a short pass inside, Vinícius took a controlling touch before bludgeoning a 25-yard shot into the top corner with a flash of his right foot.

Haaland got his first sight of goal in the 55th minute, but his shot was blocked by David Alaba. He then smiled to himself when the Austrian defender was given high-fives by Rüdiger, Courtois and Dani Carvajal. When City levelled matters in the 67th minute, Real's complaints that the ball had gone out of play 30 seconds earlier ended in Ancelotti being booked. But it was a wasteful pass by Camavinga that was the home side's undoing. Rodri stepped in to feed Jack Grealish and when the ball was played inside to Gündoğan, it prompted Rüdiger to leave Haaland to confront the danger. Gündoğan simply laid the ball back for De Bruyne to lash a lethal low drive from 22 yards past Courtois's right hand. When Ederson saved from Benzema and Aurélien Tchouaméni in the closing stages, the narrative in the Spanish media suggested City had been lucky to escape with a draw. The reality was that they appeared to be learning from past mistakes and were now a seasoned team capable of dealing with the dark arts often employed by the very best.

Haaland only managed 22 touches of the ball – the fewest of any player that started the game. Even Ederson touched it 29 times. Influential Spanish sports newspaper *Marca* gave him a score of three out of ten – and Rüdiger demanded to know what all the fuss was about. 'At the end of the day, City were not dangerous,' he said. 'They had possession, but we knew that would happen. The goal from De Bruyne was quality, but I don't think they gave us any problems. We can go to Manchester with confidence.'

Guardiola felt Ancelotti had set his team up specifically to neutralise the threat of his number nine. He said, 'The pockets, the distance between the central defenders and full-backs, was occupied by Real's attacking midfielders. They sat [Luka] Modrić, Toni Kroos and (Fede) Valverde in there and put both central defenders close to Erling. It was not easy for him, but he moved well and had chances. Congratulations to Rüdiger, but we cannot forget that Erling is 22 and it's the first time he has played in the semi-finals of the Champions League. It was also his first time at the Bernabéu, on one of the biggest stages, against a top-class club with good defenders, midfielders and strikers. Next time, it will be a little easier.' Even Guardiola wouldn't have believed how much easier.

Erling wasn't the only Haaland to have a tough evening in the Bernabéu. Alfie was removed from a VIP box along with some friends after being accused of throwing peanuts at Madrid fans. He insisted that he had done nothing wrong.

'I did not throw food,' he said. 'We had some good banter with the Madrid fans, but they were not happy when Kevin De Bruyne scored. Typical. We then had to be moved 50 metres away. Nothing more. All happy. Well, nearly.' Spanish journalist Inaki Angulo, however, insisted that the behaviour of Alfie had been provocative. Angulo told TalkSport, 'He didn't behave like a man of his experience. He lost control a little bit. The version he gave that everything erupted after De Bruyne's goal is not true. He was out of his mind in the first half. He was throwing peanuts and small food items. People are not used to this kind of behaviour in this part of the stadium. He was in the VIP area. It was a little bit disgusting. I saw Alfie's tweets and I expected a little more like "I misbehaved". He tried to manipulate a little bit saying the Real Madrid fans acted poorly after the equaliser from De Bruyne. That wasn't the story. People in this area are in charge of making the VIP people comfortable. They don't have to know who that guy was. When they realised he was the father of the best striker in the world, it turned a lot of heads. His son did not show up in the Bernabéu ... but his father did.'

Two days later the Football Writers' Association confirmed that their members had voted Haaland as their Footballer of the Year. He polled a record-breaking 82 per cent of the votes for an award first won by Stanley Matthews in 1948. The FWA had been formed on a cross-channel ferry by a group of journalists returning home from an England international in Belgium in September 1947. Three of them – Charles Buchan, Frank Coles and Roy Peskett – drafted the rules of the association and at a meeting the following month it was decided to make an annual award 'to the player, who by precept and example on and off the field, shall have been considered to have done most for football during that season'. Haaland's case to become only the fourth foreign player to win the award in his first season in England was compelling – and he duly followed in the footsteps of team-mate Rúben Dias, Jürgen Klinsmann and Gianfranco Zola. Haaland's close friend Martin Ødegaard was second, with his Arsenal team-mate Bukayo Saka third; De Bruyne and Manchester United's Marcus Rashford made up the top five.

Only four City players had won the poll previously, starting with goalkeeper Bert Trautmann, who was the FWA choice in 1956 after a season in which he had helped the Blues win the FA Cup despite playing with a broken neck in the 3-1 win over Birmingham at Wembley. Captain Tony Book shared the honour with Derby County's Dave Mackay in 1969, again when City were FA Cup winners. Raheem Sterling was the choice in 2019 after playing a key role in City becoming the first club to lift a domestic treble of Premier League, FA Cup and League Cup, while Dias's role in the 2021 title win was recognised with the English game's oldest individual trophy. Haaland said, 'To win the Football Writers' Award in my first season in English football is an honour. I try every single day to be the best I can be, and to be recognised like this means a lot to me. I have loved my time at City so far – my team-mates are incredible, and they provide me with the chances to score goals. I want to thank all of them, because I could not have won this award without them. I also owe so much to Pep and the team behind the team here at City. Everybody has been so good to me since I joined and I have never worked with such top professionals. Thank you to everyone who voted for me. It's a real honour to have won this award. I am now focused on ensuring I finish the season as strongly as possible and helping City win trophies.'

When City travelled to face Everton at Goodison Park on Sunday, 14 May, it would prove to be a pivotal day in the title race. By the time, the team bus had travelled east on the M62 to transport Guardiola and his players back to the Etihad Campus, they were just three points away from being crowned champions for a third successive season. City's 3-0 win over the Toffees had cranked up the pressure on Arsenal to an intolerable level ahead of their home game with Brighton & Hove Albion – and Mikel Arteta's team cracked before disintegrating completely as Albion romped to a 3-0 victory of their own. Guardiola had impressed upon his players the need to be ruthless. Arsenal's impressive 2-0 triumph at high-flying Newcastle a week earlier had cut City's lead at the top to a point, albeit with a game in hand. But City's run-in after their visit to Merseyside would pit them against a Chelsea team that was packed with quality despite their disappointing form under returning caretaker Frank Lampard, followed by two tricky away games at Brighton and Brentford. The City boss did not want to give the Gunners any hint of encouragement – and their ruthless demolition of an Everton side battling relegation was a statement of intent that Arteta could not come up with an answer to. Guardiola was unhappy that his team had not been scheduled to play the game 24 hours earlier to give him more time to prepare his players for the return with Madrid, and mistakenly blamed the issue on the Eurovision Song Contest being held in Liverpool that week. 'I am pretty sure the Premier League wants to help the teams,' he said. 'I don't think they want to make it uncomfortable. The schedule is the problem, with so many competitions. I don't think we could play on Saturday because of Eurovision in Liverpool and they cannot have two important events at the same time. In France and Germany, they play on Friday to help teams. Here it is the opposite.'

City certainly hit all the right notes in the Beatles' hometown. Captain İlkay Gündoğan broke the resistance of an Everton team that had battered Brighton 5-1 at the Amex Stadium six days earlier, when he controlled Mahrez's 37th-minute cross on his thigh as he arrived in the home side's six-yard box, before improvising brilliantly to hook a volley past England keeper Jordan Pickford. Two minutes later, Gündoğan crossed from the left for Haaland to leap high and score with a header that carried too much power for Pickford to keep out. When Gündoğan completed the scoring with a wonderfully floated free kick into the top corner just before the hour, Guardiola decided against risking Haaland further and brought him off with 12 minutes remaining.

Haaland had stepped out on to the Goodison pitch wearing a pair of boots that had been customised by Nike to mark his record-breaking exploits in the Premier League. They had the number 35 stitched into the side. When his team-mates started ribbing him about his footwear, Haaland joked that they would only last 90 minutes before becoming obsolete. Sure enough, after scoring his 36th – and final – league goal of the season, he was handed a magic marker by a member of the backroom staff and the number was duly altered to 36. Everton may have finished the afternoon just one point above the bottom three but that didn't prevent a group of their fans handing Haaland a trophy in the design of a boot, with the inscription 'E Haaland Record Premier League goals'. He had, of course, taken the 38-game record from Liverpool's Mo Salah.

Most of the talk afterwards was about whether Gündoğan would sign a new contract at the end of the season. The midfielder was Guardiola's first City signing, arriving from Borussia Dortmund. He would eventually turn down City's offers and move to Barcelona. Haaland also left Merseyside with another less-welcome souvenir – a series of scratches and lacerations on his ribcage and lower abdomen – something Guardiola blamed on the dirty tricks employed by Everton's aggressive central defender Yerry Mina. The striker showed off his battle scars when he stripped off his shirt in front of

City's celebrating travelling fans, while Guardiola was giving the Colombian a few choice words of advice. 'What Yerry Mina does is unnecessary,' he said. 'He does it every single game. I told him, "You're a good player, it's unnecessary to do those things." It wasn't just with Erling, but also with Jack [Grealish] and Aymeric [Laporte].'

20

A Third Consecutive Success for City Gives Haaland his First Premier League Winners Medal

IT WASN'T Erling Haaland who scored the goal that clinched the Premier League title for Manchester City for a third successive season. When Nottingham Forest striker Taiwo Awoniyi's 19th-minute winner condemned Arsenal to defeat at the City Ground the day before the Blues were due to face Chelsea, it meant the Nigerian had not only ensured his own club's top flight status, but he had also ensured that Pep Guardiola's team would be crowned champions in their final home game of the season. Awoniyi, who had spent three years with Liverpool without making a single appearance, had given Forest as much value for money as Haaland following his £17m arrival from Union Berlin. He may have only scored ten goals – but they accounted for 17 precious points as Steve Cooper's side ensured Forest's 23-year quest for the top flight would last more than a single season.

It would have been a bittersweet moment for the Haaland family. Brian Clough had tried to sign Alfie from Bryne in 1992 but by the time the deal went through the following year, the East Midlands club had been relegated from the Premier League and Frank Clark was in charge following the retirement of their greatest-ever manager. Haaland senior signed for Leeds four years later and was part of the United team that reached the semi-finals of the UEFA Cup in 2000 before moving to Manchester City. His career explained his family's allegiances.

In a twist of fate, Leeds' two-year spell back in the Premier League came to an end on the final day of the season when they were beaten 4-1 by Tottenham at Elland Road.

With City confirmed as champions, it meant Guardiola could shuffle his pack for the last three games of the Premier League season. Haaland gave an insight into Guardiola's genius during an interview with former Liverpool midfielder Jan Mølby that was screened on Viaplay. He said, 'Pep is fantastic. It's a pleasure to work with him every single day and I was so happy when he signed a new contract. That was very good news because I am really looking forward to the next years with him. Pep is a detail freak – and that's what I like about him. Sometimes we go through some things the day before a game and during the game it actually happens. I look around thinking, "How could he know?" He is so smart. It's difficult to explain.'

City still had too much for a Chelsea team temporarily being managed by Frank Lampard after new owner Todd Boehly had sacked Champions League winner Thomas Tuchel and then successor Graham Potter. Lampard's final year as a player in England had seen him join City from Chelsea after he had initially signed for their MLS sister club New York City. The former England international was given a warm reception as a carnival atmosphere swept around the Etihad. City took all three points when youth-team graduate Cole Palmer , who was to join the Londoners at the start of 2023-24 season, served up a delicious pass for Julián Álvarez and the World Cup-winning Argentine swept a lovely first-time finish into the bottom corner. Haaland came on for the final 16 minutes before the festivities really started with a trophy presentation which saw former City keeper Alex Williams do the honours alongside Richard Masters, the Premier League chief executive who was given a cold reception by fans who blamed him for the 115 charges hanging over the reigning champions.

Haaland was so swept up in the euphoria that he broke off a live interview with Sky Sports presenter Geoff Shreeves to dance in front of the more boisterous City fans in the South Stand who had adapted a terrace chant that had once paid tribute to Yaya and Kolo Touré to reflect their love for Erling and Alfie Haaland. 'Just listen to this for 30 seconds,' Haaland told Shreeves, who maintained his professionalism brilliantly under pressure. 'I feel unreal,' he added. 'I honestly don't know what to say. You see me smiling? I am so happy. These are the memories I'll remember for the rest of my life. We have been fighting so hard. I am going to enjoy this day. It's amazing. Debut season, 36 [Premier League] goals so far, the Premier League trophy and two finals left. Not a bad start.'

The striker then moved on to hang his Premier League medal around the neck of his dad before urging him to take a swig from a bottle of champagne. Elsewhere on the Etihad pitch stood Roy Keane, the former Manchester United nemesis of Alfie Haaland. The two midfield combatants hadn't shared the same pitch since Keane had gone barrelling into a revenge mission that took him studs first into Alfie's right knee at Old Trafford 22 years earlier. Keane was there in his role as a Sky Sports pundit and was interviewing an exuberant Jack Grealish alongside fellow guests Micah Richards, Jamie Redknapp and presenter Dave Jones when the younger Haaland appeared on the scene. Grabbing hold of Grealish, Erling clearly muttered to the midfielder and the watching nation, 'I fucking love you, you know that?' After he had wheeled away, Jones offered an apology to viewers.

It was a moment of stupidity from a 22-year-old caught up in the moment of becoming a Premier League winner. But within minutes, Manchester United fans with long memories were posting on social media calling for the FA to lay a disciplinary charge against the City striker. In 2011, Wayne Rooney had been hit with a two-match ban that ruled him out of United's FA Cup semi-final with City for shouting an obscenity into a TV camera as he manically celebrated scoring a hat-trick at West Ham. The England striker was sat stewing on the Wembley bench as Yaya Touré's goal took City through to a final against Stoke and towards the club's first trophy in 35 years. That semi-final win over their greatest rivals is now viewed as a breakthrough moment in the club's history.

Journalists making enquiries with the FA were told that there would be no action taken against Haaland. But it was another reminder to the striker that he was now under a spotlight that would never be dimmed. A Manchester United fan had filmed him from a car on a mobile phone as he took a stroll through the city centre shortly after his arrival in Manchester. 'You've gone to the wrong side of Manchester,' shouted the United fan. 'Come to United next season.' Haaland takes it all in his stride and good-naturedly answered, 'But they love me here.' There was a more sinister incident in March 2023 when another passerby secretly filmed Haaland appearing to use his mobile phone while he was driving. The footage was sold to a tabloid newspaper and Greater Manchester Police released a statement confirming they would be questioning the player. Haaland said, 'I haven't had any problems so far with United fans. I try to live as normally as possible. Obviously, there are things I can't do anymore or things I have to do differently. I am who I am. I'm the big, tall blond guy with the long hair who everyone sees wherever I go. But I am still the same guy

I was when I was 15 years old. I'm still the same guy from Bryne. The only thing that has changed is that people ask for pictures and autographs.'

* * *

Football Writers' Association winner

City's early title win meant Haaland was granted permission to attend the Football Writers' Association's gala dinner at the Landmark Hotel in London on 26 May to collect the Footballer of the Year award, 75 years after Stanley Matthews became the first recipient. Chelsea's Australian international striker Sam Kerr won the women's award for the second successive year. Former England strikers Alan Shearer and Gary Lineker were among those who were there to honour the winners. Haaland said, 'It was a special moment when I found out I had won [the award] a couple of weeks ago. But I must also thank my team-mates because they create the chances to help me score the goals.'

Haaland was to later be awarded in August 2023 the PFA men's players' player of the year award, with Bukayo Saka named young player of the year. He was also selected as the 2022/23 UEFA Men's Player of the Year.

Having wrapped up the Premier League title and celebrated with a party afterwards it was now a case of negotiating the final two matches at Brighton and Brentford for Pep Guardiola's squad, all of them desperate to make the final 20 for the FA Cup Final while for the 23 players still at the club who had been registered in the Champions League squad in September it was a case of staying fit and in form.

This would not be easy as both opposition teams had something to play for. At the same time Brighton were already celebrating because their victory over Southampton meant they had qualified for Europe for the first time. This was a tremendous achievement especially considering back in 1997 the Seagulls had needed a late equaliser at Hereford United to avoid dropping out of the Football League and into the Football Conference.

Having guaranteed themselves a Europa Conference League spot, City's opponents were after going one better by securing a Europa League spot.

A point would do for Brighton and they would have to earn it after Guardiola chose to play an experienced team full of attacking intent including Haaland who was restored to the starting line-up.

The striking Viking might have even opened the scoring moments into the game but his close-range header from Phil Foden's cross flew over the bar.

On 25 minutes, however, the pair combined again and Foden put his side ahead. Brighton were to record the point they required 13 minutes later when 19-year-old Julio Enciso equalised with a curling strike into the top corner from 25 yards. It was a goal in keeping with a thrilling first 45 minutes.

Although the pace slackened after the break Danny Welbeck hit the bar and İlkay Gündoğan dragged a shot narrowly wide from a tight angle.

There then arose a moment of controversy that resulted in Guardiola being yellow-carded when a 37th Premier League goal of the season for Haaland from a header from Cole Palmer's cross on 79 minutes was overruled because VAR official Chris Kavanagh felt he had pulled Levi Colwill's shirt. Referee Simon Hooper agreed after making an on-screen check and disallowed the goal. Guardiola was booked for arguing with fourth official Graham Scott about the decision.

Action replays showed the Brighton defender had earlier tugged his opponent.

In typical fashion, Haaland sought to take the positives out of having a goal disallowed due to VAR, stating, 'VAR is good for me because it makes me concentrate more on not running offside.'

Haaland was kicked and manhandled all night by Brighton defender Jan Paul van Hecke. Van Hecke was finally booked in injury time for a foul on Haaland but Guardiola felt it was too little too late. Haaland later posted a pic on Instagram showing several deep cuts on his right shin.

Guardiola had made the same point when Foden had a goal disallowed in the 1-0 defeat at Liverpool in October for a foul by Haaland on Fabinho. He felt Haaland got penalised for having too much power and strength and wasn't being afforded the same protection when similar challenges were made on him. Guardiola said, 'For every action Erling makes, it is a foul. I complained about the disallowed goal because if that's a foul then there are 25 fouls made by defenders when they go for the ball. If it's a foul by Erling, then every time it's a foul. Come on, it's ridiculous. The goal being disallowed was ridiculous – but at least this one didn't matter.'

Guardiola also argued, 'That's why it's "show me again what you have done this season", because nobody gave us absolutely anything in this competition on the pitch. Watch it! If it's a [foul], then every action for Erling is a [foul]. Every single time for the central defenders.'

He was nevertheless full of praise for Brighton's achievements, 'Exceptional game. Congratulations to Brighton for their deserved qualification to the Europa League.'

There was also praise for his players' abilities to still play so well after they had let their hair down following the victory over Chelsea, 'The game we played, 40 hours after I think we drank all the alcohol in Manchester, showed the reason why we are the champion. I didn't see a drop of intensity in our idea. They had chances, we had chances.

'This team destroy the other opponents, the way they play, and they did in certain moments tonight, especially the last ten or 15 minutes of the first half, when we struggled. But the second half, we adjusted and we did really well.'

The question now was would there be other celebrations to come after the matches against Manchester United and Inter Milan?

The draw brought to an end Manchester City's run of 12 consecutive Premier League victories, and they ended the Premier League season by losing out to Brentford who thus became the only team to record a double over their illustrious opponents in 2022/23.

When the sides had last clashed in west London at the end of December 2021 a Foden goal in a 1-0 success took City's tally over those 12 months up to 113 Premier League goals, the most by a top-flight team in a single calendar year since 1960.

Eighteen months on and with bigger days on the horizon a much-changed City side, with Haaland on the bench, started the game. There was no chance that the Norwegian would stay there for the forthcoming finals and although Kevin De Bruyne, Jack Grealish and Rúben Dias were all left out of the matchday squad they too were, if fully fit, certain to start in the FA Cup and Champions League finals.

Nevertheless, the 90 minutes was an opportunity for several players to impress their manager and convince him they should be considered for the two deciders. They, Mahrez in particular, did not take it as City slumped to a first defeat in 25 matches in what was only the second time that they had failed to score in the Premier League throughout the season.

Youngsters Cole Palmer and Rico Lewis both operated alongside Kalvin Phillips and Foden in midfield with Álvarez up front alongside Sergio Gómez and Mahrez. None could be certain of starting at Wembley. That was also true of the captain for the day, Kyle Walker, and although Walker did, in fact, start against Manchester United he was to join Foden and Mahrez, both substitutes at Wembley, on the bench in Turkey when the Champions League Final began.

Before kick-off Brentford knew that if they could win and both Aston Villa and Tottenham Hotspur failed to do so then they would secure a place in the 2023/24 Europa Conference League. In the event both Spurs and Villa took all three points from their games against Leeds and Brighton respectively.

None of which prevented great celebrations when Ethan Pinnock grabbed a late winner to ensure that Brentford finished ninth, three places behind their record sixth-placed finish in the top league of English football in 1936/37 and 1937/38.

Asked afterwards about whether De Bruyne, Grealish and Dias would be fit for Wembley, Guardiola remarked, 'I think they will be ready but it's hard to get ready in training … that's why I had to see the players who played today.' He would not have been impressed by what he was watching.

Haaland thus ended the Premier League season on 36 goals. It made him City's second-highest scorer in a top-flight season behind Tommy Johnson's 38 goals in 1928/29.

21

City's Greatest Game?

ERLING HAALAND had no doubts. When Manchester City destroyed Real Madrid to reach the 2023 Champions League Final, the first 45 minutes was a masterclass the likes of which he had never seen before. So breathtakingly dominant, in fact, that for weeks afterwards he watched it on a continuous loop in his city-centre apartment. It said something about the brilliance of City's performance that Haaland, the striker who scored 52 goals during arguably the greatest season ever produced by an English club, didn't get on the scoresheet. That was down to a quite magnificent demonstration of the art of goalkeeping by Thibaut Courtois, the Belgian international who was the only Madrid player to excel as City threatened to run riot before doing exactly that. 'The first half, when I watched it again, was one of the few games I have watched again and again,' said Haaland. 'I think it was the best first half I have ever seen myself from a football team.'

It was indeed arguably the greatest performance in the club's 143-year history – certainly the best in the living memory of most supporters. City fans of a certain vintage might still claim that the Blues have never played better than when Joe Mercer's team hammered Tottenham 4-1 on an icy Maine Road pitch in December 1967 on their way to winning the Football League championship for the second time. The game is known as 'The Ballet on Ice' and the grainy black and white footage of the occasion captured by the *Match of the Day* cameras, complete with Kenneth Wolstenholme on commentary, only adds to the legend. Two seasons later, after the Blues had won the 1969 FA Cup, more than 46,000 saw the same Mercer team of Colin Bell, Francis Lee and Mike Summerbee thrash Schalke 04 5-1 in the second leg of the Cup Winners' Cup semi-finals with another stellar display that was shown on BBC's midweek *Sportsnight* programme. But this was sublime 21st-century football watched all around the world in full HD glory.

Pep Guardiola once guided Barcelona to a 6-2 victory over Real in the Bernabéu in May 2009; two years later he masterminded the 5-0 destruction of José Mourinho in the Camp Nou. But this was a Real Madrid team who were the reigning European champions, with a coach in Carlo Ancelotti who had won the Champions League four times, and world-class players in every position. The sight of a master technician like Luka Modrić booting the ball aimlessly up the pitch in the early exchanges, such was the efficiency of City's press, illustrated the relentless stranglehold Guardiola's tactical plan exerted on the Spaniards. Former Manchester United defender Rio Ferdinand, who was at the Etihad in his role as a pundit for BT Sport, revealed that the City manager had sent him a message earlier that day predicting an overwhelming victory for his team. 'Pep texted me before the game after I had sent him a "good luck" message,' said Ferdinand. 'He replied, "Listen, believe me, we beat them two years ago and we'll beat them again."'

Guardiola had sensed something special in the Manchester air, even before the teams emerged to 53,000 blue and white flags and an explosion of streamers. 'It's probably the most important game since I came here,' he said in the pre-match press conference. 'But I have told the players to enjoy the moment. I have an incredible feeling about this team. When I signed the contract seven years ago, they didn't tell me I had to win the Champions League – but of course we want it. It's a dream come true to be here again, so let's go for it from the first minute to the end.'

Ancelotti admitted that he was worried about the prospect of facing Haaland and Kevin De Bruyne at their best. 'Today I'm very calm, full of hope and faith,' he said. 'Tomorrow, on game day, that's when the worries come in and you think things through, whether Erling Haaland will score or Kevin De Bruyne will hurt you. You try to put it out of my mind, it's all about managing thoughts. In the first leg we managed to stop Haaland by having possession of the ball. It was tough for City to get hold of it. If we can do that again then Haaland is less of a risk.' Ancelotti decided to recall Éder Militão after suspension at the expense of Antonio Rüdiger, the German who had got into Haaland's face at the Bernabéu to such great effect that he was a shadow of the striker who had terrorised the Premier League. Militão and central defensive partner David Alaba were given a torrid examination by Haaland as City steamrollered Real into total submission.

* * *

Walker's pace

Many observers felt that Kyle Walker's duel with Vinícius Junior would be key to the outcome – and it was. The Brazilian winger was neutralised by the England full-back's blistering pace and ability to sniff out danger. The previous day, Walker had been asked if, at the age of 32, he was starting to slow down, despite being clocked at the same 35.2kph speed as Haaland by statisticians during the Champions League. The Yorkshireman, who is officially the fastest player the Premier League has ever seen given that records only started in 2022, wasn't having it. He said, 'One of our sports science team told me I hit 37.5kph during speed tests in training so I'm not getting any slower. Erling is very, very quick as well. Sometimes he creates chances just with his strength and speed. But [in a race with Haaland] I would still have to back myself.' For comparison, Usain Bolt would average around the same speed as Walker in a 100m race, although the Jamaican world-record holder would hit around 44kph when he was close to the finishing line.

Haaland gave a demonstration of his leg speed after just six minutes when he was sent clear by De Bruyne. But he was cleverly forced wide of goal by Courtois and there was no team-mate on hand to convert the chance when he pulled the ball back across goal. Then, after Rodri had dragged a decent chance wide, Jack Grealish teased a tantalising cross to the far post for Haaland to direct a header from point-blank range into the stomach of the Real keeper. Courtois's next save might have had Guardiola wondering if the fates were once again conspiring against his team. De Bruyne crossed from the right after working a short corner and Haaland muscled his way in to meet Manuel Akanji's header back across goal with a meaty nod of his brow only to look on in disbelief as Courtois contorted in midair to produce a miraculous save.

* * *

Courtois with a ten but unable to protect his net

Courtois defied Haaland again early in the second half when the striker fastened on to İlkay Gündoğan's back-heel only to see his shot deflected up and on to the crossbar by the Belgian. By then, though, City were 2-0 up and putting Madrid through the wringer. Bernardo Silva scored both goals, his first a ruthless rocket into the near post after casting a glance towards the opposite corner to unbalance Courtois; his second was a looping header after Gündoğan's shot had been blocked by Militão. When Toni Kroos shuddered City's bar with a long-range strike that Ederson got the slightest of fingertips to just before half-time, it was still a case of how many City would score such was their grip on the game. There were two more goals after the break; Akanji's flicked header beat Courtois with the aid of a deflection off the demoralised Militão and Julián Álvarez found the bottom corner from Phil Foden's pass 104 seconds after replacing Haaland. Haaland, with a Norwegian flag draped around his shoulders, joined his team-mates for a lap of honour at the final whistle – but not before paying a personal tribute to Courtois with a pat on his back.

At the same time, former Manchester United defender Patrice Evra was becoming involved in a verbal spat with Guardiola's confidante Manuel Estiarte. The 61-year-old Olympic water polo gold medalist had been made aware that Evra had reported for duty with a French TV station wearing a red suit to confirm that his allegiances were still with the only club from Manchester to have completed the fabled Treble. Estiarte wasn't the only City employee who felt Evra's choice of attire lacked class and dignity – and the Frenchman's explanation confirmed it. 'I asked him [Estiarte] why he was so agitated,' said Evra. 'He said, "Because last year you said on TV that they [City's players] shit themselves – and this year they didn't shit themselves."'

Spanish newspaper *Marca* gave Courtois a perfect ten for his performance. No other Madrid player earned above a five – the same mark given to Haaland. Thierry Henry, the former Arsenal striker who won the Champions League with Guardiola's Barcelona in 2009, has always credited the Catalan for reprogramming his understanding of the game. He felt that the same was now happening with Haaland. Henry told CBS viewers in the United States, 'We were all right at the start of the season when we said Haaland hadn't adapted to the City team off the ball. Tonight, he didn't score, but that was a great game for a number nine. Not only did Thibaut Courtois make three great saves from him, but the way he held the ball, the way he was putting pressure on, the way he was dropping back in to create overloads ... Once Pep Guardiola finds the right formula for his team, you're in trouble. Until now they couldn't do it in Europe, but now they have that special man who can score goals. And, I repeat, he is now way better off the ball since the Leipzig game when Pep said he didn't want a striker who stays in the box.'

The Treble was now a very real possibility – and before City played again, they would be confirmed as Premier League champions for a third successive season. Rivals Manchester United would stand between them and a seventh FA Cup triumph at Wembley on 3 June. And they were favourites to conquer Europe for the first time after a run which had seen them finish top of a Champions League group that included 1997 winners Borussia Dortmund. They accounted for Bayern Munich and Real Madrid, winners of 20 titles between them, to reach the final on 10 June and would now have to navigate a route past Inter Milan, the Italian club who had been European champions in 1964, 1965 and 2010. Inter had overcome city rivals AC Milan 3-0 over two legs for the right to meet City in Istanbul's Atatürk Stadium.

22

FA Cup Success

WHEN MANCHESTER United completed the Treble in 1999, Erling Haaland was still 14 months away from being born. The magnitude of United's achievement cannot be underestimated – and over one million people packed the streets of Manchester to pay tribute. The heartbeat of Sir Alex Ferguson's squad was an incredible group of players who had graduated from the club's fabled 'Class of '92' youth team, such as Ryan Giggs, Paul Scholes, David Beckham, Nicky Butt and the Neville brothers, Gary and Phil. Ferguson had also used United's wealth wisely to recruit established internationals like Roy Keane, Peter Schmeichel, Jaap Stam, Denis Irwin, Dwight Yorke, Andy Cole, and Teddy Sheringham – and there were also three Norwegians in the Old Trafford ranks, including a goalscoring substitute called Ole Gunnar Solskjær, who years later was one of the first to recognise Erling Haaland's huge resource of natural talent, as well as Ronny Johnsen and Henning Berg.

It was ironic, then, that the first club to do the Treble were given the opportunity to prevent their nearest rivals from emulating their feat in the first Manchester derby FA Cup Final in the famous old competition's storied history of more than 150 years.

City and United had met at Wembley before, with the Blues prevailing 1-0 in the 2011 FA Cup semi-final on their way to lifting the club's first trophy in 35 years and sparking a revolution that would change the face of English and European football. The following season, in the showpiece Community Shield curtain-raiser for the new campaign, Premier League champions United came from two goals down to win 3-2 against the FA Cup holders.

The importance of the FA Cup has diminished since clubs began concentrating most of their resources towards their Premier League fortunes, with even the side finishing bottom now earning in excess of £100m. Even the top clubs only tend to become interested in the latter stages of the world's oldest knockout competition, with the prospect of Champions League bounty focussing the mind during the early rounds.

But the magnitude of the 2023 FA Cup Final was clear to see – history makers against history chasers, old money versus the nouveau riche.

Pep Guardiola has always professed his love for the FA Cup. When City lost the 2016/17 semi-final to Arsenal in his first season as manager it meant he would finish without a trophy for the first time in his managerial career. He did get his hands on the glittering piece of silverware when City completed a domestic treble by beating Watford 6-0 in 2019. The scoreline equalled a record set by Bury in 1903 when the Shakers hammered Derby County at the Crystal Palace. But City lost three successive semi-finals from 2020 to 2022 when each time the Catalan had shuffled his squad resources rather than going with his strongest team.

It was a surprise to see Haaland on the bench for the 4-0 home win over Chelsea in the third round, given the rest he had enjoyed during the World Cup. He got his first taste of the FA Cup when City beat title rivals Arsenal at the Etihad 1-0 in the next round before sitting back down with the substitutes for the 3-0 victory at Bristol City. Haaland's first goals came in the competition arrived in the form of a hat-trick in the 6-0 execution of Vincent Kompany's Championship leaders Burnley in the quarter-finals – and he then played 68 minutes of the 3-0 semi-final win over promotion-chasing Sheffield United when he walked out at Wembley for the first time in his career. Guardiola had kept faith with stand-in goalkeeper Stefan Ortega during City's route to the final and the 30-year-old German – following in the gloves of his countryman Bert Trautmann who played in the 1956 final – retained his place ahead of regular number one Ederson for the clash with United after keeping clean sheets in all five ties. Of the ten outfield players named by Guardiola for the big Wembley derby, only Kyle Walker would not start in the following week's Champions League Final.

Haaland's first Wembley experience had been as a 13-year-old fan watching with his father as City came from behind to beat Sunderland 3-1 in the 2014 EFL Cup Final. 'It was very special,' he told the Football Association's official website during an interview that would be printed in the matchday programme for the final. 'It was also a special moment to win here in the semi-final against Sheffield United and a great feeling that we want to share again. Now we want to do the same in the final, but we know we have tough opponents ahead of us. We're excited and ready for this match.

'Everyone who follows football knows how historic and special this competition is, especially in England. Of course, Yaya Touré's goal against Stoke City to win City the FA Cup in 2011 is a moment I remember and one that was so special for our fans. When you play for a club like Manchester City you have to fight for every single trophy. The FA Cup is a trophy the club hasn't won for four years and we want to change that. Everyone is really excited to get to Wembley to play this final. We know how important this match is for the fans. We want to make them proud and we will give everything to try and make them happy.

'We had an amazing result at the Etihad in the Premier League which was a very special day in my first Manchester derby, before a frustrating result in the away fixture. We need another big performance to try and get the win. After lifting the Premier League a few weeks ago in front of our fans, our focus turned to the next challenge straight away. It would be unreal to make history and I will do all I can to achieve it. United will be motivated. They will be ready and we have to play at our best. If we do that then we have a really great chance. Every game against United is not easy because of the history. It's a final at Wembley and we have to make sure we play our game.'

Guardiola told his players on the eve of the game that they had to be so superior to United that they would take any controversial refereeing decisions out of the equation. 'Guys, guys,' he beseeched his players during dinner. 'Remember what happened at Old Trafford when you lost your focus after United equalised. We cannot let that happen again. If we feel there has been a bad decision, we don't let it change the way we play. You have to make sure that you are so good over 90 minutes that whatever the referee decides doesn't matter in the end.' He also felt his team had suffered at the hands of officials in the defeat at Liverpool the previous October and the victory over Arsenal at the Etihad the previous month. Events would prove he was right to go to Wembley with his suspicions.

All the talk before the game was how United could stop their rivals – and in particular Haaland. The discussion was more like a David v Goliath tie rather than a meeting of equals – but United's World Cup-winning French defender Raphaël Varane was bullish about his forthcoming battle with the Norwegian, 'Yes, Haaland is a very good player, we all know that, but the danger from City is everywhere. They are very complete. They can score from set plays, from a possession game and from a transition game. We know we have to stop them as a team and collectively as a group. As a defender, the connection especially with De Bruyne that Haaland has, with that special kind of pass is complicated to defend, so we try to cut that connection. We try to stop them earlier and not at the end because sometimes it's too late. We know we have to be strong as a team.' Brazilian midfielder Fred added, 'From my point of view, City play the best football in the world at the moment. They know how to maintain possession, so it's tough to face them – but not impossible. I agree that Haaland is the world's best forward right now, but we are Manchester United. We beat City at home when Haaland was on the pitch – and if we play our best football, I don't see why we can't win.'

It was a monumental occasion that provided a monumental moment after just 12 seconds when İlkay Gündoğan put City ahead with the fastest goal in FA Cup Final history. Gündoğan played the ball back to Ortega straight from the kick-off and the keeper launched it towards Haaland, who leapt above Casemiro to flick on. When United defender Victor Lindelöf challenged Kevin De Bruyne, the ball looped up invitingly towards skipper Gündoğan who connected with a sweet first-time volley from 25 yards that carried so much dip and direction that United keeper David de Gea could only watch as it flashed into the top corner. While the City fans in the West End of Wembley erupted, the 30,000 United supporters behind de Gea's goal wearing red, white and black bucket hats given out by their club appeared paralysed in disbelief. Everton's Louis Saha had held the official record previously, his strike in the 2-1 defeat by Chelsea in 2009 having been clocked at 25 seconds. This was United's worst nightmare.

Haaland just failed to get enough power on his shot after stretching to meet a Gündoğan cross and then sent a powerful effort spinning over after slipping on contact. Then, after 33 minutes of City pressure, United equalised when Guardiola's premonition came true. Aaron Wan-Bissaka got in behind Jack Grealish on the right flank when Bruno Fernandes found him with a cleverly floated pass and the full-back's attempted header across goal flicked the hand of Jack Grealish. The midfielder wasn't even looking at the ball and was making a natural movement after leaping in a failed attempt to cut out the pass. But VAR official David Coote advised referee Paul Tierney to take a look at his pitchside monitor – and Bruno Fernandes duly sent Ortega the wrong way from the penalty spot to ruin City's hopes of becoming the first club since Bury in 1903 to lift the FA Cup without conceding a single goal. Howard Webb, the newly appointed head of Professional Game Match Officials Limited, the company that oversees match officials, was in Wembley's Royal Box. 'It was a joke,' said Grealish afterwards. 'I wasn't even looking at the ball. It was never a penalty – but luckily Gundo [Gündoğan] saved me.'

Indeed, City went ahead again five minutes into the second half when De Bruyne picked out Gündoğan lurking on the edge of United's box with a free kick from wide on the right – and although the German didn't connect so cleanly with his left foot, his volley bounced up through a crowd of players blocking de Gea's sight and found the corner of the goal.

Sixty-seven years after former German POW Bert Trautmann played with a broken neck to help City lift the FA Cup, one of his countrymen was following in his footsteps. Gündoğan was denied a hat-trick after straying offside to score after de Gea had palmed Haaland's shot into his path. But apart from a late United flurry that saw Scott McTominay strike the crossbar with a deflected close-range shot, the Premier League champions maintained complete control. One of the biggest cheers of the afternoon boomed out from the City fans when Haaland chased down Phil Foden's pass deep into injury time to play the ball off Varane and buy his team a corner and kill a few more precious seconds. At the final whistle, Haaland could be seen roaring 'one more, one more' at his team-mates to remind them that the week's Double could become a Treble in seven days' time.

* * *

United 1999 or City 2023?

The debate about whether Manchester City's 2023 team were superior to Manchester United in 1999 began even before the Blues had added the FA Cup to the Premier League title. There was an assumption, particularly in the UK, that if Erik ten Hag couldn't halt Pep Guardiola at Wembley, then it was a formality that City would beat the third-best team in Serie A to lift the Champions League. The Treble was indeed duly completed in the Atatürk Stadium, but only after a titanic struggle in which the English side struggled to break down the organisation and resistance of an Inter team that called up the ghost of *catenaccio*, quite literally a defensive 'door bolt', which had been perfected in Italy in the 1940s.

Football, of course, like beauty is in the eye of the beholder. Statistics can help shape an argument. It's impossible to suggest that a team from the last century would beat one from the current era, given the ongoing improvements in coaching, sports science, fitness, even pitches. But the reality is that Guardiola's Barcelona gave Sir Alex Ferguson a schooling in two Champions League finals, when the Catalan was a virtual novice in coaching terms compared to the seasoned Scot. The numbers do make a compelling case that Guardiola had indeed produced the greatest team in the history of English football if winning the Treble was the first benchmark.

United played 63 games in 1998/99, including the old Charity Shield in which they lost 3-0 to Arsenal. They won 34, drew 24 and lost just five. Ferguson's side scored a total of 138 goals and conceded 63. In comparison, City lost 3-1 to Liverpool in the Community Shield and emulated United in the League Cup by reaching the fifth round. Of the 61 games they played, the Blues won 44, drew seven and lost seven, scoring 152 goals and conceding 46. City had started the season as reigning champions, whereas United had finished second in 1997/98 and had to enter the Champions League qualifying round. City's Premier League points tally was 89 – ten more than United in 1999. They scored 14 more goals in winning the title and conceded four fewer.

In the FA Cup, United prevailed in two replays – and still scored seven fewer goals, while the only goal City conceded was that disputed penalty in the final, where they beat their biggest historical rivals and the only club to have completed the Treble in a unique derby occasion.

The Champions League comparison is just as stark. City topped their group with four wins and two draws; United were second behind Bayern Munich with two wins and four draws. In the knockout stages, City beat Bundesliga champions Bayern 4-1 on aggregate and Champions League holders Real Madrid as well as scoring eight in two games against RB Leipzig. United produced memorable performances at Inter Milan and Juventus, clubs who finished eighth and seventh in Serie A that season. Both teams enjoyed some luck in the final, United winning 2-1 against Bayern in Barcelona and City emerging 1-0 victorious over Inter in Istanbul.

Numbers, of course, don't capture the essence of football – but the explosion in statistics in recent years now fuels scouting and coaching at every level of the game as well as the huge billion-pound markets of gambling and the Fantasy Football industry.

Figures are arguably the most efficient way of comparing teams from two different eras. What else is there?

23

Immortality – Istanbul 2023

ERLING HAALAND knew his mission was to make Manchester City champions of Europe. He spoke about it on his very first day at the club – and again when he faced the media just 72 hours before City met Inter Milan in the Champions League Final, when he was honest enough to admit he was feeling the pressure despite already adding Premier League and FA Cup medals and the Golden Boot to a collection where Austrian league and cup honours took pride of place next to a DFB-Pokal medal.

Haaland had scored just one goal in his last seven appearances. 'Of course, I feel pressure,' he said. 'I would lie if I said I didn't. City brought me here to win the Champions League. They won the Premier League without me, they won every other trophy except the Champions League without me, so I'm here to try to do a thing that the club has never done before and I'll do my best. If I can make the difference, it would mean everything to me.

'But I don't feel stressed about goals. You can think of it in one of two ways. You can think of it as one goal in my last seven games or 52 goals in 52 games. Oh, and eight assists, I think. I think it's important to speak good about yourself to yourself. I know what I have done this season – but there is still one game left so let's keep my feet on the ground. My biggest dream is to win the Champions League. Hopefully I will do it in my life and it [the Champions League anthem] will stay as my ringtone. It's a tournament I have been watching since I can remember and it's a tournament where the best teams win it because you are playing against the other best teams.'

Haaland would also fail to find the back of the net in the Atatürk Stadium on a night when defensive midfield lynchpin Rodri capped a wretched performance of his own by emerging as the unlikely match-winner. The Norwegian's only sight of goal was when he fastened on to Kevin De Bruyne's pass in the first half, but chose to aim to beat André Onana with power at his near post rather than with the precision needed to find the opposite corner and saw the Cameroon international – who would join Manchester United later that summer – beat the ball to safety. At that point he had managed as many touches of the ball in City's box as Inter's.

Haaland finished the game with just 18 touches – the fewest of any player to feature in a Champions League Final since the statistic had first been recorded in 2004. Haaland wasn't helped by the departure of assist king De Bruyne with a hamstring tear six minutes before half-time. The Belgian had been quite literally knocked out of the 2021 final by a brutal challenge from Chelsea defender Antonio Rüdiger and now the gamble which had seen him nurse his damaged muscle through the final weeks of the season had backfired.

* * *

Surrounded

But Inter coach Simone Inzaghi's game plan involved surrounding Haaland with central defensive trio Matteo Darmian, Alessandro Bastoni and Francesco Acerbi. Inzaghi also detailed midfielder Marcelo Brozović to patrol the space in front of Haaland to prevent balls into the striker. It was a hugely effective strategy that might have worked against previous City teams.

On the eve of the game, Guardiola had urged his players to be patient. He told them, 'The difference between English teams and Italian teams is that when it's 0-0, Italian teams think they are winning and English teams think they are losing.' John Stones recalled, 'It was Pep's way of saying to us "don't get frustrated". Something as simple as that makes you realise the importance of sticking to your game plan – because sometimes in the past we haven't. I thought it was a great bit of advice for settling us and making us realise that it's a 95- or 100-minute game plus extra time if needed, and that we shouldn't get disheartened.' It was City's patience that crafted the winning goal for Rodri in the 68th minute.

When İlkay Gündoğan seized on to a loose ball on the left edge of Inter's penalty area and reached the byline, the obvious option would have been to send in a cross out of hope rather than expectation. But instead, the captain recycled the ball back to Phil Foden – and when he was closed down by tenacious Croatian midfielder Brozović, it appeared as though Inzaghi's team had squeezed the life out of another City attack. But Foden's square pass found Manuel Akanji advancing into space – and instead of holding his position, centre-back Bastoni was tempted into engaging the right-back. In the blink of an eye, Bernardo Silva had sped into the space Bastoni had left behind and with five Inter defenders and four City attackers drawn into the six-yard box waiting for a cross, when the Portuguese's ball struck Acerbi's backside it dropped perfectly for Rodri to pick his spot and find the corner with a measured shot from 16 yards. The moment earned Rodri the man of the match award, even though the Spaniard's assessment after the game was, 'I played shit.'

* * *

Below their best

City as a team were well below their best – but the credit for that should go to Inzaghi. Ederson, Stones, Rúben Dias, Nathan Aké, Akanji and Silva were Guardiola's standout performers on a night which showed the Catalan had grafted a razor-sharp edge on to his talented team. Inter created the better chances both before and after Rodri's strike, but were toothless upfront, where 37-year-old former City striker Edin Džeko partnered Lautaro Martínez. Argentine international Martínez literally brought Guardiola to his knees on the touchline in the 58th minute when he raced clear down the left after Silva's wayward pass, only for Ederson to make the first of several outstanding saves. Inter wing-back Federico Dimarco saw his looping header bounce back off the crossbar just after his team had gone behind – and his goalbound follow-up was blocked by team-mate Romelu Lukaku, who had replaced Džeko just before the hour. Foden should have given the Blues breathing space but shot too close to Onana after leaving Dimarco for dead, before the Italians launched a frantic finale. Ederson reacted instinctively to block Lukaku's header from point-blank range and then saw team-mate Dias divert the loose ball inches wide of his own goal. The Brazilian saved again, punching away Robin Gosens's header in what was the last act of the final, with all 11 City players within 12 yards of their own goal when Polish referee Szymon Marciniak blew the final whistle.

Haaland dashed towards the City fans at the opposite end of the stadium, realised what he had just helped to achieve, and then clutched both hands to his face as the tears came freely. 'I haven't cried like that in a long time,' he admitted. 'In fact, I can't remember the last time I even cried. The first thing I thought of was my mum and dad and the sacrifices they have made for the last 15 years. I was just so full of emotion. I knew City had bought me to help win the Champions League, so it feels like a weight of 100 kilos has been taken off my shoulders. But this shows that anything is possible no matter where you come from. From a small town in Norway to be on the biggest stage and to win the biggest trophy in football has always been a special motivation for me.' Just over 2,000 miles away in his hometown of Bryne, thousands of locals had gathered in the town square to watch the game on a big screen. Among them was the striker's maternal grandmother, Inge Asse Braut, wearing a City shirt with Erling's name and number on the back.

It was over an hour before City's players made it back to their dressing room with the spoils of victory. Haaland enjoyed an impromptu kick-about with Foden's young son, Ronnie, who himself now boasts 3.5 million Instagram followers at the age of four. It was just past 2.30am when City's team boarded the coach that would take them back to the five-star JW Marriott Hotel overlooking the Marmara Sea – and a party that would last for the next four days. The players and coaching staff were joined by family, friends and a 400-strong group of club employees who had been treated to an all-expenses-paid trip to the final by a club that prides itself on nurturing a holistic approach. Jack Grealish, still wearing the kit he had played in, led the festivities, clutching a bottle of Grey Goose vodka. He dragged Haaland, Stones and Kyle Walker to their feet to join him in singing the terrace chants that were echoing throughout the streets of Istanbul as the 40,000 City fans who had made the trip partied like it was 1999. Haaland posted a picture of himself puffing on a huge cigar just as the sun was coming up before jumping on one of the DJ decks that had been provided by the hotel to blast out some Europop. Earlier in the season, Haaland had been invited by the City-mad former Oasis frontman Liam Gallagher to help him arrange a reunion with his equally blue-eyed but estranged brother Noel, who had promised to get the band back together if Guardiola's team completed the Treble. 'Maybe they just need a Norwegian peacemaker,' said the striker.

Some players didn't make it to bed before being summoned for the noon journey to the airport to catch the flight back to Manchester. As soon as they touched down in England, a group of players including Haaland and Grealish were whisked away on a private jet for a 12-hour bender on the party isle of Ibiza. Unfortunately for Manchester United defender Lisandro Martínez, they chose the same £550-a-night Ushuaia Ibiza Beach Resort Hotel in Playa d'en Bossa that he was spending a few days in with his wife.

* * *

Open-topped bus parade

City's players reported back at the Etihad the following day for an open-topped bus parade of the city that was in danger of being cancelled when a weather warning predicted that Manchester was going to be sluiced by a violent thunderstorm just as Guardiola and his players were scheduled to be heading down Deansgate. Players and staff were transported to the city-centre rendezvous on one of the Metrolink trams that take fans to the stadium on matchday, Guardiola embracing all three trophies for the 15-minute trip. The downpour only added to the occasion, with soaked players and an estimated 250,000 supporters embracing the typically Mancunian deluge with gusto. One iconic photograph captured Grealish in a biblical pose, bare-chested with arms outstretched, appearing to be giving thanks to the heavens. At one point the England midfielder donned a hi-viz jacket and started directing supporters towards some shelter. The players later moved on to the Depot Mayfield, once a Victorian railway yard that has been revamped into a 10,000-capacity venue. It had been packed to the rafters for the final by fans watching the action on a giant screen.

By the time Haaland boarded another flight later that week to take him to his holiday home in Majorca, he would have been thinking about what was to come next. His exploits in Manchester have made him a short-odds second favourite to win the 2023 Ballon d'Or by the time of publication. It's unlikely that the coaches and journalists who vote for the award will see past handing Lionel Messi the accolade for an eighth time after the Argentine led his country to World Cup glory in Qatar. But Messi now plays for MLS side Inter Miami while his long-time rival Cristiano Ronaldo is now earning football's biggest fortune in Saudi Arabia. It's unlikely that either will feature in the Ballon d'Or poll going forward. 'Messi and Ronaldo are two big legends,' said Haaland. 'How old are they now, 35 and 37? They both inspired me – and I think they inspired the whole football world. To reach those numbers, not for one year but every single year. I was really happy to be able to watch both of them when I was younger.'

* * *

Mentality and learning

Haaland was still on the pitch at the Atatürk Stadium, Champions League medal glistening around his neck, when he gave a real insight into what makes this Mentality Monster tick. He agreed to be interviewed on CBS Sports by former City defender Micah Richards and Champions League winners Thierry Henry, Peter Schmeichel and Jamie Carragher. Carragher asked him if there was one thing he would like to ask Henry, a masterful forward who won the Premier League with Arsenal, the Champions League with Barcelona and the World Cup with France. Haaland asked, 'If you could give me one piece of advice what would it be?' He watched intently as Henry responded, 'I just think that in the box there is nothing you can learn. What you do is second to none. But, back to the goal, going on to your right foot sometimes and making the runs you don't want to make – these are the things you can learn. But if you do that, City will win the Quadruple. If you start to finish with your right foot like you do with your left, then it's all over.'

* * *

Every 79 minutes

Haaland scored 52 goals from the 4,129 minutes he spent on the pitch in his debut season in Manchester. That works out at a goal every 79 minutes. He scored 34 with his left foot, ten with his right and eight with his head. Just one of his goals came from outside the box. Haaland said, 'I go into the areas where you can score the most goals. It's a good quality to tap goals in. Take the game against Leipzig, when I scored five times. In the game, it felt like I had a magnet in my foot. Last season I watched City send crosses through the box with no one there and I imagined myself being there to slide the ball in. I'm not going to create chances. My job is to put the ball in the back of the net. But I'm still young and so I am still going to develop. There is so much I can learn. In three years, I will probably think back to now and how I was thinking.

'When I think how I am now to when I signed for Dortmund there is such a big difference in how I think after games, how I think before games, how I motivate myself and speak to people. You get experience from other people and from out on the pitch and I know I can develop much, much more. I should have scored more goals this season. I missed a lot of chances. I think what will happen is that in a few days I will feel all the emotions of winning the Treble – and then I will want to do it all over again. I also think that, when I look back on my career, I will have had to play in a World Cup or at a Euros.'

24

Playing for his Country

LEEDS-BORN ERLING Haaland began his international career at under-15 level, playing and scoring four times for his country. Further appearances followed for the under-16s (17 games, one goal), under-17s (five games, two goals), under-18s (six games, six goals), under-19s (six games, six goals), under-20s (five games, 11 goals), and under-21s (three games, no goals). This is a total of 46 appearances with 30 goals.

The undoubted highlight of these many games was Haaland's nine goals versus Honduras at the Under-20 World Cup that not only meant he captured the Golden Boot but also helped his country establish a new record 12-goal victory at the tournament.

But even in the process of getting to the World Cup, Haaland was showing that on the highest stage for young players he was the number one scorer.

* * *

Dramatic late winner earns qualification and an award

When the draw for the 2018 UEFA European Under-19 Championship qualifying competition was made to establish eventually which seven sides would join hosts Finland at the finals in July 2018, Norway were placed alongside Ukraine, Albania and Montenegro in Group 12. The games were played in October 2017 in Albania. Norway finished in second place behind Ukraine against whom Haaland netted in a 2-1 defeat in which Vladyslav Supryaha scored the winner. Haaland also scored twice in a 7-1 hammering of Albania and once in a 3-0 victory over Montenegro.

As runners-up, Norway moved forward to the next stages, the elite round which was played in Germany. There was the shock of being trounced 6-1 by the Netherlands with Donyell Malen scoring twice. There were also seven goals in the game against the hosts who lost 5-2 with Haaland scoring twice. Any hopes of going further appeared to have ended when Scotland's Glenn Middleton scored his second of the game to put his side 4-2 up on 66 minutes. Haaland had scored both of the Norway goals and in a highly dramatic ending he followed up goals from wide man Jens Petter Hauge (82 minutes) and Eman Markovic (84) to score Norway's fifth with a penalty on 91 minutes. Not only did this third of the match put his side into the finals but as it was Haaland's ninth of the tournament it meant he finished as the top scorer, a goal ahead of Alexandru Mățan and three ahead of a group including Eddie Nketiah and Kai Havertz. By finishing in first place in their group, Norway progressed to the eight-team finals in Finland.

* * *

Three in three for World Cup qualification

Haaland played in all three group games of the finals in Finland in July 2018.

After losing their opening game 3-1 to eventual winners Portugal, Norway, making their fourth appearance at the finals, beat Finland 3-2 thanks to two added-time goals. Norway then drew 1-1 with Italy where Haaland and his striking colleague Markovic had a real tussle with central defenders Gianmaria Zanandrea and Davide Bettella. When

Haaland opened the scoring on 62 minutes with a penalty, both sides knew that another goal would put them into second place in the group and a place in the semi-finals but it was Italy who were next to score through Moise Kean on 83 minutes as the game ended level.

Disappointment was tempered by knowing that by finishing in third place Norway would get an opportunity to qualify for the Under-20 World Cup in Poland if they could beat England in a play-off.

A slight injury kept Haaland out of the squad for the big game but his side won easily 3-0 to ensure they would make the trip to Poland in May and June 2019.

* * *

Golden Boot and a record win

Norway were drawn alongside Uruguay, New Zealand and Honduras in Group C in Poland. After losing 3-1 against Uruguay, with Darwin Núñez opening the scoring, and then being beaten 2-0 by New Zealand, any hope of making it through to the last 16 depended upon hammering Honduras, who also had no points, and hoping to end up as one of the four best third-placed finishers from the six groups.

It was a case of attack, attack, attack and with few of the defenders in front of him getting anywhere near Haaland during the game, José García in the Honduras goal endured a horrible night. It did not help that two of his team-mates managed to get themselves sent off and to his credit the goalkeeper never gave up trying.

Garcia had no chance for the first of what proved to be Haaland's nine goals as the number 19 was unmarked in front of goal following a cut-back from Markovic. The second was from a ball over the top with Haaland beating the keeper with a fierce shot through his legs. On 36 minutes Haaland picked himself up after being fouled in the box to complete his hat-trick from the spot. Before then centre-back Leo Skiri Østigård scored with a downward header, and on 43 minutes came the goal of the night when Haaland brilliantly controlled a ball slightly behind him before swivelling and from 15 yards out hitting a powerful left foot shot beyond García.

His fifth after the break came following more good balance and control. The sixth was the only one with his right foot, the seventh – a new tournament record – was from ten yards, while the eighth, which García should have saved, was from a tight angle and for the ninth his shot flew high beyond García as the score became Norway 12 Honduras 0. There was even a very late chance for the Salzburg player to take his total into double figures but he just failed to net.

It was though this final opportunity that Haaland commented on afterwards, stating, 'It annoys me a little bit that I didn't score with my last kick of the game. I'll have to sit down and think a little bit about it and maybe I'll work out what happened.'

Nevertheless, it had been some occasion with the 12-0 win also representing the largest margin of victory for a team in Under-20 World Cup history, eclipsing the 10-0 thrashing Brazil handed Belgium in the 1997 edition.

The goals he had scored were to result in Haaland winning the Golden Boot but even that last result was not enough to put his country into the next stages as they finished with the poorest record of the six third-placed finishers.

Under FIFA's eligibility rules, dual nationality players can transfer allegiances until capped at senior level in a competitive match. Rather than follow in his father's footsteps, Haaland could therefore have decided to play for England.

However, as a Salzburg player he made his full debut for Norway when he was selected by Lars Lagerbäck, the former manager of Sweden, Nigeria and Iceland for Norway, at the age of 19 on 5 September 2019 against Malta.

Gareth Southgate believes that the player was always unlikely to play for the country where he was born. Speaking to *The Independent* the England manager said, 'Obviously at the young age groups at the time, that wouldn't have been on my full radar, because when he broke into first-team football he was pretty much already in the Norwegian youth system. We recruit early, but we wouldn't have been into him when he was still in Yorkshire, that's for sure. We are always trying to monitor these cases, but I think in that instance he was tied up pretty early by Norway and I think also, with players like him, they're quite clear where they want to play as well. He feels that allegiance to the country that he's playing for now and you're always respectful of that.'

For Haaland's debut, Norway lined up as follows: Rune Jarstein, Haitam Aleesami, Omar Elabdellaoui, Even Hovland, Sander Berge, Stefan Johansen, Håvard Nordtveit, Martin Ødegaard, Ole Selnæs, Joshua King, Erling Haaland.

Playing up alongside Joshua King in a 4-4-2 formation, Haaland, who was later replaced by Tarik Elyounoussi on 66 minutes, was immediately into action with a fourth-minute header from a Stefan Johansen cross from the centre of the box. Goals from Sander Berge and King, from the spot, marked a winning full international debut.

Haaland scored his first international goal on 66 minutes with an assist from his fellow frontman, Crystal Palace's Alexander Sørloth, in just his second game, a 2-1 defeat in Oslo against Austria in the UEFA Nations League on 5 September 2020.

Two days later in the same competition he put his side ahead again and completed the scoring in a 5-1 hammering of Northern Ireland at Windsor Park. He also provided the assist for Sørloth's second of the match. It was classic centre-forward play and left Daniel Ballard and Craig Cathcart floundering with both central defenders booked.

Before kick-off, Ballard, who had yet to play for Arsenal, had told reporters he was relishing the opportunity to test his wits against one of football's brightest prospects, 'If I have to face the best players in the world then I will be ready. I am up for the challenges.' After a tough first period Ballard was replaced at the break.

At 1-1, Sørloth managed to direct a loose ball towards Haaland who opened up his body and unleashed a sweetly-struck left-footed strike beyond a helpless Bailey Peacock-Farrell into the bottom-left corner.

Then just before the break Johansen drove infield before laying the ball off to Haaland, who sprayed it over to the left for full-back Haitam Aleesami who delivered a first-time cross in towards the far post, which Sørloth knocked into the top-right corner from close range for 3-1.

For the fourth goal, Johansen lifted a smart, lofted pass over the top of Ireland's defence and Haaland beat Cathcart to the ball before picking his head up and steering it across the box for Sørloth, who tapped it into the bottom-left corner for his second.

For the fifth Johansen clipped another ball forward which Sørloth knocked down for Omar Elabdellaoui whose first-time header beyond the hosts' defence was seized upon by Haaland who opened up his body before curling a powerful shot into the bottom-left corner from the centre of the box.

Haaland went one better to record his first international hat-trick in his sixth game as Romania left for home beaten 4-0. Both his first and third were created by his good friend Martin Ødegaard, the youngest Norwegian international ever at 15 years and 253 days. All three goals were scored with his left foot from inside the area.

In December 2020 the Copenhagen manager Ståle Solbakken, who had played very briefly for Wimbledon in the Premier League in the late 1990s before falling out with manager Joe Kinnear, being banned from training and being quickly sold to Danish side Aalborg SK, was appointed to replace Lagerbäck, who had resigned, as Norwegian manager. Solbakken had played for Norway at the 1998 World Cup. 'I am proud and honoured to have been offered the job as the new national team manager. For me, this is a good time to take over,' he said. 'Lars Lagerbäck and [assistant] Per Joar Hansen have done a solid job and developed a foundation that will be exciting to work on.'

Having scored his first hat-trick there followed a four-game spell in which Haaland failed to score, and there was then the only goal of the game in a friendly against Luxembourg in Málaga.

In qualification for the 2022 World Cup in Qatar, Norway were drawn to play in Group G against the Netherlands, Turkey, Montenegro, Latvia and Gibraltar.

Against the Netherlands, Latvia and Gibraltar in September 2021, Haaland – now with Borussia Dortmund – scored five goals over seven days in the 1-1 draw with the Netherlands in Oslo, the 1-0 success in Riga and, wearing number 23, three in the 5-1 defeat of minnows Gibraltar in Oslo.

In the latter game his first came after he seized on a through ball from Kristian Thorstvedt and hit a left-footed shot from the centre of the box to the bottom-left corner. His second on 39 minutes was almost an exact repeat except this time he was assisted by Sørloth. On 91 minutes Haaland wrapped up the scoring when from Marcus Pedersen's assist he drove home with his right foot from the centre of the box. He also had four other attempts during the match.

Norway had gone into these games having taken six points in March 2021 from victories away to Gibraltar and

Montenegro, but at home they had been easily beaten 3-0 by Turkey.

After six qualifying games, Norway had 13 points, equal top with the Netherlands and two ahead of Turkey.

Amid the on-field success there had been off-field calls that should Norway qualify for Qatar they should stay at home. This was because some supporters wanted to boycott the tournament over deep concerns about human rights abuses allied to the estimated 6,500 deaths of migrant building workers.

Tom Høgli, a former Tromsø player, and the club captain William Kvist had led a successful nationwide boycott campaign that only failed when senior officials at the Norwegian Football Federation, where every year the country's 1,850 clubs and 19 county associations can send delegates to the general assembly, won a hotly contested debate.

While a boycott dominated public discourse, Solbakken rallied to have his players, including Haaland, protest at the treatment of migrant workers in Qatar, displaying a human rights message in every qualifier. Solbakken opposed a boycott, stating it wasn't 'the right means' for improving conditions in Qatar. His criticism of the gulf state's treatment of its labour force was sincere. Other countries made similar protests.

The grassroots uprising against Qatar forced the NFF to raise the issue with both FIFA and the 2022 World Cup organising committee in joint statements with the other Nordic federations.

With Haaland injured he missed out on Norway's next two qualifying matches in October in which they took four points from a 1-1 away draw in Istanbul in which Thorstvedt was dismissed, and a 2-0 defeat of Montenegro with Elyounoussi scoring both. Norway had 17 points, Turkey 15 and the Netherlands 19.

He was also missing for the two games in November in which Norway drew 0-0 with Latvia before losing 2-0 to the Netherlands in Rotterdam in a match played behind closed doors.

Norway were to finish in third place with the Netherlands topping the group and automatically qualifying for the first Middle East World Cup finals. In second place Turkey, who finished three points ahead of Norway, advanced to the play-offs where they lost 3-1 to Portugal.

Having scored five times in Group G, Haaland finished level with Burak Yılmaz in second place in the goal charts but well behind Memphis Depay who netted 12 for the Netherlands.

In March 2022 and amid speculation he was leaving Germany, Haaland returned to international action and scored once in a 2-0 victory in a friendly against Slovakia and twice in a 9-0 hammering of Armenia in a friendly where he earned his 17th full cap.

Norway were drawn in Group B of the 2022/23 UEFA Nations League and in an 11-day period in June 2022 the new Manchester City striker scored the only goal with a left-footed shot from a Pedersen pass against Serbia in Belgrade.

* * *

Double victory over bitter rivals

There was then the thrill of scoring four in two victorious games against neighbours Sweden, Norway's first international opponents.

In a 2-1 win in Stockholm, Haaland converted an 18th-minute penalty with his left foot to the bottom left-corner and then on 69 minutes he doubled Norway's advantage when he fastened on to Sørloth's pass and delivered a right-footed shot from the right side of the box to the bottom left corner. The decision by Solbakken to play with a front three of Haaland, Sørloth and Elyounoussi was fully justified by the result and the performance in which Norway enjoyed 58 per cent possession in a famous victory.

Haaland had appeared to single out Alexander Milošević when he scored his second by celebrating in front of him. During the game it looked like the AIK defender had been talking to Haaland, who afterwards told reporters that his opponent had 'called me a whore, which I can assure you I'm not, and told me he was going to break my legs. Then I scored a minute later.' Despite his threats, Milošević did not thereafter seek to carry them out.

In the return match in Oslo, Haaland put his side ahead in a 3-2 win with a header from the centre of the box into the bottom-left corner, from a Fredrik André Bjørkan cross. He doubled the lead when from a penalty awarded following a VAR review he converted with his left foot. He then turned provider with a cross that Sørloth headed home from very close range.

If the Swedes had been hit hard by Haaland on the pitch he also inadvertently hit them off it when he later joined Manchester City.

He had been signed up by Visit Norway to help promote tourism. But there were complaints from Sweden's tourism board that the coastal county of Halland was losing its online presence because of Erling's success. Visit Halland director Jimmy Sandberg said, 'We are Halland. He is Haaland. The popularity of the football phenomenon is completely suffocating our online presence. To our despair, we now see that all of our efforts promoting Halland are rapidly being wiped away. Since Haaland arrived at Manchester City and scored all those goals, we have been overwhelmed by his presence in our hashtags and in search engines.'

Following his successes in June there was then a great disappointment on 24 September 2022 when Norway lost 2-1 in Slovenia after Haaland had put his side ahead.

He had been accompanied on the trip by Mario Pafundi, Manchester City's first-team sports therapist who was present to help specifically ensure Haaland's fitness was preserved.

The final group match was at home to Serbia three days later. With both teams on ten points from their opening five games, whoever won the game would advance to the next stages. A draw would put the visitors through on goal difference.

Haaland was played up front on his own and he started well with a first-minute left-footed shot. But the Serbs proved to be the better side and when Aleksandar Mitrović scored their second on 68 minutes it was no more than they deserved. Haaland never stopped trying and his battle with Getafe defender Stefan Mitrović was one of the highlights of the game and he had a very late attempt saved when he was put through. It was, though, the Serbs who qualified for the next stages in a tournament that Spain eventually won.

Injuries then put Haaland out for Norway's next two friendlies, against the Republic of Ireland and Finland in November. 'Erling has had a few troubled weeks [with injury],' Solbakken said on Haaland's withdrawal from the squad. 'We have been in dialogue with Manchester City … Everyone has seen how it has been lately for Erling. City have not used him unless they absolutely had to. He played the last 25 minutes against Fulham, nothing against Copenhagen and Sevilla. He's still not quite there.'

Having suffered an injury against Burnley in the FA Cup, Haaland also missed Norway's two European Championship qualifying Group A games in March 2023. They did not go well with group favourites Spain winning 3-0 in Málaga's La Rosaleda Stadium and Norway drawing 1-1 in Georgia with Sørloth scoring in a game his side dominated.

It meant that the games in June at home to group leaders Scotland on 17 June and away to Cyprus three days later were must-wins.

Things looked like they were going to plan when, despite Angus Gunn going the right way, Haaland's spot-kick in the second half beat the goalkeeper for power as Scotland fell behind. Having earlier stayed on his feet following a rash challenge in the box by Jack Hendry, Haaland had won the penalty after going down in a tussle with Ryan Porteous.

Haaland though was unable to prevent a Scotland victory when three minutes after he was substituted off, Lyndon Dykes scored a late equaliser. A fine curling finish from substitute Kenny McLean then won the game. It was a typical smash-and-grab end to an exciting game and provided Scotland defender Liam Cooper with a small measure of revenge for Haaland's two goals at Elland Road in December 2022.

It was a reward for Scotland focusing on their own efforts, with manager Steve Clarke saying beforehand when asked about trying to stop Haaland, 'As we always do, we concentrate on ourselves. We prepare properly for the game, we respect our opponents. We play Norway the team, and hopefully Scotland the team are a little bit better on the night.'

Haaland had, in fact, asked to be substituted with Solbakken telling the press that he was exhausted after such a long season, 'He asked to be changed. We kept him on the pitch ten, 12 minutes longer. In the last few minutes he was on the field, we played with one less man. He was completely empty. He has only played 60 minutes several times before. We're talking about it being 30 degrees, it's applied. He ran out of steam.'

Despite his distressed condition, Haaland was still determined to go out with a bang in his final game of a lengthy, highly successful season against Cyprus on 20 June 2023. Just as in his first competitive match of 2022/23 against West Ham United in August the Norwegian maestro scored twice, including a penalty on 55 minutes after Cyprus defender Nicholas Ioannou had handled, as Norway won 3-1.

His second to make it 3-0 saw him again link up with Martin Ødegaard whose fine through ball allowed the Premier League winner to beat Joël Mall with a left-footed shot from the centre of the box. Despite this victory Norway had little chance of qualifying for the European Championship finals as of July 2023 when they were eight points behind Scotland with just four games to play.

It begs the question: will the big man ever play at a top international tournament and was the Norwegian a little too hasty in deciding to not seek to play for the country of his birth?

It is very much hoped that Erling Haaland does get the opportunity to play at a World Cup as most really great players have done so, with some of the exceptions being Eric Cantona, George Best, Ian Rush and the best of them all, Real Madrid's Alfredo Di Stéfano. Born in Argentina, Di Stéfano scored 216 goals in 282 league games for *Los Blancos* and, alongside strike partner Ferenc Puskás, won five European Cups and eight La Liga titles. He also won the Ballon d'Or in 1957 and 1959.

Di Stéfano switched his international allegiance to Colombia and then Spain after becoming a Spanish citizen in 1956.

In 1962, Di Stéfano helped Spain to qualify for the finals in Chile before missing the tournament through injury, thus depriving the greatest football stage of one of its finest.

Haaland's goals against Cyprus meant he ended the 2022/23 season having scored 58 goals in club and international appearances in this most momentous of seasons.

* * *

Set to become Norway's top international scorer
Haaland's goal against Cyprus was his 24th for Norway in 25 games. It must surely only be a matter of time before

he advances to overtake the current record of 33 goals held by Lyn's Jørgen Juve, a bronze medal winner at the 1936 Olympics in Berlin, who made 45 international appearances.

25

Money and Image

WITHIN FOUR months of Erling Haaland's arrival at Manchester City, his agent was already boasting that he had the potential to become the world's first £1bn footballer. 'If you put together Erling's football value, his image value, his sponsor value, it is for sure already £1bn,' said Rafaela Pimenta. 'It is normal to compare Erling with [Kylian] Mbappé, so you have a little bit of an idea of the market – and I think Erling would be the first player to achieve a transfer that would be around £1bn.'

When highly respected media and marketing company Sportspro 50 published their 2022 rankings of the top 50 most marketable athletes in the world, Haaland was in 25th place, with Liverpool's Mohamed Salah the only Premier League player ahead of him in 18th. Cristiano Ronaldo, Serena Williams, Lewis Hamilton, LeBron James and Lionel Messi made up the top five.

Haaland has certainly been worth his weight in goals for City – and by the end of his first season at the Etihad he was also worth his weight in gold. After the Treble campaign that had seen City plunged into a fight against the Premier League to clear accusations of financial irregularities, chief executive Ferran Soriano revealed that the Blues were about to become the first club to announce annual revenues in excess of £700m. By emulating rivals Manchester United by winning the Champions League, Premier League and FA Cup in the same season, City had banked £294m in prize money alone. But their success off the pitch has been just as impressive – helped in no small part by the arrival of a Norwegian striker being spoken about as a generational talent set to follow in the footsteps of Messi and Ronaldo.

Soriano said, 'It's been spectacular. We know that this year our revenues are going to be above £700m. This is the British record and we are probably number one in Europe and also the world. This has happened over the last decade and it's based on the football that we play. We have a good football club, we play very good football – and we win. That helps us sell more merchandise.

'Our sales last season were 80 per cent more than the previous season. We thought that was spectacular. But guess what? In the first few weeks ahead of the coming season, we are selling 80 per cent more merchandise again. These are real numbers. Four days after winning the Champions League, our sales were as high as what we usually sell in a month. We play the best football in the world. People watch us, they fall in love with our football, and they become fans. That brings commercial opportunities and more money to invest in better players and better facilities. It's a virtuous cycle.'

City have made some major signings since Abu Dhabi's Sheikh Mansour bought the club for £200m when disgraced former Thailand prime minister Thaksin Shinawatra needed cash to fight a legal battle to extradite him back to the country he had governed. Brazilian superstar Robinho was the first, a daring £30m purchase on deadline day 2008 when the takeover was hours away from being completed. One claim suggested Robinho assumed he was flying to Manchester to sign for United and couldn't understand why the shirt he was asked to pose with alongside Mark Hughes wasn't red. Another piece of gossip insisted he thought he was leaving

Real Madrid for Chelsea. There's been Yaya Touré and Kevin De Bruyne. Vincent Kompany, Sergio Agüero and David Silva served City with such great distinction that they have been cast in bronze outside the stadium.

And in 2009, when Carlos Tevez swapped United for City, the huge 'Welcome to Manchester' poster that the Blues pasted on a billboard on Deansgate, close to the bridge that takes people over the Irwell and into the city centre from the Red heartlands of Salford, caused uproar in the city.

Yet the capture of Haaland was different. This was the first time City had beaten all of the world's biggest clubs to a player who was going to be the next big thing – both on the pitch and off it. A potential Ballon d'Or winner. When his arrival in Manchester was confirmed, City were shocked by a frenzy which saw fans buying replica shirts with Haaland's name and number on the back at a rate of one every 12 seconds.

There were suggestions from Germany, once it became clear that Haaland wasn't leaving Dortmund for Bayern, that Mino Raiola was demanding a £1m-a-week pay packet. Newspaper reports pitched his earnings at the Etihad at £865,000 a week when a lucrative package of bonuses and image rights were included. But when City were in negotiations for the transfer, they made it clear that they were not willing to wreck a wage structure which made £375,000-a-week De Bruyne their highest earner.

Haaland predicted that the narrative behind the move to Manchester would be monetised even before he had passed his medical, 'It's not true that they [City] offered the most money. That's the first thing I wanted to say.' Soriano insisted that the Norwegian was signed for his prowess on the pitch – and that his commercial power is a natural consequence of being the best in the world at putting the ball in the net. He also dismissed suggestions that City had broken the bank.

Soriano said, 'All the football decisions are taken through a football lens. Not a marketing lens, not a celebrity lens. So Txiki Begiristain, Pep [Guardiola] and the whole group think very carefully about the players that they need. Haaland could have gone anywhere. There were many clubs. It was a transparent situation because he had a release clause. That meant he could leave Dortmund without any negotiation. A lot of clubs wanted to sign him, so he made the decision and he made a well-informed decision with the main emphasis a football criterion. He asked, "Where am I going to play? How are we going to play? How am I going to work with this coach?"

'It was a football decision because the financial decision was not a big challenge. The fee with Dortmund was agreed in the release clause and a lot of clubs wanted to pay the salary he gets.'

Haaland has always preferred to do his talking on the pitch rather than into a microphone. Some of his interviews in Germany were excruciatingly awkward – which Haaland and the people who know him insist doesn't give a true reflection of the nature of the man. His apparent arrogance when being questioned has been explained as a reluctance to give the world an accurate view of who he is. Haaland has even been accused of dressing in an outlandish way to provoke his critics. Older brother Astor said, 'You have to be special to rock some of his clothes. Not everyone can – so they criticise him.' Sister Gabrielle added, 'People may think they know him from what they see in the media. But that is not always him.'

Haaland is unapologetic about only playing media games when they are contested on his terms – but he still reckons it's better to be spoken about than not. He said, 'I have to think it's good when someone is writing about me, even when I'm being criticised. In front of a camera, I do not feel like showing who I am. Why should people know who I am? So I prefer putting on a front.'

Haaland is a hugely popular member of the dressing room at City. His impressions of his team-mates have gone down a storm, notably the viral social media clip of him copying John Stones's Yorkshire accent when the defender brought the Louvre Museum up in a conversation.

Haaland struck up a close friendship with Jack Grealish and Phil Foden on his arrival at the club and Foden's young son Ronnie joined the striker as he lifted the Champions League trophy in front of fans at the Atatürk Stadium. Foden junior became an instant social media star when a microphone picked him up teasing the striker. 'I thought you were a girl,' said the four-year-old, referencing Haaland's plaited hairstyle. 'Did ya?' replied the Norwegian.

Guardiola observed, 'In every press conference, I get 50 questions and 45 of them are about Erling. For me it is OK – but what I like is that the guys [players] here accept it perfectly. I have had players before who wouldn't have liked it. Here, they are delighted. We don't have incredible players here who say "all the time they talk about him". This is why it is a joy to train this team.'

That hasn't always been the case. Arsenal captain Martin Ødegaard is now such a close friend of Haaland's that he appeared in the player's documentary *The Big Decision*. In it, Ødegaard recalls the first time he met the striker when he was called into Norway's squad for a European Under-21 Championship qualifier against Germany in October 2018. 'You have changed a little bit,' says Ødegaard. 'At the beginning you were a bit of a bastard when I first met you. At the beginning, you were childish. You have grown up a lot in the last couple of years. You see videos of the first camp, where you sing and dance. It was like you were 12 years old

– the biggest little bastard. But something has happened in the last couple of years.'

Later in the film, Ødegaard recognises that Haaland's private persona is very different to his public one. He says, 'I don't think he always does things because he thinks they're really cool. I think that sometimes he likes to get a little reaction and be a little funny. I just laugh. I don't take these things seriously. He can come in with some sick shoes or a bag, but I don't think, "This is Erling, he really loves this." I think more like, "What does he want from this?" The media contribute to the way you are portrayed. If you do one thing wrong, it creates 10,000 headlines. Even though it is not a mistake but just a funny thing, it is still written about. It is something you think about and try to protect yourself from.'

The number of Haaland's Instagram followers almost doubled to 33.4 million during his first season at City, but he still has some work to do to break into football's top ten. Cristiano Ronaldo has a staggering 596 million followers – and can bank a cool $2.3m for every sponsored post. Lionel Messi is next on 478 million, while Neymar and Kylian Mbappé make up the top four. Gareth Bale, Zlatan Ibrahimović, Paul Pogba, James Rodríguez, Sergio Ramos and Marcelo are also well ahead of Haaland.

Haaland has sponsorship and endorsement deals with luxury watchmaker Breitling, communications company Samsung Norge and Nordic streaming service Viaplay, and had a stake in the sports tech company Hyperice in 2021. But an illustration of his growing stature came in March 2023 when sportswear giants Nike agreed to pay him £20m for a ten-year link-up. Haaland had been contracted to the American company since the age of 14 but had allowed the agreement to expire in January 2022 to spark a bidding war that also included Adidas and Puma, the company that manufactures City's kit.

Haaland was wearing Adidas X Speedportal boots when he scored his first City goal on his debut in a pre-season friendly against Bayern Munich in July 2022 and again in the Community Shield defeat to Liverpool. But eight days later, he got off the team bus at West Ham wearing Adidas trainers before changing into Nike Mercurial Vapor 14 boots to score twice on his Premier League debut. His constant changes of footwear put him in the biggest shop window in sport.

He insists he didn't realise the social media stir he was causing – but his dad did. Erling said, 'I don't check online – but my father Alfie tracks it. Normally, it is not allowed to wear Adidas and Nike together and I got a couple of hate comments about wearing [Nike] Jordans and an Adidas hoodie. It was just for fun. It was a nice hoodie and I've got a couple of pairs of Jordans so I paired them together.'

It was reported that Haaland returned to a Nike stable that includes sporting superstars like Cristiano Ronaldo, Kylian Mbappé, Tiger Woods, Rafael Nadal and LeBron James because the company promised to make him the face of their 'No 9' boot range, the line that was launched in 1998 by the Brazilian World Cup legend Ronaldo. Nike announced the deal by proclaiming, 'Erling's record-breaking scoring has put a stamp on the future of the game, and makes him the heir to No 9 – the next-generation striker.'

Haaland's deadly swoosh boots are the Phantom GX Elite model, a custom-made shoe that weighs just 204g, manufactured by a workshop in the tiny town of Montebelluna in northern Italy using moulds of the customer's feet. It is a service offered to all of Nike's sponsored athletes. Players can sometimes go through a pair every two weeks, but Haaland prefers to wear the same boots for up to three months before switching to a different colour at Nike's behest.

Nike sent Haaland a commemorative pair when he smashed the 34-goal Premier League record held by

Alan Shearer and Andy Cole when he netted his 35th of the campaign in a 3-0 win over West Ham on 3 May. Emblazoned with the number 35, he wore them for the game at Everton four days later and scored again in another 3-0 win. Told by City's backroom team that his boots were now behind the times, Haaland took out a magic marker and made his own alterations. When he posed wearing just a pair of oversized Calvin Klein Y-front underpants with City-mad rock star Noel Gallagher and fan Jonathan Mowatt in the dressing room after the Blues had routed Arsenal 4-1 at the Etihad in April, sales rocketed by over 45 per cent.

Haaland confesses to having a weakness for shoes, bags, watches and cars.

When it comes to watches he's a brand ambassador for Breitling and wears a Breitling Chronograph Automatic GMT 40. But he also has an extensive collection of Rolex, Patek Philippe, Vacheron Constantin and Audemars Piguet.

He also has an extensive collection of cars and owns a sky blue Rolls-Royce Cullinan (£300,000), Range Rover Sport (£120,000), and Audi RS6 Avant (£120,000). However, he usually goes to training in a £90,000 Mercedes-AMG GLE Coupe.

He has over 200 pairs of training shoes and an extensive collection of Louis Vuitton luggage that covers him for every occasion. One holdall he uses for away games retails at £8,000.

Haaland was reportedly swayed to sign with Nike because of their long-term affiliation with Brazil legend Ronaldo. And they aren't the only company who pay staggering sums to be associated with the superstar striker.

Haaland, who turned 23 in the summer of 2023 and having signed a multimillion pound deal with Nike, is almost always used for commercial shoots because that is what the partners want – him and Jack Grealish.

His career has been meticulously mapped out by his advisers – and Alfie revealed the long-term plan is for him to play in all the top leagues around Europe. He said, 'I think Erling wants to test his capabilities in every league for a maximum of three or four years. Maybe he has two-and-a-half years in Germany, England, Spain, Italy and France. He cannot stay for more than that in each league. We do not know if it will be like that. But I think he would like to test his capabilities in all the big leagues. I absolutely believe that.'

When news broke in Spain in October 2022 that Haaland had a release clause of €200m in his City contract, it appeared that Mino Raiola's parting gift before his death was to give the player some degree of control on his future. The suggestion was that it would allow Real Madrid to sign Haaland once Karim Benzema's career was over, but the small print meant he could only join a club outside England and that the clause would not kick in until 2024. The buy-out would then be reduced after every year until his contract expired in 2027.

Guardiola dismissed the report as 'not true'. But he had insider knowledge. He was less than a month away from signing a two-year extension to take his reign at the Etihad to nine years – and by putting pen to paper on 23 November he effectively deleted the buy-out in Haaland's contract. It appeared the Norwegian had wedded himself to Guardiola by allowing the clause to be removed if the Catalan extended his own stay. City's next step was to open talks aimed at persuading Haaland to commit himself to the club beyond 2027.

There will have been delight from sponsors in Abu Dhabi when it became clear that Haaland would travel there with City's under-23 squad for a warm-weather camp during the World Cup. He was filmed cooking with Riyad Mahrez and relaxing on a hammock for video content. They had him greeting young locals and he gave a quick interview too.

Haaland – whose viral clip spontaneously mimicking Stones's Yorkshire accent came from a promotional video – apparently takes this sort of thing in his stride and accepts it is part of the job.

He will also surely be aware of his pull when it comes to merchandising. City wore their new kit at Brentford on the final day of the 2022/23 Premier League season, modelled as ever by Haaland and Grealish in the unveiling promo, and saw a surge in sales.

2023 was proving to be a record year for Manchester City's retail department and the pace of sales of the new shirt led to the highest 24 hours of trading they have ever encountered.

The Norwegian Football Federation have been some of the most outspoken critics of human rights abuses in Qatar during World Cup qualifying and some in the country questioned Haaland moving to City given Amnesty International's criticism of their Abu Dhabi owners. However, such is the hope and hype that Norway finally have their own Zlatan Ibrahimović that many are more focused on how Haaland can get them firing to major tournaments again for the first time since the turn of the millennium.

'The vast majority in Norway still believe that you cannot blame Haaland and the players at City. This is at an overall political level,' says Norwegian journalist Tore Ulrik Bratland.

'If you ignore the owners, most Norwegians want Haaland to succeed at the club. It is due to a desperate desire over several years to get a world-class player. Norway has never had this before. Ole Gunnar Solskjær and John Arne Riise were good at Manchester United and Liverpool respectively, but they were never world-class players. For years we have envied Sweden's Zlatan Ibrahimović.'

Statistics

2022/23

Manchester City results

20 July	Manchester City 2 Club América 1 Friendly
23 July	Manchester City 1 Bayern Munich 0 Friendly
30 July	Liverpool 3 Manchester City 1 Charity Shield
7 August	West Ham 0 Manchester City 2 Premier League
13 August	Manchester City 4 Bournemouth 0 Premier League
21 August	Newcastle United 3 Manchester City 3 Premier League
24 August	Barcelona 3 Manchester City 3 Friendly
27 August	Manchester City 4 Crystal Palace 2 Premier League
31 August	Manchester City 6 Nottingham Forest 0 Premier League
3 September	Aston Villa 1 Manchester City 1 Premier League
6 September	Sevilla 0 Manchester City 4 Champions League group stage
14 September	Manchester City 2 Borussia Dortmund 1 Champions League group stage
17 September	Wolverhampton Wanderers 0 Manchester City 3 Premier League
2 October	Manchester City 6 Manchester United 3 Premier League
5 October	Manchester City 5 Copenhagen 0 Champions League group stage

8 October	Manchester City 4 Southampton 0
	Premier League
11 October	Copenhagen 0 Manchester City 0
	Champions League group stage
16 October	Liverpool 1 Manchester City 0
	Premier League
22 October	Manchester City 3 Brighton & Hove Albion 1
	Premier League
25 October	Borussia Dortmund 0 Manchester City 0
	Champions League group stage
29 October	Leicester City 0 Manchester City 1
	Premier League
2 November	Manchester City 2 Sevilla 1
	Champions League group stage
5 November	Manchester City 2 Fulham 1
	Premier League
9 November	Manchester City 2 Chelsea 0
	EFL Cup third round
12 November	Manchester City 1 Brentford 2
	Premier League
17 December	Manchester City 2 Girona 0
	Friendly
22 December	Manchester City 3 Liverpool 2
	EFL Cup fourth round
28 December	Leeds United 1 Manchester City 3
	Premier League
31 December	Manchester City 1 Everton 1
	Premier League
5 January	Chelsea 0 Manchester City 1
	Premier League
8 January	Manchester City 4 Chelsea 0
	FA Cup third round
11 January	Southampton 2 Manchester City 0
	EFL Cup quarter-final
14 January	Manchester United 2 Manchester City 1
	Premier League
19 January	Manchester City 4 Tottenham Hotspur 2
	Premier League
22 January	Manchester City 3 Wolverhampton Wanderers 0
	Premier League
27 January	Manchester City 1 Arsenal 0
	FA Cup fourth round

5 February	Tottenham Hotspur 1 Manchester City 0
	Premier League
12 February	Manchester City 3 Aston Villa 1
	Premier League
15 February	Arsenal 1 Manchester City 3
	Premier League
18 February	Nottingham Forest 1 Manchester City 1
	Premier League
22 February	RB Leipzig 1 Manchester City 1
	Champions League last 16 first leg
25 February	Bournemouth 1 Manchester City 4
	Premier League
28 February	Bristol City 0 Manchester City 3
	FA Cup fifth round
4 March	Manchester City 2 Newcastle United 0
	Premier League
11 March	Crystal Palace 0 Manchester City 1
	Premier League
14 March	Manchester City 7 RB Leipzig 0
	Champions League last 16 second leg (8-1 on aggregate)
18 March	Manchester City 6 Burnley 0
	FA Cup quarter-final
1 April	Manchester City 4 Liverpool 1
	Premier League
8 April	Southampton 1 Manchester City 4
	Premier League
11 April	Manchester City 3 Bayern Munich 0
	Champions League quarter-final first leg
15 April	Manchester City 3 Leicester City 1
	Premier League
19 April	Bayern Munich 1 Manchester City 1
	Champions League quarter-final second leg (4-1 on aggregate)
22 April	Manchester City 3 Sheffield United 0
	FA Cup semi-final
26 April	Manchester City 4 Arsenal 1
	Premier League
30 April	Fulham 1 Manchester City 2
	Premier League
3 May	Manchester City 3 West Ham United 0
	Premier League

6 May	Manchester City 2 Leeds United 1
	Premier League
9 May	Real Madrid 1 Manchester City 1
	Champions League semi-final first leg
14 May	Everton 0 Manchester City 3
	Premier League
17 May	Manchester City 4 Real Madrid 0
	Champions League semi-final second leg (5-1 on aggregate)
21 May	Manchester City 1 Chelsea 0
	Premier League
24 May	Brighton & Hove Albion 1 Manchester City 1
	Premier League
28 May	Brentford 1 Manchester City 0
	Premier League
3 June	Manchester City 2 Manchester United 1
	FA Cup Final
10 June	Manchester City 1 Inter Milan 0
	Champions League Final

Haaland's goals:

Premier League – 36

West Ham United (A) 2, Newcastle United (A) 1, Crystal Palace (H) 3, Nottingham Forest (H) 3, Aston Villa (A) 1, Wolverhampton Wanderers (A) 1, Manchester United (H) 3, Southampton (H) 1, Brighton & Hove Albion (H) 2, Fulham (H) 1, Leeds United (A) 2, Everton (H) 1, Tottenham Hotspur (H) 1, Wolverhampton Wanderers (H) 3, Arsenal (A) 1, Bournemouth (A) 1, Crystal Palace (A) 1, Southampton (A) 2, Leicester City (H) 2, Arsenal (H) 1, Fulham (A) 1, West Ham United (H) 1, Everton (A) 1
22 at home, 16 away. Scored against 16 teams but did not score against Liverpool, Chelsea and Brentford

Premier League top scorers in 2022/23
Erling Haaland – 36
Harry Kane – 30
Ivan Toney – 20

Champions League – 12
Sevilla (A) 2, Dortmund (H) 1, Copenhagen (H) 2, RB Leipzig (H) 5, Bayern Munich (H) 1 (A) 1

Champions League top scorers in 2022/23
Erling Haaland – 12
Mohamed Salah – 8
Vinícius Junior – 7
Kylian Mbappé – 7

FA Cup – 3
Burnley (H) 3

EFL Cup – 1
Liverpool (H) 1
Total in competitive club matches – 52

Manchester City top scorers in all competitions in 2022/23:
Erling Haaland 52, Julián Álvarez 16 + 1 in Community Shield, Phil Foden 15, Riyad Mahrez 15, İlkay Gündoğan 11, Kevin De Bruyne 10

Appearances

Premier League: Rodri 36, Haaland 35, Ederson 35, Silva 34, De
   Bruyne 32, Foden 32, Gündoğan 31, Mahrez 30, Álvarez 30,
   Grealish 28, Walker 27, Aké 27, Dias 26

Overall: Rodri 56, Silva 55, Haaland 53, Gündoğan 51, Grealish 50

Haaland's goals in friendlies – 2

Bayern Munich (N) 1, Girona (H) 1

Norway international goals in 2023 – 4

Slovenia (A) 1, Scotland (H) 1, Cyprus (A) 2

In 2022/23 Haaland thus scored 56 goals in competitive matches
   for club and country.

Golden Boot

Haaland became the fifth Manchester City player to win the
   Golden Boot by finishing as top scorer in the top division of
   English football:

Frank Roberts 1924/25 – 31 goals

Francis Lee 1971/72 – 33 goals

Carlos Tevez 2010/11 – 21 goals – equal with Dimitar Berbatov
   of Manchester United

Sergio Agüero 2014/15 – 26 goals

Erling Haaland 2022/23 – 36 goals

Bibliography

Books

Balls, P. & Martin, L., *Pep's City* (Backpage Polaris Publishing, 2019)

Crawley, S. & James, G., *The Pride of Manchester* (ACL Colour Print and Polar Publishing, 1990)

Gardner, P. (Ed.), *Manchester City Football Book* (Stanley Paul, 1969)

Gardner, P. (Ed.), *Manchester City Football Book No 2* (Stanley Paul, 1970)

Gardner, P. (Ed.), *Manchester City Football Book No 3* (Stanley Paul, 1971)

Gardner, P. (Ed.), *Manchester City Football Book No 4* (Stanley Paul, 1972)

Harding, J., *Football Wizard: The Billy Meredith Story* (Robson Books, 1998)

Hesse, U., *Building The Yellow Wall: The Incredible Rise and Cult Appeal of Borussia Dortmund* (W&N, 2019)

Hesse, U., *TOR! The Story of German Football* (Polaris Publishing, 1992)

James, G., *The Manchester City Years* (James Ward, 2010)

James, G., *Manchester City: The Complete Record* (Breedon Books Publishing, 2006)

James, G., *Manchester: A Football History* (James Ward, 2008)

Keith, B., *Dixie Dean: The Inside Story of a Football Icon* (Robson Books, 2001)

Kidd, A. & Wyke, T., *Manchester: Making the Modern City* (Liverpool University Press, 2016)

Matthews, T., *Manchester City Player by Player* (DB Publishing, 2013)

Metcalf, M., *Frank Swift: Manchester City and England Legend* (DB Publishing, 2013)

Metcalf, M. & Matthews, T., *The Golden Boot: Football's Top Scorers* (Amberley Publishing, 2012)

Perarnau, M., *Pep Confidential: The Inside Story of Pep Guardiola's First Season at Bayern Munich* (Arena Sport, 2014)

Perarnau, M., *Pep Guardiola: The Evolution* (Arena Sport, 2016)

Rich, T., *Caught Beneath The Landslide* (de Coubertin, 2018)

Steves, R., *Pocket Munich and Salzburg* (Second Edition by Rick Steves, 2019)

Documentaries

Haaland - The Big Decision – by Viaplay

Haaland Conquers England – by Viaplay

Newspapers and magazines

Birmingham Mail

Blizzard Magazine

Daily Mirror

Sunday Mirror

Daily Express

Daily Star

The Sun

Sunday Mail

The Guardian

The Times

Daily Telegraph

Evening Standard
Liverpool Echo
Manchester Gazette
The Chronicle
When Saturday Comes
Yorkshire Post
The Scotsman

Broadcast media
CBS Golazo
BBC Sport
Sky Sports
talkSPORT
ESPN

Websites
YouTube
Football Writers' Association
The Athletic
Goal.com
The Gooner
Wikipedia
Scorebar
Gary James' Football Archive
Sportsmole
Soccerway
Be Soccer
Borussia Dortmund
Champions League
EFL
FA
FIFA
Liverpool FC

Manchester City
Molde FK
Norwegian Football Federation
Premier League
RB Salzburg
UEFA
England Online
Bundesliga